EL FELIZ INGENIO NEOMEXICANO

 PASÓ POR AQUÍ SERIES ON THE
NUEVOMEXICANO LITERARY HERITAGE
A. Gabriel Meléndez and Genaro M. Padilla,
Series Editors

The Pasó por Aquí Series emerged in the 1990s from the Recovering the U.S. Hispanic Literary Heritage Project, a gathering of scholars from universities across the United States engaged in recovering Hispanic works of literature and history that were published before 1960. While the goal of the series is the recovery of the Hispanic literary heritage of greater New Mexico, the editors recognize that part of the project also includes publishing new fiction and poetry in order to preserve a literary tradition that is often thematically, linguistically, and culturally interconnected. Moreover, scholarship in allied fields lends greater intellectual coherence to the series, and we therefore encourage the collection of photography, historical documents, religious artifacts, and other aspects of expressive culture in varied forms.

Also available in the Pasó por Aquí Series on the Nuevomexicano Literary Heritage:

Defying the Inquisition in Colonial New Mexico: Miguel de Quintana's Life and Writings edited by Francisco A. Lomelí and Clark A. Colahan
The Life and Writing of Fray Angélico Chávez: A New Mexico Renaissance Man by Ellen McCracken
Juan the Bear and the Water of Life: La Acequia de Juan del Oso by Enrique R. Lamadrid and Juan Estevan Arellano
The Legend of Ponciano Gutiérrez and the Mountain Thieves by A. Gabriel Meléndez and the Paiz Family
Fray Angélico Chávez: Poet, Priest, and Artist edited by Ellen McCracken
The Writings of Eusebio Chacón edited by A. Gabriel Meléndez and Francisco A. Lomelí
Amadito and the Hero Children: Amadito y los Niños Héroes by Enrique R. Lamadrid
The Daring Flight of My Pen: Cultural Politics and Gaspar Pérez de Villagrá's Historia de la Nueva Mexico, 1610 by Genaro Padilla
Santa Fe Nativa: A Collection of Nuevomexicano Writing edited by A. Gabriel Meléndez, Enrique R. Lamadrid, and Rosalie C. Otero
Big Dreams and Dark Secrets in Chimayó: A Novel by G. Benito Córdova

For additional titles in the Pasó por Aquí Series on the Nuevomexicano Literary Heritage, please visit unmpress.com.

"La Voz del Pueblo Office, 1900." Courtesy of the City of Las Vegas Museum and Rough Rider Memorial Collection (Object ID #0799).

El feliz ingenio neomexicano

Felipe M. Chacón and *Poesía y prosa*

Edited, Translated, and Introduced by

ANNA M. NOGAR *and*

A. GABRIEL MELÉNDEZ

University of New Mexico Press / Albuquerque

© 2021 by the University of New Mexico Press
All rights reserved. Published 2021
Printed in the United States of America

First paperback printing 2023 | ISBN 978-0-8263-6565-1

Library of Congress Cataloging-in-Publication Data

Names: Chacón, F. M. (Felipe Maximiliano), 1873– author. | Nogar, Anna M., editor. | Meléndez, A. Gabriel (Anthony Gabriel), editor. | Chacón, F. M. (Felipe Maximiliano), 1873– Obras de Felipe Maximiliano Chacón, el Cantor neomexicano. | Chacón, F. M. (Felipe Maximiliano), 1873– Obras de Felipe Maximiliano Chacón, el Cantor neomexicano. English.
Title: El feliz ingenio neomexicano: Felipe M. Chacón and Poesía y prosa / edited, translated, and introduced by Anna M. Nogar and A. Gabriel Meléndez.
Other titles: Pasó por aquí.
Description: Albuquerque: University of New Mexico Press, 2021. | Series: Pasó por aqui series on the nuevomexicano literary heritage | Includes bibliographical references.
Identifiers: LCCN 2021033417 (print) | LCCN 2021033418 (e-book) | ISBN 9780826363275 (cloth) | ISBN 9780826363282 (e-book)
Subjects: LCSH: Chacón, F. M. (Felipe Maximiliano), 1873—Translations into English. | LCGFT: Poetry.
Classification: LCC PQ7079.C5 A2 2021 (print) | LCC PQ7079.C5 (e-book) | DDC 861/.62—dc23
LC record available at https://lccn.loc.gov/2021033417
LC e-book record available at https://lccn.loc.gov/2021033418

Founded in 1889, the University of New Mexico sits on the traditional homelands of the Pueblo of Sandia. The original peoples of New Mexico—Pueblo, Navajo, and Apache—since time immemorial have deep connections to the land and have made significant contributions to the broader community statewide. We honor the land itself and those who remain stewards of this land throughout the generations and also acknowledge our committed relationship to Indigenous peoples. We gratefully recognize our history.

COVER ILLUSTRATION BY Mindy Basinger Hill
DESIGNED BY Mindy Basinger Hill
COMPOSED IN 10.75/14.8 point Fanwood.

CONTENTS

List of Poems and Prose   ix

Acknowledgments   xiii

Felipe Maximiliano Chacón: A Literary Genealogy   1
A. GABRIEL MELÉNDEZ

Poetics and Their Politics in the Lyric Work of Felipe M. Chacón   27
ANNA M. NOGAR

Notes to the Spanish and English Editions of *Poesía y prosa*   75
ANNA M. NOGAR AND A. GABRIEL MELÉNDEZ

Spanish Transcription of *Poesía y prosa*   77

English Translation of *Poesía y prosa*   259

Appendix   441

POEMS AND PROSE

Spanish

Una agudeza 148
A los legisladores 140
Al enviudar mi madre 173
Al explorador del oeste 128
Alternados 105
A María ante su altar 109
A mayo 121
A mi ahijada, Rosa Córdova 203
A mi ahijado, Jacobo Aragón, hijo 205
A mi amada hermanita, Lucía 207
A mi Elvira 200
A mi hija, Elvira 198
A mi hija, Herminia 189
A mi hija, Josefina 194
A mi hija, Julieta 196
A mi hijita, Melba 202
A mi hijito, Buenaventura 201
A mi hijo, Felipe 191
A la niñez 131
El angel de la guarda 170
Anita 172
A Nuevo México 124
A la patria 101
A Santa Fe 103

A la Señora Adelina Otero-Warren 116
A la Srta. Adela Cruz 174
Asunto enredado 139
El ateo y la verdad 167
Axiomas 171
Ayer y hoy 112
Un baile de caretas 234
Un bello ideal 214
Caso doloroso 165
Caso florido 111
Caso singular 135
Celos y amor 107
Complacencia 157
La creación 176
Desencanto 138
Desengaños 115
Devoción 158
Don Julio Berlanga 237
En la muerte de una joven 217
Es el amor 147
Eustacio y Carlota 240
La fénix 212
Filosofando 118
Fragmentos 106

Una ilusión 133
Indiferente 159
El ingrato 123
In memoriam 150
María Estuardo y su doliente 219
Mi escogido y mis razones 160
La navidad 136
Nocturno a... 142
El obrero 113
Oda a los héroes 95

Otoñal 119
Paradoja 149
Prólogo 85
Un republicano real 227
Un sabio 213
Salmo de la vida 210
Se aleja y se vá 166
Sueños y realidades 153
La vida 127
La visión de Baltasar 215

English

Anita 354
The Atheist and the Truth 349
Autumn 301
Axioms 353
Christmas 318
Creation 358
Deception 320
Deceptions 297
Devotion 340
Don Julio Berlanga 419
Dreams and Truth 335
Eustacio and Carlota 422
A Flowery Circumstance 293
Fragments 288
Guardian Angel 352
Here's to Childhood 313
Here's to the Month of May 303
Hobnobbers 287
The House by the Side
    of the Road 396
An Illusion 315
Indifferent 341

The Ingrate 305
In Memoriam 332
In Mexico 87, 269
It's Love 329
It Withdraws and Disappears 348
Jealousy and Love 289
Life 309
Mary Stuart and Her Mourner 402
A Masquerade Ball 416
My Candidate and My Reasons 342
My Mother's Widowhood 355
A Nocturne to... 324
Ode to the Heroes 277
On the Death of a Young Lady 400
A Painful Affair 347
Paradox 331
Parting 87, 269
Philosophizing 300
Pleasure 339
Prologue 267
Psalm of Life 392
A Real Republican 409

A Sharp Edge 330
A Singular Moment 317
A Tangled Affair 321
To the Duchess of York 394
To the Homeland 283
To the Lawmakers 322
To Mrs. Adelina Otero-Warren 298
To Ms. Adela Cruz 356
To My Beloved Little Sister,
    Lucía 389
To My Daughter, Elvira 380
To My Daughter, Herminia 371
To My Daughter, Josefina 376
To My Daughter, Julieta 378
To My Elvira 382
To My Goddaughter,
    Rosa Córdova 385
To My Godson,
    Jacobo Aragón, Son 387
To My Little Daughter,
    Melba 384
To My Little Son,
    Buenaventura 383
To My Son, Felipe 373
To New Mexico 306
To Santa Fe 285
To the Virgin at Her Altar 291
To the Westward Explorer 310
Vision of Belshazzar 398
A Wise One 395
The Worker 295
Wouldst Thou? 88, 270
Yesterday, Today 294

ACKNOWLEDGMENTS

The authors wish to acknowledge the following individuals and institutions for their assistance in bringing this project to fruition. A special thank you to Spanish and Portuguese graduate students Debra Nieto and Monica Mancillas, who worked under the supervision of Dr. Nogar on early stages of the research on Felipe M. Chacón. We thank Isaiah Romo, an undergraduate intern at the University of New Mexico's Center for Regional Studies working under the supervision of Dr. Meléndez, for finding and transcribing copies of the poems in English on which Chacón based his translations. We also thank Dr. Anselmo Arellano, a pioneering researcher on New Mexico letters, for granting us permission to use his 1996 interview with Herminia Chacón González. Thanks to Dr. Nicolás Kanellos of the Recovering the U.S. Hispanic Literary Heritage project for permission to cite portions of Dr. Nogar's article. Finally, a subvention grant to Dr. Nogar from the Center for Regional Studies provided partial support for this book's publication.

EL FELIZ INGENIO NEOMEXICANO

A. GABRIEL MELÉNDEZ

Felipe Maximiliano Chacón

A LITERARY GENEALOGY

In 1924, Felipe Maximiliano Chacón published a collection of writings he titled *Obras de Felipe Maximiliano Chacón, "el cantor neomexicano": Poesía y prosa*. The work, as far as can be determined, appears to be the first collection of poetry published by a Mexican American author. Readers of the Spanish-language weekly *La Bandera Americana* were asked to remit an order form along with $3.50 in cash to obtain a copy of the book. This approach points to the fact that a system of self-publishing and self-distribution of books was the sole means of issuing creative writing in Chicano communities nearly eighty years after New Mexico became a US possession.

Chacón released his book while living in the Barelas neighborhood of Albuquerque and serving as the editor of *La Bandera Americana*. *Poesía y prosa* appeared six years after both the outbreak of the so-called Spanish influenza pandemic and the signing of the armistice that brought World War I to a close. The year 1924 was not particularly remarkable in terms of the history of the United States. News for the year included the fact that Johnny Weissmuller, who would later star in Tarzan movies, won three gold medals at the Paris Summer Olympics. In 1924 Calvin Coolidge was president, J. Edgar Hoover was appointed director of the FBI, there were calls to close Ellis Island, and the Indian Citizenship Act, a measure that applied to all Indigenous people born in the United States, was passed.

As the editor of *La Bandera Americana*, Chacón would have been more acutely aware of issues in New Mexico where, for example, public health was a serious problem. In the aftermath of the "Spanish" influenza pandemic, tuberculosis became the leading cause of death in the state and would remain so until the advent of World War II, and other serious health issues raged.

New Mexico had long registered a high infant mortality rate, the result of poor sanitation and the prevalence of infectious diseases and parasitic outbreaks. To address these issues, the Division of Public Health Services had been created by former governor Octaviano Larrazolo only a few years prior, but by 1924 it employed only four public health nurses to cover the needs of a state roughly five times the size of Ireland.

Other regional issues would have also concerned Chacón. The US Congress in 1924 passed the Pueblo Lands Act, which sought to put to rest competing land claims in areas where non-Indigenous people had encroached on lands that were part of the Pueblo reservations. Democrat James Hinkle was serving in his first term as governor. Following the death of Lieutenant Governor José Albino Baca in the summer of 1924, Governor Hinkle named Soledad C. Chacón acting governor for the two weeks he would be away attending the Democratic National Convention. Soledad Chacón was a cousin of the up-and-coming Democrat Dionisio "Dennis" Chávez, who would become a US senator in 1935. Soledad was also Felipe M. Chacón's sister-in-law, having married his younger brother Ireneo Eduardo Chacón. Felipe summed up the year in a small editorial he placed in *La Bandera Americana* titled "Siempre la Chicana, paga el pato." He noted:

> Mientras que se reporta que sólo cuatro pagadores de tasaciones reportaron sus rentas en exceso a $5,000 por el año de 1924 mas de 2,000,000 de americanos reportaron rentas de $2,000 y estos son los que mantienen las ruedas del gobierno en movimiento.

> [It has been reported that while only four taxpayers reported earnings in excess of $5,000 for the year 1924, more than 2,000,000 Americans reported earnings of $2,000 and these are the ones who keep the wheels of government turning.]

In light of this snapshot of 1924, the common trope of the Roaring Twenties may be best understood as a few years of prosperity coupled with a general loosening of conventional mores and a zest for fashion, mainly by urban residents on the East and West Coasts of the country. By contrast, the New Mexico Felipe Chacón knew was decidedly outside and beyond the world of flapper girls, jazz clubs, and well-heeled, socially influential leisure classes. Whatever prosperity Chacón experienced would come to a dramatic and painful halt five years after the publication of *Poesía y prosa* with the stock market crash of 1929 and the Great Depression that followed.

After 1929, Felipe M. Chacón and his book fell into obscurity for the next half century, consigned to the dustbin of history. Notice of Chacón only reemerged with the publication in 1977 of Doris Meyer's article "Felipe Maximiliano Chacón: A Forgotten Mexican-American Author" in the *New Scholar*. Meyer reproduced in English translation a handful of the poems in *Poesía y prosa* and a translation of "Don Julio Berlanga," one of three prose pieces in the book. Using Benjamin Read's ten-page prologue, which every researcher since has agreed provides a "solid basis for the study of Felipe Chacón" (Nogar 339), Meyer made the first foray into the mind and talent of this early *nuevomexicano* writer, characterizing him as both a forgotten voice and a precursor to Chicano/a literature. Meyer's scholarship is the starting point for any critical study of Felipe M. Chacón, a subject she returned to by adding a full chapter on Chacón to *Speaking for Themselves* (1996), her comprehensive study of the nuevomexicano press movement.

I offered my first sustained look at Chacón in *So All Is Not Lost* (1997), amplifying his biography and documenting mentions of him in the Spanish-language press going back to 1894, when as a boy he would visit the offices of *La Aurora*, a newspaper his father, Urbano, operated in Santa Fe. There was also mention of his first cousin Eusebio in the same paper four years earlier in an enthusiastic report that Eusebio, though only a boy of thirteen, had recently addressed the Trinidad Mutual Aid Society. Uncle Urbano, eager to spur on the next generation of Chacóns in the arts of oratory and letters, remarked of his nephew Eusebio, "The lad is only thirteen years old. He exhibits surprising talent that promises great things; a future in which he will gather the laurels of a happy and bright career."[1] In preparing this literary genealogy, I combed through the pages of a dozen or more newspapers published in New Mexico and southern Colorado for reports of Felipe M. Chacón's activities between 1894 and 1930. To my surprise, many of Felipe's activities, movements, and achievements in journalism and writing, overlooked in previous studies, surfaced.

Another major source on Felipe are the recollections of his eldest daughter, Herminia Chacón González. I was incredibly fortunate to meet and interview doña Herminia in 1996 when I was completing my book *So All Is Not Lost*. Doña Herminia was eighty-three years old and living in El Paso, Texas. Our conversation ranged over several topics during a couple of meetings. Herminia provided me with information on her father and mother's courtship, marriage, and early years in El Paso. She confirmed the working relationship Felipe M. Chacón had with Felix Martínez and with other nuevomexicanos. She registered her concern over the lack of awareness of the history of Spanish-language journalism and of her father's contributions, reflecting on the language shift from Spanish to English in the Southwest. She spoke of her close friendship with the major New Mexican figure Aurora Lucero-White, with whom she worked at the US Censorship Office during World War II. She reluctantly (not wanting to draw attention away from the newspapers) agreed to talk about submitting her own writings for publication in newspapers, journals, and magazines specializing in New Mexico history and culture. Finally, she asked if I had a copy of her father's book. I answered that I had a photocopy of it from the rare book collection at the University of New Mexico's Zimmerman Library. She then simply handed me an original copy, one of perhaps a dozen that lined a small bookshelf in her apartment.

In 2012, Francisco Lomelí of the University of California at Santa Barbara and I published *The Writings of Eusebio Chacón*, a book that we had determined, based on our combined experience and search of archives, brought together all the known published and unpublished works written by Eusebio Chacón. We noted, "This book could only have been written through a close and lengthy collaboration, given the nature of the 'lost' documents we sought. By joining forces, we think we have managed to properly represent, as well as recreate Chacón as a leading voice of ideas and concerns. Thus, we provide a more complex profile of what he embodied during his respective era" (Meléndez and Lomelí 10).

Eusebio and Felipe Maximiliano stand at each end of the most active period in the nuevomexicano cultural and literary arts movement that accompanied the rise of Spanish-language newspaper publication. Eusebio's lasting literary achievement, the 1892 publication of the novelettes *El hijo de la tempestad* and *Tras la tormenta, la calma* [The Son of the Storm and The Calm after the Storm] in Santa Fe's *El Boletín Popular*, is at one end. His novelettes were prefaced by his clear-eyed declaration announcing the "liberating possibilities of what he termed, *una literatura nacional* (a national literature)" (*Writings*, 5). Eusebio dared to announce a project that would register the achievements of Mexican Americans as full citizens in the US public imagination. In his novelettes, he proclaimed his literary credo as he urged his fellow nuevomexicanos to seize control of their social and cultural destiny. While Lomelí suggests that early students of Chacón viewed the novelettes as an isolated case of Eusebio Chacón's formal debut, we now know their publication was part of a larger literary movement. Indeed, Lomelí, Meyer, and I happened upon the work of Eusebio Chacón, José Escobar, and Felipe M. Chacón at roughly the same time, and we came to appreciate how the work of each author led back to the full corpus of the nuevomexicano literary and cultural scene.

Writing in 1996, Meyer was cognizant of the achievement *Poesía y prosa* represented, seeing the book as a doorway leading back to that corpus. She assessed the work as "a book whose importance is as much sociohistorical as literary. Forgotten for decades, its rediscovery confirms the existence of an early *neomexicano* literary tradition and makes the case for reexamining the multicultural roots of American literature, and what it can tell us about the American experience, even stronger" (*Speaking for Themselves*, 164). Meyer was writing at the point of the initial rediscovery of *Poesía y prosa* in 1977; we certainly know more now about both Felipe M. Chacón and the movement he was a part of.

More than four decades after Meyer's keen observation, my coeditor, Anna M. Nogar, and I now bring forth this first bilingual recovered edition of *Poesía y prosa* with the aim of finally making the work available to contemporary readers and to students of Chicano/a literature. Working as a team, we have split our task. I take up the work of adding to the sociohistorical understanding of Chacón as an author and of *Poesía y prosa* as a publication. Professor Nogar's focus is on examining the aesthetic and creative dimensions of Felipe M. Chacón's writings.

Feisty Instigator of New Mexico Letters

In examining Felipe M. Chacón as a subject, some additional context about his personal story is important. I begin with the details of his early career as an aspiring journalist along with his concerns as a citizen deeply engaged in electoral politics in both the Democratic and Republican Parties. Next, I consider how others have characterized Chacón as a person, a writer, a member of a prominent family, and a citizen of New Mexico at the moment of its political transition from a US territory to the forty-seventh state of the Union.

The Spanish-language press kept tabs on the activities and movements of Felipe Chacón in personal columns, public information notes, editorials, opinion pieces, poems, and other forms of creative writing with great consistency between 1894 and 1925. Various facets of Chacón's endeavors emerge with sufficient detail to sense the variable nature of his relationship to his community.

The Child Prodigy

Felipe's first appearance in print casts him as a child prodigy, as shown by Pietre Balducci, an editor hired by Urbano Chacón at *La Aurora*. Balducci's column, "El testamento del redactor" [The Editor's Last Will and Testament], is a colorful, tongue-in-cheek account meant to entertain the readership. The conceit of the piece is to have the editor reply to the in-house *gacetillero*'s [copyboy] questions and publicly announce what he intends to leave as an inheritance to the paper's office staff. After going through the organizational chart, Balducci turns to Felipe, then a boy of eleven who had been working at his father's side as an apprentice in the offices of *La Aurora*, and says, "To *La Aurora*'s poet, so young, so valiant, so courteous a young man, to him I pass on the recommendation that he unfold his wings and that they guide his imagination toward the world of ideas" (Meléndez, *So All Is Not Lost*, 185).

Felipe shadowed his father as he went about his newspaper work, but only for a short time since Urbano died quite suddenly in 1886, Felipe just having turned twelve. A decade later, Eusebio Chacón, employing the pseudonym Adelfa, heaped praise on his cousin, lauding a speech he had given for the Fourth of July celebrations held in Hillsboro, New Mexico, in 1897. Eusebio was effusive in his high praise: "The speech provides a glimpse of what this young man will be in time. We believe that great men come from the people. Local communities produce great teachers and soldiers and even in their youth great men show who they will become. From a very young age Felipe has shown signs that his spirit rises high above the common masses" (Adelfa cited in Meléndez and Lomelí 175).

Felipe's appearance in southern New Mexico prefigured the next stage of his life and career when he joined efforts with Felix Martínez, a noted businessman and the owner of the Spanish weekly *La Voz del Pueblo* (for more on Martínez, see Meléndez, *So All Is Not Lost*). Chacón worked for Martínez in El Paso between 1898 and 1904. In an interview in 1996, Herminia Chacón (1913–2003) recalled her family history and details about her father's association with Martínez: "Sí, mi papá vino aquí con don Manuel Aragón, su tío. Vineron con Felix Martínez. Se trajo al doctor Romero, a Manuel Aragón y mi papá. Establecieron una tienda aquí en El Paso" [Yes, my father came here with don Manuel Aragón, his uncle. They came with Felix Martínez. He brought Doctor Romero, Manuel Aragón, and my father. They established a store here in El Paso] (Chacón, "Interview"). Martínez had a decisive influence on a group of nuevomexicano editors and businesspeople who picked up and moved with him to El Paso at the turn of the twentieth century. While working at the store, Felipe and others attended a gala event sponsored annually by the Mexican, British, German, and US consulates in Ciudad Juárez, and there he met Otila Cristina Domínguez, a native of Rosales, Chihuahua. The two married soon after in 1902.

Felipe returned to Las Vegas two years later, and the English-language paper *Las Vegas Daily Optic* reported that he was opening up a brokerage business on Bridge Street. Felipe also continued to work as a journalist, sending items to various newspapers during this time, including an editorial published in the *El Paso Times* in 1911 endorsing Octaviano Larrazolo for governor of New Mexico. The piece was reprinted in Chacón's hometown paper, *La Voz del Pueblo*, and presumably served to keep him in good stead with the paper; he became an associate editor of *La Voz* in 1911.

Political Agitator

Felipe Chacón maintained running disputes with various politicians that lasted for months and even years. He was known for casting criticism in highly partisan ways, as either a supporter or a detractor of particular political causes. Chacón supplied enough vituperation in his columns to put him at odds with some elected officials for years. Felipe feuded with Casimiro Barela, the president of the Colorado Senate and the owner of two newspapers, *El Progreso* (Trinidad,

Colorado) and *Las Dos Repúblicas* (Denver, Colorado). Barela was also Eusebio Chacón's father-in-law. The enmity between them seems to have stemmed from political differences, but whatever the precise nature of those disagreements they were aired nearly in the language of personal vendetta.

The initial clash was bitter enough to erupt again years later and harden into a political matter when Felipe took the job of associate editor of *La Voz del Pueblo*, a paper published by Barela's political rival, Felix Martínez. Chacón, assigned to cover the most recent session of the state legislature, had, according to Barela, libeled him and misrepresented him to the public. In January 1913, Barela publicly admonished Felipe for his lack of judgment and professionalism, placing a letter in *El Independiente* of Las Vegas and in *La Revista de Taos*. The piece was meant to cut down Chacón the journalist and was titled "Con el fin de que el pueblo sepa la conducta pública de Felipe M. Chacón, editor(?) de *La Voz del Pueblo*, doy las siguientes explicaciones personales" [So That the Community Is Aware of the Public Conduct of Felipe M. Chacón, the Editor of *La Voz del Pueblo*, I Offer these Personal Explanations].

Ostensibly, Barela's chief gripe was that Chacón provided a spurious account of Barela's visit to the New Mexico legislature. Chacón told his readers in *La Voz* that the Colorado senator was in Santa Fe to promote himself in the hope that the Republicans would draft him to be a US senator for New Mexico, a vacancy the New Mexico legislature was charged with filling. Barela wrote that his motives were completely aboveboard: "Como siempre he sido un defensor del pueblo hispano-americano y pongo esto sobre cualquier vínculo de partido; durante mi estancia en Santa Fe me empeñé para que la legislatura nombrara un neo-mexicano como senador al congreso nacional, el Sr. Larrazolo, o algún miembro del partido republicano que fuera competente para tan alto puesto" [I have always been a defender of the Hispano community and I place this over any party association; during my time in Santa Fe I worked so that the legislature would name a nuevomexicano to be a senator in Congress, be that Mr. Larrazolo or some other member of the Republican Party]. Barela said his motives were disinterested and that he put forth the idea that the Mexicans should form a union in both chambers of the legistlature to elect a Hispano as senator, either Republican or Democrat.

What really set Barela off was a report Felipe had circulated earlier in the year suggesting that Barela had lost his reelection bid to the Colorado Senate.

Barela was so incensed that readers would buy this false report that, in an attempt to set the record straight, he put the matter before Chacón's boss, Felix Martínez. Barela reported that Martínez appeared to side with him by responding that his views differed greatly from that of the reporter. Perhaps feeling that there was a wedge between Chacón and Martínez, Barela clearly hoped his letter would dislodge Felipe from *La Voz*. Barela's lengthy, four-column letter was a barrage of insults, name calling, and impolite invectives. "Felipillo" (a disparaging diminutive of "Felipe") was called "morongo" [lazy], "solapado" [crafty], "sátrapa" [sly], "chiflado adulón" [mad sycophant], "alacrán" [scorpion], and "bufón"[jester]. Barela was effusive: "Chacón es tan menguado en tamaño como en conocimiento natural" [Chacón is as short in stature as he is of common sense]. Barela declared that he was at a loss to understand why after years of knowing each other, Chacón would attack him without provocation: "no tengo idea del por qué de su mala fe, pues nunca le he hecho daño alguno, ni a él, ni a su familia" [I have no idea where his bad faith comes from, since I have never done anything to harm him or his family].

Barela reasoned that Chacón's character flaws were the result of having grown up without the direction of his father, who died when Felipe was a boy. But Chacón alone was responsible for his despicable ways, Barela believed, since he had known and worked collaboratively with Felipe's father: "Su padre, el Hno. Urbano Chacón fue hasta su muerte, íntimo amigo mío. Fue republicano como lo es la familia Chacón, pero se cambió Demócrata a sugestion mía y de Jesús Ma. García. Le ayudamos para que publicara el primer periódico en español en Trinidad. Lo elegimos como represntante a la primera legislatura del estado y al tiempo de su muerte estaba en deuda conmigo" [His father, the honorable Urbano Chacón, was up to his death, a close personal friend. He was a Republican but changed to Democrat at my suggestion and that of Jesús María García. We helped him publish the first newspaper in Spanish in Trinidad. We elected him as a representative to the first legislature of the state, and when he died he owned me money].

Barela may have drawn first blood, but Felipe did not let the matter rest and counterpunched by publishing a short ditty about Barela in *El Anunciador de Trinidad* in April 1918. *El Anunciador*, a rival in business and politics to the Barela political machine, readily accepted the submission. Felipe titled his verse "El viejo babas" [Old Man Spittle] and laid in to Barela (see table 1). Despite

TABLE I

Estás muy flaco para buen cochino	You are too skinny to be a good pig
Porque eres cerdo sin estar cebado,	Not having been fattened yet, you're still a pig,
Y ni las gentes que aman el tocino	Even folks who love bacon
A un cerdo como tú AMANCEBADO.[a]	Don't like you, fattened pig.
Tu ser en cuerpo y alma está viciado,	Your entire being, body and soul, is empty
Y de amasar su pan con tu manteca,	Buttering her loaves of bread with your fat,
Aun cuando estabas menos atenuado,	Even in times when you were slim
Se escapa de morirse la Re-B-K.	Rebecca, more dead than alive, barely squeaks by.
Max Fel y Pilyo[b]	

a. Chacón plays on the verb "to love," amar. "They love" [aman] is the first half of the compound noun amancebado. Amancebado means to shack up or live with a woman outside of marriage. The second half of the noun, cebado, means "to fatten," more emphatically "to layer in fat."

b. Chacón's wordplay here requires the reader to decipher the identities of the people the verse alludes to, including the identity of the poet who is spinning the lines. Readers must first decide who "el viejo babas" is and then Felipe adds a modernist twist. "Re-B-K" stands for the mistress, Rebecca, and "Max Fel y Pilyo" for the bard's first two names, Felipe Maximiliano (something like Max Little Phil). There's an added twist since "Pilyo" can also be rendered in standard Spanish as pillo [rascal].

the outward playfulness of the verse, the jest was a bullet aimed at the heart of Casimiro Barela's reputation. It outed Barela, a family man and pillar of the mexicano community in southern Colorado, and besmirched his honor by accusing him of having a mistress whom he kept—poorly, despite his obvious wealth (for more on Barela, see Meléndez, *Biography of Casimiro Barela*).

On three other occasions, Felipe was at the center of scandal and public squabble. In November 1913, the *Las Vegas Daily Optic* reported that Manuel C. de Baca, the editor of *El Sol de Mayo*, had filed a charge of libel against Felipe for defaming him in *La Voz*. In February of the following year, Manuel's brother, Ezequiel C. de Baca, an editor at *La Voz* and the lieutenant governor of New Mexico, was arrested on charges of having accosted Felipe. Herminia Chacón recalled having heard as a child that, although the two men were *compadres* (Felipe and Otila Cristina had earlier served as godparents to Ezequiel's daughter Natalia), they got into a row over "una cosa que no vale la pena" [a small, useless thing]. Herminia attributed the problem to the habit of Ezequiel C.

de Baca of claiming that he was a blueblood and a direct descendant of the famous sixteenth-century Spanish explorer-trekker Álvar Núñez Cabeza de Vaca. Felipe eventually tired of Ezequiel's presumptions and in one conversation retorted that "he had in his line at least two knights of Santiago and one of Calatrava." Ezequiel responded by punching Felipe in the face and bloodying his nose. This ended Felipe's employment as business manager and associate editor of *La Voz*. Chacón left Las Vegas to work for Elfego Baca at *La Opinión Pública* in Old Town Albuquerque before going on to establish *El Faro del Río Grande*, a paper Chacón issued for a time in Bernalillo and Socorro, New Mexico. The remaining editors at *La Voz* got the last word in print on Felipe in an item they titled "De faro a farol, hay gran distinción" [There's a Huge Difference between a Lantern and a Lighthouse]. The staff at *La Voz* jabbed at Felipe in prose and verse:

> Felipito, el del Farol, se ha metido a mata piojos, y en sus afanes espulgadores revisa de arriba y abajo a *La Voz del Pueblo*, sacando a colación todos los errores en caja, que puidiera haber en la misma, dizque para desmostrar al público que, de acuerdo con *La Estrella* los que escriben en *La Voz* son unos solemnes papanatas.

> [Little Felipe of *El Farol* has decided to go into the business of killing lice and is using his lice-picking talent to check *La Voz del Pueblo* from head to toe, gathering together all its typos in a box, and, as he says, to show the public that *La Estrella* has it right when that paper writes that all who write for *La Voz* are a bunch of simpletons.]

> Chaconcito, Chaconcito
> Habla bien y despacio
> No sea que por grámatico
> Vayan a dejarte extático.

> [Little Mr. Chacón, Little Mr. Chacón,
> Speak slowly and with care,
> So you are not taken for a grumpy grammarian
> And left bereft and bewildered.]

Felipe was back in Las Vegas in 1917 working as an editor for *El Independiente*, a paper owned and operated by Enrique Salazar. Chacón, it seems, could not free himself from his prior reputation and found his name sullied in the papers again, this time due to an altercation in public with José Jordí, a Catalan editor on staff at *La Voz*. The *Albuquerque Morning Journal* reported that after exchanging insults in their respective papers, the pair clashed on a street in town at which point Chacón called Jordí a *tamalero* (translated in the *Journal* as "tamale vendor") and took up a rock to defend himself. Jordí, who also was a mounted policeman, brandished a pistol and attempted to arrest a defiant Chacón. Jordí later added a resisting arrest charge to his complaint. The judge dismissed the latter charge and found that Jordí had no right to be carrying a gun in public since officers could only be armed if they were in the process of serving a warrant.

Beyond any personal animus, political affiliations were at the core of this matter since Chacón's new employer, *El Independiente*, was, despite its name, staunchly aligned with the Republican Party and Jordí's *La Voz* was Democratic. The clash with Jordí might have been the reason Felipe headed to Trinidad, Colorado, at the end of December 1918, as was noted in the press: "donde se hará cargo del periódico que se publica en español en dicha ciudad" [he will take charge of the newspaper that's published in Spanish in that city].

Felipe M. Chacón was at the helm of several papers over his career. In 1914 he had announced the establishment of *El Faro del Río Grande* in quite figurative terms:

> Como un pequeño retoño de esta magna institución, fresco y lleno de vida, nos es grato presentarle al público lector del condado de Sandoval en particular, y al de Nuevo México en general, *El Faro del Río Grande*, periódico independiente, de ilustración y novedades, que verá la luz pública el jueves de cada semana, repleto de todas las nuevas de más interés a nuestro pueblo, y realzado por vivos e interesantes editoriales artículos de fondo y obras de mérito literario poéticas y prosáicas.

> [As a small offshoot of this great institution, fresh and full of life, we are happy to present to the reading public of Sandoval County, in particular, and of New Mexico in general, *El Faro del Río Grande*, an independent

newspaper of learning and news, which will be out on Thursday of each week, replete with the most important news to our community and enhanced with lively and interesting in-depth editorials, in-depth articles, and quality literary works of poetry and prose.]

Journalists like Chacón occupied a central space in nuevomexicano society, and the causes they espoused often became the object of popular scorn and ridicule, which at times found an outlet in the very newspapers they were associated with. As an example, Ignacio S. Duarte's contribution to *La Bandera Americana* in anticipation of Christmas 1920 consisted of a thirty-five-strophe *décima* or corrido he called "La Cucaracha: Santa Clos, nos trajo Chrismas" [Cockroach: Santa Brought Us Gifts]. The verses start out with a local figure, "The Roach," fretting over the prospect of a dismal and giftless Christmas. Around midnight, Santa, who is traveling through southern Colorado and New Mexico towns, appears. The Roach decides to follow along as the bearded visitor stops at the offices of several Spanish-language newspapers, doling out gifts to writers, editors, staff members, owners, and politicians:

Ayer ya entrada la noche,
Nuestra buena cucaracha,
Se puso su mejor hilacha
Y se fue a pasear en coche.

Muy triste y desconsolada,
Andaba zurciendo chismes
Y pensando la desdichada
Que naide le traería "crismes."

Eran a punto de las dos,
Y al cruzar en callejón
Se encontró con Santa Clos
Con regalos de á montón.

[In the wee hours of the night
Our good roach
Got dressed in her best rags,
And went out to cruise by car.

Very sad and disheartened
She was about mending gossip
And thinking as she went,
Ain't nobody bringing me Christmas.

As the clock struck two
And crossing through an alley
She bumped into Santa
With his bag loaded with gifts.]

The individuals and newspapers Duarte named were known to Chacón and were the settings for and participants in many of his newspaper antics. Below are a few of the gifts Santa delivered, all, of course, given with zest and biting satire.

To Antonio Lucero, associate editor of *La Voz del Pueblo*:

A Toño Lucero,
Yo bien lo sé
Por ser su buen aparcero,
Le trajo unas medias y un corsé.

[To Tony Lucero,
This I know that for being
the sharecropper that he is,
He brought him some socks and a corset.]

Gifts for Nestor Montoya and Francisco Hubbell as they feuded over *La Bandera Americana*:

Para Don Nestor Montoya
Trajo un grandísimo tanque,
Dos cañones y hasta una olla
Para que le atore a Franque.

[To Sir Nestor Montoya,
He brought a big tank,
Two pieces of artillery and a big pot
To stick these to Frank [Hubbell].]

Al director(?) de la Banda,
Al maestro, Juan Faschico,
Le trajo una cara panda
Y un diploma de borrico.

[To the editor(?) of *La Bandera*,
The maestro of simpletons, Juan Faschico,
He brought a panda bear mask
And a diploma on his graduation to donkey.]

Three gifts, to José (Pepé) Jordí, associate editor; to Anastacio Cobley, head typesetter; and to the staff of *La Voz del Pueblo*:

Para don Pepé Jordí,
Que es tan "corto" de nasals,
Trajo cincuenta tamales
De chivo y jabalí.

[For Sir Joey Jordí
with his nasally voice,
He brought fifty tamales
Filled with goat and wild boar meat.]

Para Cobley, el impresor
Más competente y activo,
Trajo un gran "componedor"
Forado en cuero de chivo.

[For Cobley, the most
able and active typesetter,
He brought a great, goatskin-lined
composing table.]

A los "Voz de los Encierros,"
Santa Clos les trajo sopita,
Un "guey" y doscientos cueros,
Y un editor con "pepita."

[For those at the "Voice of the Corralled,"
Santa brought bread pudding
and an ox, two hundred lambskins,
And a nugget of an editor.]

Two gifts to the staff of *El Independiente*:

De los pobres "independientes"
Santa Clos no se olvidó
Pa que se curen les dio,
Cien rechinidos de dientes.

[Santa didn't forget
Those poor "independent" cats.
To help them get back on their feet,
He gave them one hundred gnashing teeth.]

Al viril "Independiente,"
Le trajo un perrito "cuete"
Para que muerda a la gente,
Demócrata del chisgueta.

[To that very macho *Independiente*,
He brought a spiffy little hound
Trained to bite Democrats
As they take a snort.]

To *El Progreso* of Trinidad, Colorado, and its owner, Casimiro Barela:

Un bolsheviki travieso,
Socialista y bravucón
Trajo para "El Progreso,"
El pobre Viejo barbón.

[The poor, bearded old man
Brought to *El Progreso*
A rambunctious Bolshevik,
a socialist and a bully boy.]

To *El Boletín Popular* of Santa Fe, New Mexico:

Y al "Boletín Popular,
que tanto quiere "gachuza"
le trajo un hermoso
par de loros y una lechuza.

[And to *El Boletín Popular*,
so in love with packs of cats
He brought a beautiful pair
Of parrots and a night owl.]

To *El Anunciador de Trinidad* of Colorado:

Para el pobre "Anunciador,"
Vino un frasco con "vampiro"
Para curarle el ardor
A su "trampe" que no olvido.

[For the wretched *Anunciador*,
There's a jar with some vampire juice
To cure the burning itch of its roving tramp
The one I can't shake from my mind.]

To *Revista Ilustrada* of Santa Fe and its editor, Camilo Padilla:

Al bueno de don Camilo,
Le trajo dos piernas "gueras"
Para que les agarre el hilo
Y pueda hasta echar carreras.

[To good old Sir Camilo,
He brought two blond legs
So he can latch onto them
And even be able to run some footraces.]

Chacón's employment stabilized by the end of 1922 after he became the managing editor of *La Bandera Americana* in Albuquerque. The position came to him following years of litigation between Francisco and Santiago Hubbell, who headed the board of La Bandera Corporation, and Nestor Montoya, the paper's founder, who continued to claim a stake in the business.[2] In November 1922, *La Bandera Americana* announced, "La Corte Suprema acaba de pronunicar en el asusto, 'La Bandera Americana' vuelve otra vez al dominio de su dueño original que es la Corporación de ese mismo nombre" [The Supreme Court has just made a pronouncement on the subject, *La Bandera Americana* will return to the control of the original owner that is the Corporation of the same name]. The same column provided Chacón with the opportunity to lay out the aim and purpose of *La Bandera* under his editorship. In terms of electoral politics, *La Bandera Americana* without apology embraced the platform and goals of the Republican Party but vowed to respect other political views: "En nuestras polémicas políticas, por consiguiente, jamás nos olvidaremos que la caballerosidad, el decoro y el respeto debido a las opiniones de otros, deben siempre caracterizar toda discucion [sic] entre gentes decentes y de amplio criterio" [Therefore, in our debates, we shall never forget to be polite and keep to the ideal that decorum and respect for the views of others should measure all discussion among decent, open-minded people] ("Nuestro saludo").

In April 1923, Chacón reaffirmed the work of his paper and took the opportunity to announce that *La Bandera Americana* was installing a new press and would be sharing offices with the *Albuquerque Herald*. Chacón wrote that improvements to the press, linotype, and graphics would make it possible for *La Bandera* to turn out an eight-page, seven-column weekly with state-of-the-art graphics. Chacón again announced that *La Bandera Americana* would keep to its principles and "seguira siendo un fiel adalid y compeón de los intereses del pueblo hispanoamericano, los cuales vigilará con celo en todo tiempo" [will continue to be a faithful defender and champion of the interests of the

Hispano community, which it will watchfully guard at all times] ("Será un grande empresa periodística").

It was during Chacón's time at *La Bandera Americana* that his reputation as a writer and poet of talent solidified. Soon after his arrival at the paper, praise from the desks of other editors in New Mexico began to tumble onto the pages of *La Bandera*:

El Independiente (Las Vegas), November 3, 1922:
Seguros estamos que no somos nosotros los únicos que nos alegramos de ver empuñar la pluma de nuevo al Sr. Chacón sino miles de lectores se sienten del mismo modo, pues conocen sus escritos y saben que es competente y capaz de ilustrar al pueblo. Bienvenido seas amigo y ojalá que nuestra humilde pluma pudiera un día igualar la vuestra.

[We are sure that we are not the only ones glad to see Mr. Chacón take up his pen again, but so too thousands of readers who feel exactly the same; they are aware of his writings and know him to be competent and very able to enlighten the community. Be ever welcome, my friend, and here's hoping my humble pen might one day equal yours.]

La Revista Popular, December 15, 1922:
Felicitamos de todo corazón a nuestro colega por la magnifica adquisicion que hizo al conseguir los servicios de un periodista de la capacidad del Sr. Chacón con lo que no damos por pronto adquirirá mayor fama el referido semanario.

[We congratulate with all our heart our sister newspaper for its coup in acquiring the services of a journalist with the skills of Mr. Chacón, and by this we can see that in a short time the newspaper will acquire even greater fame.]

El Nuevo Estado (Tierra Amarilla), December 7, 1923:
Bajo la pluma de oro del escritor Neo-Mexicano, don Felipe Chacón, *La Bandera Americana* se ha colocado por ensima [sic] de las publicaciones

escritas en el bello y clásico idioma de Cervantes, pues Felipe, empuña una pluma de oro y diamante y sus frases castellanas son filigranas y flores jardines retóricas y palabras que tocan el sentimentalismo del alma de nuestro buen pueblo.

[With the golden pen of the nuevomexicano writer, Mr. Felipe Chacón, *La Bandera Americana* has risen above all the papers written in the beautiful and classic language of Cervantes; thus, Felipe holds a pen of gold and diamonds, and his expressions in Spanish (Castilian) are filigree and florid gardens of splendid rhetoric and words that touch the emotions of our good people.]

Nuestro ilustre poeta [Our Illustrious Poet]

Chacón began to publish poems, which would later be reprinted in *Poesía y prosa*, with regularity soon after arriving at *La Bandera*, although he had often submitted his verses to other newspapers previously. Before having an official tie to the paper, Chacón had sent the holiday poem "La navidad" to *La Bandera*, where it appeared in the December 21, 1917, issue. The poem was reprinted several more times by *La Bandera* and other papers as a seasonal piece. Another poem, the patriotic laud "A la patria," appeared on the Fourth of July in various years. In November 1922, Chacón's poem "A la Señora Adelina Otero-Warren," a tribute to the first nuevomexicana candidate for Congress, was published in support of her campaign. A number of other *Poesía y prosa* poems appeared in *La Bandera* in 1924 and 1925.[3]

In an article entitled "Escritores neo-mexicanos," Isidoro Armijo, a contributor to *La Revista de Taos*, produced a tally of the best-known and active nuevomexicano writers (for more on Armijo, see Meléndez, *So All Is Not Lost*). Armijo began with a lament for the lack of public acknowledgment of these writers and their work: "Nuevo México cuenta con algunos genios hispano-americanos. Pero debido a que uno en su propio suelo desmerece a merced de sus paisanos, estos ilustres hombres carecen de encomio popular" [New Mexico has a number of Hispano intellects. But because we in our own land undervalue our countrymen, these illustrious men work without praise, unknown to the public]. Armijo mentioned authors Luis Tafoya, Camilo Padilla,

Aurelio Espinosa, Eusebio Chacón, Benjamin Read, and Felipe M. Chacón, providing a short note in tribute to each. Concerning Chacón he said, "poeta contemporáneo, periodista y selecto escritor de muchas obras inéditas" [a contemporary poet, journalist, and exquisite writer of many unpublished works]. In an addendum, the editor of *La Revista de Taos* suggested that Armijo had failed at his task and missed a name, saying, "Mas nosotros en calidad de justicieros e imparciales, era imposible que pasara desaprecibido este punto, y por cierto nos hemos permitido agregar a la lista de los brillantes escritores con que cuenta Nuevo México, el nombre de Isidoro I. Armijo" [However, for us, being just and impartial, it was impossible for us to let the point slip by, and we give ourselves permission to add to the list of brilliant writers that New Mexico has the name of Isidoro I. Armijo].

Several of the writers in the group were regular contributors to the literary, history, and culture sections that populated *La Bandera* even prior to Chacón becoming the paper's editor. The various projects and research into New Mexico history taken up by Benjamin Read over the course of a decade found mention in *La Bandera*,[4] as did the works of Armijo, who would become Chacón's most avid supporter, advancing the lauds he believed Chacón rightly merited. Armijo, for example, contributed "Meditaciones inspiradas por las obras literarias del bardo de Nuevo México FMC" [Meditation Inspired by the Literary Works of the Bard of New Mexico FMC] (*La Bandera Americana*, September 19, 1924), "Un libro en cada hogar de Nuevo México" [A Book in Each New Mexican Home] (*La Bandera Americana*, February 13, 1925), and "Nuestro ilustre poeta" [Our Illustrious Poet] (*La Bandera Americana*, June 5, 1924).

Chacón's reputation and that of his community were mutually constitutive, as one colleague put it: "a cuyo pueblo el autor dignifica y enaltece con pertenecer" [a people the author dignifies and raises up by being part of it]. Six months after the publication of *Poesía y prosa*, someone—likely Isidoro Armijo—provided a lengthy summation of Chacón's merit and the importance of his book for the Spanish-speaking community of the greater Southwest. Armijo remarked on the high quality of the book as a publication, "a work of 183 pages, excellently bound," and then spoke of how from the earliest times the art of poetry has been judged to be the best measure to understand the stature of a society. He reminded readers, "Un pueblo que tiene poetas dotados y solo estando dotados pueden serlo—es un pueblo superior" [A people that has gifted poets—and only by having gifts and talents can they be called poets—is a superior community]. Armijo offered the sort of praise that would today appear as a back cover blurb recommending the book and its author:

> El pueblo hispano de todo el Gran Suroeste debe sentir justo orgullo de tener entre sus hermanos un poeta tan brillante como el autor Chacón; la extirpe [sic] de hombres con su poesía inspiran la formación de grandes naciones y poderosos Imperios; que formaron la base de la civilización y que fueron el orgullo de la humanidad.

> [The Spanish-speaking people of the greater Southwest should feel just pride to count as a brother a poet as brilliant as the writer Chacón, one of that lineage of men who through poetry inspire the building of great nations and powerful empires that have always been seen as the foundation of civilization and have been the pride of humanity.]

Following the logic of the times, Chacón's lyric contribution was representative of the highest achievement in the arts. To drive home the point, Armijo dropped the names of poets high in the canon of Western civilization: Virgil and Lord Byron. He then contended that the Spanish-speaking community, the Mexican Americans of the Southwest, should aspire to "la norma respectable de vida que los pueblos blancos deben ocupar" [the respectable norms of life that the white communities occupy], "en vez de seguirnos gradualmente resblando al nivel del peonaje y la esclavitud al cual nuestro pueblo lenta pero seguramente ha ido caminando en los últimos años" [instead of the gradual slip toward peonage and slavery, the direction in which our community has been headed in recent years].

Some key touchstones have continued to lead me back to Felipe M. Chacón's story. The first was the early reprinting of Chacón's work by Anselmo Arellano in *Los pobladores nuevo mexicanos y su poesía: 1889–1950*, where eleven of the original poems from *Poesía y prosa* appear. Next was the scholarship of Doris Meyer, as I have noted. Two uncanny connections came from the words of Felipe's daughter Herminia, which were imparted to me in person and by letter when I was working on *So All Is Not Lost*. In a sense, doña Herminia's interests neatly coincided with her father's efforts in letters and journalism. In an October 1995 letter, she noted, "I am very happy someone is finally recognizing our old Spanish-language newspapers and editors. I look forward to your book and would be happy to contribute what information I may have." She did contribute mightily and not just by recalling aspects of her father's activities but through her own contributions to *La Bandera Americana* in the 1920s, to the El Paso Historical Society quarterly in the 1970s, and finally to *La herencia del norte* in the 1990s (see Meléndez, "Herminia Chacón"; Meléndez, *So All Is Not Lost*).

Finally, there was a small yet most personal link, one occasioned by Arellano, a good friend and researcher, who brought to my attention an item from the *Santa Fe New Mexican* that he thought would be of special interest to me. It was a short article published in May 1919 that reported on the closing exercises for the eighth-grade graduation at the public school in Mora, New Mexico, a school then run by the Sisters of Loreto. Chacón, at the time the editor of the Spanish weekly *El Eco del Norte*, had given a rousing talk exhorting the young graduates to continue their education. Among the twelve graduating eighth-graders sat my father, Manuel Santos Meléndez. The children listened to Chacón deliver a talk in eloquent and formal English. He exhorted, "Don't be contented and satisfied with the degree of education you have thus far attained. It is but one of the first steps in the stairway of life" ("High School Education"). Chacón's speech was filled with moralizing zest, including a passionate condemnation of sloth, typical of the motivational talk one would expect to hear at such ceremonies across the United States in 1919. It is important to note that this was coming from a respected and accomplished member of the nuevomexicano community whose achievements had been aided by education, and it is equally important to understand that the students, parents, and teachers in attendance were residents of one of the poorest Hispano rural communities in the nation.

Manuel Santos would indeed complete his high school education and kept turning to books for the rest of his life. In his stories of growing up, my father frequently mentioned how there had been a generation of orators in New Mexico: "tenían el don de la palabra" [they had the gift of words]. By this he meant that they could captivate an audience and by wit, grace, and conviction win over listeners, all the while educating, enlightening, and entertaining through the dexterity of their verbal artistry. With the recovery of *Poesía y prosa*, and having the full measure of Felipe M. Chacón's work to consider, I most especially value this last touchstone. It permits me to imagine, and almost hear, Felipe's voice, his cadence rising and falling, his inflections cascading and sonorous, his exhortations clear in defense of his most cherished activity: poetry.

Works Cited

Arellano, Anselmo. *Los pobladores nuevo mexicanos y su poesía, 1889–1950*. Albuquerque, NM: Pajarito, 1976.
Chacón, Herminia. "Interview," March 2, 1996. Video interview conducted by Anselmo Arellano and Arsenio Córdova. Used with permission of Anselmo Arellano.
Meléndez, A. Gabriel. *The Biography of Casimiro Barela*. Albuquerque: University of New Mexico Press, 2003.
———. "Herminia Chacón." In *The Greenwood Encyclopedia of Latino Literature*, vol. 1, ed. Nicolás Kanellos. Westport, CT: Greenwood, 2008, 220–21.
———. *So All Is Not Lost: The Poetics of Print in Nuevomexicano Communities, 1834–1958*. Albuquerque: University of New Mexico Press, 1997.
Meléndez, A. Gabriel, and Francisco Lomelí, eds. *The Writings of Eusebio Chacón*. Albuquerque: University of New Mexico Press, 2012.
Meyer, Doris. "Felipe Maximiliano Chacón: A Forgotten Mexican American Author." *New Scholar* 6 (1977): 111–26. Reprinted in *New Directions in Chicano Scholarship*, ed. R. Romo and R. Paredes. San Diego: Center for Chicano Studies, University of California, 1984.
———. *Speaking for Themselves*. Albuquerque: University of New Mexico Press, 1996.
Nogar, Anna M. "Navigating a Fine Bilingual Line in Early Twentieth-Century New Mexico: *El cantor neomexicano* Felipe Maximiliano Chacón," in *Writing/Righting History: 25 Years of Recovering the U.S. Hispanic Literary Heritage*, vol. 10, ed. Antonia Castañeda and Clara Lomas. Houston, TX: Arte Público Press, 2020, 337–49.

PERIODICAL SOURCES

"Acróstico a don Felipe Chacón," *La Bandera Americana*, Albuquerque, NM, February 8, 1924.
"La Bandera Americana," *La Bandera Americana*, Albuquerque, NM, December 28, 1923.
"Con el fin de que el pueblo sepa la conducta pública de Felipe M. Chacón, editor(?) de *La Voz del Pueblo*, doy las siguientes explicaciones personales," *El Independiente*, Las Vegas, NM, January 30, 1913, and *La Revista de Taos*, Taos, NM, January 31, 1913.
"La cucaracha: Santa Clos, nos trajo Chrismas," *La Bandera Americana*, Albuquerque, NM, December 21, 1920.
"De faro a farol, hay gran distinción," *La Voz del Pueblo*, Las Vegas, NM, September 26, 1914.
"Escritores neo-mexicanos," *La Revista de Taos*, Taos, NM, August 11, 1922.

"High School Education of Prime Importance, Speaker Tells Student Pupils at Mora Graduation," *Santa Fe New Mexican*, Santa Fe, NM, May 9, 1919.

"Un libro en cada hogar de Nuevo México," *La Bandera Americana*, Albuquerque, NM, February 13, 1925.

"Meditaciones inspiradas por las obras literarias del bardo de Nuevo México FMC por Isidoro Armijo," *La Bandera Americana*, Albuquerque, NM, September 19, 1924.

"Nuestro ilustre poeta," *La Bandera Americana*, Albuquerque, NM, June 5, 1924.

"Nuestro saludo: Programa de La Bandera Americana," *La Bandera Americana*, Albuquerque, NM, November 17, 1922.

"Será un grande empresa periodística en poco tiempo," *La Bandera Americana*, Albuquerque, NM, April 6, 1923.

"Siempre la Chicana, paga el pato," *La Bandera Americana*, Albuquerque, NM, *La Bandera Americana*," August 25, 1925.

"El testamento del redactor en gefe [sic]," *La Aurora*, Santa Fe, NM, August 9, 1884.

"El viejo babas Barela," *El Anunciador de Trinidad*, Trinidad, CO, April 20, 1918.

Notes

1. Eusebio's talk was most likely an instance of staged performative oratory. The mention in the newspaper illustrates how highly nuevomexicanos prized oratory and speechmaking as displays of intellectual acuity. It's also likely that bringing youths into such performativity was the main objective of this event. For other examples involving Eusebio Chacón, see Meléndez and Lomelí.

2. Nestor Montoya (1862–1923) was a publisher, editor, and president of the state press association. Montoya served as a delegate to the state constitutional convention, regent of the University of New Mexico, and chair of the Bernalillo County Draft Board during World War I. He was elected to the Sixty-Seventh Congress and served from March 1921 until his death in Washington on January 13, 1923.

3. "A la patria" (July 4, 1924; July 3, 1925), "La navidad" and "Otoñal" (December 19, 1924), "A mayo" and "A María ante su altar" (May 1, 1925).

4. Several of Read's writing projects, either proposed or completed, were mentioned in *La Bandera Americana*, including "La historia de nuestros heroes" [The History of Our Heroes], a proposal for a book on the participation of New Mexicans in World War I (January 3, 1919); an announcement that Read was proposed for the position of state historian (February 18, 1921); Read's call for his book *Popular Elementary History of New Mexico* to be used in the public schools (September 30, 1921); "Libro del historiador Read" [Read's Book of History], in which Read proposed writing on the subject of nuevomexicanos in the so-called Indian Wars (November 24, 1922); "La vida de Hernán Cortez" [The Life of Hernán Cortés], which indicated that Read's book was accepted by a well-known publishing house in Boston (January 19, 1923); and "Nuevo México en la Guerra de la Union Americana" [New Mexico in the American Civil War], which noted that Read's book was about to be published with an introduction by Octaviano Larrazolo (April 23, 1923).

ANNA M. NOGAR

Poetics and Their Politics in the Lyric Work of Felipe M. Chacón

No hallo duda de que, en curso de esta evolución del tiempo, las obras literarias de Felipe Maximiliano Chacón están destinadas a dejar como huella una época distinta en la historia literaria de los Estádos Unidos de América.

[I do not doubt that, in the course of time's passage, the literary works of Felipe Maximiliano Chacón are destined to leave as their footprint a distinct epoch in the literary history of the United States of America.]

BENJAMIN READ, "Prologue," *Obras de Felipe M. Chacón, "el cantor neomexicano": Poesía y prosa*

Ahora yo quiero, mi querido suelo,
Que digno de esa gloria, tu gobierno
Tienda sus alas por el ancho cielo
Y sepulte en el golfo de lo eterno

Leyes injustas que tu nombre manchen;
Quiero ver tus archivos relucientes
De datos limpios que tu nombre ensanchen
A través de los siglos sucedentes.

[Now I desire, dear homeland,
That your government, worthy of that glory,
Stretch its wings across the heavens
And bury in the gulf of eternity

The unjust laws that tarnish your name.
I want to see your archives gleam
With resplendent accomplishments bearing your name
Into the centuries to come.]
    —"A Nuevo México" by Felipe Maximiliano Chacón

Felipe M. Chacón wrote these words in his poem commemorating New Mexico's 1912 admission as a state into the United States. The poem's exuberant sensibility and lyric precision, which are tempered with political and social awareness, suffuse Chacón's remarkable *Poesía y prosa*. While the book enjoyed great *aprecio* [appreciation] from Chacón's *nuevomexicano* contemporaries, Chacón's significance as a writer, more specifically as a US citizen who wrote and published literature in Spanish in the late nineteenth and early twentieth centuries, has gone largely unnoticed.[1] With this volume, we seek to establish Chacón as a significant author, a unique early twentieth-century literary figure from a remarkable family lineage of nuevomexicano authors who wrote with political, cultural, and linguistic awareness for their community, including that community's evolving engagement with Spanish-English bilingualism.

As Gabriel Meléndez articulated in in the preceding historical introduction and in his pioneering book *So All Is Not Lost*, many nuevomexicano journalists and writers in the nineteenth and early twentieth centuries were engaged in the project of creating a national literature [*una literatura nacional*] in Spanish representative of Mexican Americans in New Mexico as well as in Texas, Arizona, and Colorado (Meléndez 58–59). The necessity of this literature emerged in part due to the colonizing politics imposed on New Mexico during the territorial period and after. A report made to Congress in 1902 by Indiana senator Albert Beveridge regarding the incorporation of New Mexico and Arizona into the United States argued that New Mexico was unfit to become a state at least partially based on the territory's bilingual and monolingual Spanish inhabitants (Meléndez, "Nuevo México"). This delayed the admission of the two territories by almost a decade and was part and parcel of a countrywide nativism that ultimately resulted, among other ramifications, in the appointment of state superintendents of education in New Mexico who opposed teaching Spanish in public schools to appease that national sentiment. Even New Mexicans who supported statehood recognized the critique of the Spanish language for what it was: baseless xenophobia and the imposition of a hegemonic praxis with the end of disenfranchising nuevomexicanos from political and economic spheres.

As Meléndez and Gonzales-Berry have noted, the types of literary pursuits in which Felipe M. Chacón, Benjamin Read (the author of *Poesía y prosa*'s prologue), and their colleagues participated were therefore no casual affair. Literary and intellectual brilliance expressed through autochthonous works by nuevomexicanos countered a colonizing narrative that declared that New Mexico's people were unlettered, uneducated, and/or incapable of governing themselves. Meléndez has argued that historical texts like Read's *Guerra México-Americana* (1910), *Historia ilustrada de Nuevo México* (1910), *Illustrated History of New Mexico* (1912), and *Popular Elementary History of New Mexico* (1915) were sites where nuevomexicanos ensured that they were not written out of the historical record, that their deeds were accurately recorded from their perspective, and that these histories were accessible to their own community in Spanish. John Nieto-Phillips elaborated on this in the introduction to the *Illustrated History of New Mexico*, noting that Read "felt compelled to undertake the writing of New Mexico's past to correct the inaccuracies that plagued Anglo Americans' writing [on the subject]. Knowing little Spanish, he [Read] wrote, they often resorted to incorrect translations of Spanish colonial documents.... Moreover, histories written in Spanish, he insisted, best preserved the original meaning of Spanish documents" (Nieto-Phillips 189).

In a similar manner, *Poesía y prosa*'s political valence encompasses much more than a book of Spanish poems might suggest. These are poems intentionally and brilliantly written in Spanish at a time when the public role of that language in New Mexico, as a symbol and as a behavior, existed in precarity. As nuevomexicanos faced challenges to their cultural identity, to their history, and to their religious practice, the Spanish language was another aspect of their existence under constant attack from without; it also served as a metonym for those challenges collectively. Chacón wrote in Spanish and bilingually for readers who were forced to accommodate the English language while their own majority language—Spanish—was being systematically and institutionally erased.

In the prologue, Read doubles down on the significance of Chacón's writing in Spanish, specifically in light of Chacón's identity as a US citizen. Read notes that Chacón's use of Spanish should be a point of pride for readers from the United States: "En mi humilde concepto, el pueblo de los Estados

Unidos debe sentirse orgulloso de haber producido uno de sus conciudadanos, que diera lustre a su Patria con las producciones de su talento, en la lengua de aquellos reyes, los reyes Católicos, que tan señaladamente contribuyeron al descubrimiento de América, el continente que habitamos" [In my humble opinion, the United States should be proud of having produced a fellow citizen who offers up glowing praise for his homeland through the talent of his literary production in the language of those kings, the Catholic kings, who so notably contributed to the discovery of America, the continent we inhabit].[2] Although Read resorts to the rhetoric of comparative conquest, his message comes across clearly: writing in Spanish is not a sign of lesser citizenship; rather, it should be seen as a contribution to the greatness of the United States. Indeed, neither Chacón nor his contemporaries saw themselves as anything less than full citizens of the United States. However, and as they were constantly compelled to explain in their writing, this patriotism did not require the excision of their nuevomexicano identity, history, or language, nor did it demand turning a blind eye to the injustices they suffered due to "el insulto proferido / Del prejuicio racial por la malicia" [the insults born of racial hate / So often invoked against you]. As Erlinda Gonzales-Berry noted of nuevomexicanos of the time, "How burdened Hispanics of this period must have been with the suspicion of disloyalty!" (194).

In addition to the important political and social work accomplished by *Poesía y prosa*, the lyrics themselves are priceless, displaying not only artistic skill, but also an important connection to the *modernista* literary movement and implicit messages about bilingualism in early twentieth-century New Mexico.[3] Chacón's poems fit within Latin American and Spanish poetic traditions, suggesting the extent to which he was aware of—and perhaps viewed himself as a contributor to—these literary worlds. So seamless is this continuity that a Spanish reader of these poems might not be aware of Chacón's US nationality. Indeed, Read suggests that global Hispanophone readers understood Chacón's writing as belonging to that larger sphere: "Por otra parte, los pueblos de habla española, lo mismo americanos que europeos e insulares, deben dar la más generosa acogida a las obras de Chacón, obras de uno que, desde extranjero suelo ha sabido hacer honra al dulce idioma de España: lengua de sus propios países, hecho que de suyo reviste méritos acreedores a profundo aprecio" [Moreover, Spanish-speaking people—Americans as well as Europeans and *insulares*—

should openly embrace Chacón's works, as writing by one who, though from a foreign land, has honored the sweet language of Spain—that is, the language of their own countries—an accomplishment that of itself merits profound esteem]. Read makes explicit the connection between Chacón's work and its potential readers in the Americas, Europe, and Philippines who would recognize in it not only the language, but also familiar poetic forms and tropes.

As can be seen throughout the collection, Chacón carefully reproduces the shapes and sounds of Hispanophone poetic forms and pays rigorous attention to the effects these types of poems are intended to convey. Aside from revealing his knowledge of the application of such forms—which he anticipates his readers will likewise understand—Chacón reveals his mastery of language. For example, "Al explorador del oeste" employs the *octava real* form, which lends nobility and regal pacing in this elegy to early Anglo explorers in the West. By contrast, the sweet, precisely metered *quinteto* to his daughter Elvira uses a flawlessly crafted metric to yield the tender, lilting sense Chacón wishes to convey.

In the sections that follow, I examine Chacón's writing as a groundbreaking piece of US-published Spanish-language literature, one that manifests, as the epigraph above indicates, a distinct epoch in the literary history of the United States.[4] First, I consider the poetry as a powerful statement on language maintenance, bilingual literacy, and resistance to colonization in early twentieth-century New Mexico. Next, I read it in light of its explicit political commentary on candidates for office and governance. Shifting to a literary appraisal, I then consider these artistic works in relationship to Latin American poetics, specifically the modernista movement. Finally, I analyze Chacón's creative writing on its own literary and aesthetic terms, considering specific themes and touchstones he elaborates in *Poesía y prosa*.

Bilingual Poetry with a Bilingual Critique

Conditions in New Mexico in the nineteenth and early twentieth centuries led to what may be Chacón's characteristic accomplishment: his intense, perfectly symmetrical bilingualism, which he uses to speak to an audience that likewise understands this way of communicating. Chacón uses this skill to critique Anglo incursion into New Mexico, to comment about the imposition of social conditions and political dynamics onto nuevomexicanos, and to poke fun at those who would demand that nuevomexicanos speak English, while they themselves do not learn the dominant community language, Spanish.

This dynamic is evident in the poem "In Mexico," which is included in the prologue to *Poesía y prosa* and which Read frames as an example of Chacón's command of English. Yet rather than Chacón's English-language ability, what stands out is his precise assessment of his bilingual audience and delivery of a poem that draws on their linguistic abilities as it evokes their political position. Perhaps Read could sense this, for he qualifies the poem with the following explanation: "Estos versos deben tomarse en el espíritu que el autor los intentó: como una ocurrencia de buen humor, y bajo ningún concepto, en sentido ofensivo" [These verses should be taken in the spirit in which the author intended them: as an instance of good humor and, in no sense, with the intent to offend]. I see in the poem what Read believed readers would recognize: a sharp tease in Spanish and English that both pokes fun at English-dominant-speakers who claim to speak Spanish and displays what true symmetrical bilingualism—with a skill for poetic artistry—looks like:

> We met: for me 'twas love at first sight.
> She was divine;
> I prayed her then my soul delight.
> Asked her to make my future bright,
> To be but mine,
> Said she: "No entiendo!"
>
> I love you more than tongue can tell,
> I yield supine;
> Without thee life, in sadness' spell,
> Is but a winter's barren dell,
> Won't you be mine?
> Said she: "No sabe."
>
> Unbounded wealth at your command,
> Rich, superfine,
> All at your feet, belle of this land,
> You'll find anon as you demand,
> If you'll be mine,
> Cried she: "¡Ay Dios!"

Diamonds, gold, all to surprise.
A treasure's thine;
I'll give you, love, a paradise,
A home that queens may long for twice,
Won't you be mine?
Said she: "Oh! Yes me quiere."

Chacón's command of English in this poem is superb. The lexicon impresses not only for the sophisticated words he utilizes, but also for the inclusion of terms that were no longer used in common speech in the early twentieth century, such as "anon," "thine," "'twas," and "thee." Chacón creates a particular tone while showcasing his grasp of the registers and usages of poetic English. The poem's strict conformation to rhyme and rhythm schemes further demonstrates Chacón's creative prowess in English. The first five lines of each stanza follow a strict *abaab* rhyme scheme, with all of the four-syllable lines throughout the poem rhyming with each other: "mine," "thine," "supine," superfine," and so on. Chacón's execution of the "surprise-paradise-twice" series demonstrates a particularly subtle rhyme combination. In a similar manner, the syllabification is precise and consistent throughout the English portions: a pattern of 8-4-8-8-4 carries throughout, with appropriate contractions ("'twas," "won't") and additions ("I'll give you, love, a paradise") to force the verse to fit that rhythmic scheme perfectly. Chacón indicates he can control the handles and levers of English to great poetic effect.

Given the lyricism of the English verse, the four lines of the poem that are partially in Spanish are all the more impactful. In contrast to the sophisticated vocabulary of the English, the Spanish is at best simple ("No entiendo") or stereotypical ("¡Ay Dios!"). In one of the other two cases, it is grammatically incorrect ("Won't you be mine?": "No sabe"), while the other is incomprehensibly mashed between Spanish and English ("Oh! Yes me quiere" in reply to "Won't you be mine?"). The distorted Spanish demonstrates a lack of appropriate conjugation of Spanish verbs in the first-person present tense, usually the first learned verb form, and reflects a commonly held view of how non-Spanish-speakers disfigure the language. In addition, the syllabification of the final lines is inconsistent with the precise rhythm scheme set out in the rest of the poem. The Spanish lines are of five and seven syllables, though without any particular pattern, and thus present a strong dissonance with the rest of the poem's tightly controlled rhythm.

The Spanish-language lines are jarring and interrupt the fluidity of the rest of the poem. What is the purpose behind this uncomfortable juxtaposition? The answer lies in the structure and premise of the poem and in the representative politics of language in New Mexico in the late nineteenth and early twentieth centuries. It seems well within reason that the poem could be read as "In *New* Mexico," especially given the perception of many in the eastern United States that New Mexico was, in fact, Mexico, and the various attempts to change the name of the territory to something that did not invoke Mexico (Meléndez, "Nuevo México"). Chacón might have chosen the title "In Mexico" not only as an ironic commentary on this perception, but also perhaps to neutralize his point, to keep the work from being too finely or locally critical.

Since the setting of the poem is in "New Mexico/Mexico," one can assume that the male poetic voice, which is written in English, is, in the context of the poem, actually speaking in Spanish. His poetic language can be read as a translation of what he said in Spanish to the female persona, a monolingual who responds in broken pidgin Spanish. Seen in this way, there is a disparity between the two speakers' ability to express themselves in Spanish, with the Mexican or nuevomexicano voice much more adroit.

By placing carefully metered and chosen words in the mouth of his nuevomexicano speaker, Chacón underscores the historical fact that while nuevomexicanos moved toward Spanish-English bilingualism, those newly arrived to the state remained mostly monolingual in English. The stock phrases and grammatical train wrecks of the Spanish lines are representations of the poor attempts made by newcomers to the territory to muddle through the nuevomexicanos' "barbarous tongue" rather than learn it correctly, acknowledging its legitimacy. In contrast, the male speaker (whom the reader knows to be speaking in Spanish) expresses himself in flawless English—a reflection of the nuevomexicano forced to learn English. This poetic voice displays mastery of the second language, while the English-dominant individual says only "Oh! Yes me quiere" in pidgin semi-Spanish.

Reading outside the poem as a whole, the bilingual reader would also grasp Chacón's ability to deftly deploy both languages to such cutting effect, since the message of the poem is an implicit criticism of English monolingualism in "[New] Mexico." Though primarily in English, the poem could not have been intended for a monolingual English-speaker, who would not be able to decipher the subversive and political meanings embedded in Chacón's use of Spanish. Indeed, in this poem, Felipe Maximiliano Chacón takes full advantage to express what he does not often say directly elsewhere; as Gonzales-Berry muses, "Perhaps herein lies a clue to Chacón's use of Spanish. He could do, in that language [Spanish], what he dared not do [in] English" (195). By presenting the Spanish-in-English of the primary poetic voice, Chacón addresses a long-standing political inequality in New Mexico that was especially acute for the nuevomexicano bilinguals for whom he wrote. Chacón understood the meaning in who spoke which languages and what that speech signified for nuevomexicano political agency, and used his verse as the site for its expression. The poem is remarkably controlled and strategic in its expression of an ongoing and painful dynamic for nuevomexicanos, who since 1848 had seen their language used as a political chit against them and increasingly experienced its disappearance in public spaces.

A similar bilingual approach, which again is intended for and relies on the capacity of a bilingual audience to decipher its meaning, emerges in "Un republicano real." Chacón's primary objective is to critique carpetbagger William "Bull" Andrews for his exaggerated claims of heroic military service, which he used to advance his political career at the expense of nuevomexicano political candidates. Chacón accomplishes this using the bilingual wordplay that he knows his readers will understand. He moves between different meanings for words in Spanish and in English, saying that Andrews considers himself a "real" republican (that is, as a soldier, he fought for the republic of the United States of America), but Chacón takes the English "real" and spins it into the Spanish term for a colonial-era form of money, the "real" coin. Chacón writes:

Un republicano
   que dice que es "Real,"
Pieza de cuartilla
   o claco no más.

[A republican
Who says that he is worth a "real,"
When it's more like a quarter
Or penny, no more.]

In this clever bilingual game, the "real" republican is not worth a "real"—he is at most worth twenty-five cents or a penny. Chacón sharpens this juxtaposition by using the local Spanish terms for money ("real" is still used in the present day to refer to a large coin) to contrast in a harsh joke with the English-language "real." After several stanzas critical of Andrews's exaggerated recounting of his military prowess (made by someone who "sólo exhala / vapores y gas" [only exhales / Steam and gas]), Chacón returns to the eponymous motif at the poem's close. Chacón recalls his critique of Andrews's claims, specifically of how the military paid him additional money for his service, and drops the reader into the bilingual tension of the real/real: "Persista en su tema / tan digno de 'un real'" [He persists in his subject matter / So worthy of one "real [republican]"] or "so worthy of a few cents."

Underscoring his special ability with language, Chacón purposefully includes seven translations of English-language poems. He does not provide a rationale for why these translations are included, but I propose that Chacón does so to draw attention to his symmetrical bilingualism, in effect performing knowledge of English-language poetry and translation for a bilingual audience. With the exception of one poem, which he describes as a free translation, the Spanish translations preserve the originals' meter and rhyme scheme, reproducing the content as well as the aesthetic sense of the English-language poems. This is extremely difficult to execute and requires considerable skill, as Read notes: "sólo tenemos que referirnos a las traducciones de obras de grandes poetas de habla inglesa, que aparecen en este libro, para palpar la pericia del autor; sus íntimos conocimientos de ambos idiomas" [we have but to read his translations of works by great English-speaking poets, which appear in this book, to fully appreciate the author's expertise, his intimate knowledge of both languages].

Read also alludes to other poems Chacón wrote in English: "Una de las cosas que todos los que le conocemos admiramos, es la facilidad con que escribe lo mismo el castellano que el inglés, lo mismo en poesía que en prosa. Felipe ha escrito muchas poesías en inglés, serias, festivas y de amor" [One of the things that all who know Felipe admire in him is the uniform ability with which he writes in Spanish and English, and poetry as much as prose. Felipe has written many poems in English—serious ones, witty ones, and love poems]. Only three of these—"Parting," "In Mexico," and "Wouldst Thou?"—are included in *Poesía y prosa*, which raises the question of what the rest of Chacón's English poetry was like and where he published it, or if he published it. When read in the context of a creative book written in Spanish, these English-language poems and the allusion to others draw attention to Chacón's mastery of both languages in an environment where, given the political pressure to remove Spanish from public discourse, "[hubo] pocas o ningunas oportunidades de aprender el castellano con propiedad" [(there were) few or no opportunities to learn Spanish formally]. Chacón resists and contests this in a self-evident manner through his skillful poetic transliteracy.

Politics and Poetics Intertwined

Poesía y prosa offers a glimpse into how Chacón used his poetry as a political platform to critique enemies and laud those he supported. Gonzales-Berry offered a nuanced reading of how the political nature of Chacón's poems and language played a concrete role in nuevomexicano politics: "there is no doubt that Chacón the editor (the political persona) hid behind Chacón the poet to inspire poetry that covertly testifies to a deeply entrenched Nuevo Mexicano political play that for decades has nurtured cultural survival and simultaneously ensured participation in the political machine of the dominant society" (196). Chacón had no fear of leaning in with his political opinions in (often acerbic) lyric format. He focuses on specific political figures, comments on historical moments or important turning points, critiques political conditions, and, most important, speaks up for the political perspective of nuevomexicanos in the face of increasing Anglo encroachment and open efforts to displace nuevomexicanos from the political prominence they maintained from the colonial period through the early twentieth century.

Chacón openly supports several nuevomexicano political figures, notably Octaviano Larrazolo and Adelina "Nina" Otero-Warren. In "Mi escogido y mis razones," Chacón explains why Larrazolo merits his lauds, and how he is supported by the people of New Mexico:

"¡Que viva Larrazolo y el Progreso!"
Y de orgullo entusiástico se agita;
¡Es la unánime voz del pueblo egrégico
Del histórico y culto Nuevo México!

["Long live Larrazolo and Progress!"
And with enthusiastic pride the people clamor,
The unanimous voice of the historical and erudite
New Mexico!]⁵

Chacón builds support for Larrazolo in his approbatory verse, noting his intellect and nobility and flatteringly comparing him to figures in Greek and Roman mythology (Athena, Pericles) to elevate his persona. Most significant from a political perspective, Chacón repeatedly asserts nuevomexicanos' historical importance and capacity for good judgment and governance ("Del histórico y culto Nuevo México").

In addition to praising Larrazolo as a political candidate, Chacón denounces both the open and covert subversion of nuevomexicanos as leaders on the basis of their culture and race, a xenophobic fiction perpetuated by the political opposition. Chacón openly decries how the election was stolen from Larrazolo as a result of political favoritism and how the recipient of the office, Bull Andrews, accepted his ill-won victory with no guilt at all. Chacón is bracingly direct in detailing how nuevomexicano political leadership was unscrupulously subverted. The poem's conclusion condemns the racism Larrazolo suffered, which affected his political trajectory and that of other nuevomexicanos of the epoch:

> Nos ha dado tu lógica elocuencia,
> Bello don del "nativo" predilecto,
> Para destruir la despreciable creencia
> Del que tacha al latinoamericano
> De inferior al sajón por intelecto.
>
> [It has given us your rational eloquence,
> The beautiful gift to which the "native" inclines,
> To destroy the contemptible belief
> That the Latin American is inferior to the Anglo-Saxon
> On the basis of his intellect.]

As Chacón deftly illustrates, he and other nuevomexicanos were acutely aware of how their race, language, and religious practices were leveraged against them by the Anglo minority in the state. As in other poems of the collection, Chacón's long experience in the politics of New Mexico and Spanish-language newspapers and his family's historical connections to those fields, as Meléndez details, informed his understanding of these political dynamics.

Perhaps for this reason, Chacón strongly favored the first Hispana congressional candidate, Nina Otero-Warren, a Republican who ran to represent New Mexico in 1922. He wrote "A la Señora Adelina Otero-Warren: Candidata republicana para el Congreso, 1922" in unequivocal support. In the poem, there is no prevaricating about whether her gender should inhibit participation in Congress. Her unique candidacy is described in the second stanza:

El mundo avanza con la idea humana
Y nacen nuevas cosas en la vida;
Hoy refleja la luz de la mañana
En otra esfera la mujer nacida.

[The world advances and so too human thought
And new things into this life are born;
Today reflects the morning light
Of a new dawn into which women are born.]

Chacón advances progressive pride in Otero-Warren, asserting that her election would reflect well on New Mexico and New Mexicans: "Cubrirá Nuevo México de gloria / Poniendo una mujer en el Congreso" [Will cover New Mexico in glory / By sending a woman to Congress]. The poem closes with another shout of support for Otero-Warren from the progressive quarter: "Salud! Un brindis de alegría / Placer del progresivo ciudadano" [A toast! A pledge of joy, / And gratitude from the progressive citizen], a greeting sent from "un pueblo soberano" [a sovereign people].

Besides showing New Mexico to be politically engaged and consistent with the changing political times in nominating a woman for national office, Chacón acknowledges the women's suffrage efforts that preceded Otero-Warren's nomination, as well as women's fundamental equality with men in matters of governance and their patent suitability for holding office: "Nacida en el sufragio igual al hombre, / Pero en lo espiritual, más elevada" [Born into suffrage as man's equal, / But a more spiritually elevated soul]. The combination of praise with acknowledgment of past injustice is not unique to this poem; here, Chacón recognizes that the lack of voting rights for women was an inequality foisted onto them since they were "born into suffrage as man's equal." In other instances in his political poetry, Chacón praises the United States with nationalistic pride while at the same time decrying the efforts that impeded New Mexico's acceptance as a state for almost seven decades.

Indeed, Chacón draws on the ongoing conversation about nationality that is also present in his other poems. Here, when discussing Otero-Warren, she is both a "vástago noble de español linaje" [descendant of noble Spanish lineage] (a way of asserting her nuevomexicana difference) and also "americana pura" [wholly American]. But Chacón moderates the importance of nationality and citizenship altogether by saying, in essence, that her nationality is not of particular import ("qué importa el exterior ropaje / Del que amerita distinguida altura" [Yet, of what importance is this external garb / For she who deserves such echelons]. He continues in his lauds, stating that human grandeur has nothing to do with one's country of origin, but rather with what the divine deems worthy:

> No es exclusiva la grandeza humana,
> Que no limita con nación ninguna;
> Del alto cielo su poder dimana
> Y a quien le place su belleza aduna.
>
> [Human greatness is not bounded,
> It is not limited by nation;
> From on high its power emanates
> And descends upon those whose beauty pleases it.]

Drawing from and enhancing Otero-Warren's personal character, power from the heavens is showered down on her—power that should, according to Chacón, be channeled into high office.

Beyond depicting Otero-Warren as a national political figure representative of women's right to vote and hold office, Chacón considers the specific qualities demonstrating her appropriateness for governance. Perhaps referencing her previous political and civic work, Chacón praises Otero-Warren's accomplishments, which were completed "en pureza moral [. . .] / Y la tierra va bien en su jornada" [in moral purity / And the earth profits through her labors]. She is furthermore "Habilidosa, competente, honrada / De alma gentil, de corazón sincero" [Accomplished, capable, honorable, / Of graceful soul and sincere heart], all qualities that both precipitate and reflect what Chacón frames as a divine mandate for her as a political candidate. And yet, as remarkable as her moral and personal character is, Otero-Warren is in these same respects the nuevomexicana everywoman, the "dama típica" [emblematic lady], a candidate of her people and also called by them: "la del pueblo proclamada."

Chacón not only declares his backing for Otero-Warren on the basis of justice, a justice that according to the preceding has to do with correcting the exclusion of women, but also because he envisions a justice colored with idealism, rather than empty praises and shallow lauds for Otero-Warren. In this poem, he appears to see not only an excellent candidate, but a corrective to past regressive views of women voters and of women in elected office: "Que sólo encierra mi intención altiva / Teñir en la Justicia un idealismo" [Rather my lofty aim / Is to tinge Justice with idealism]. From the very beginning of the poem, Otero-Warren is esteemed ("Ceñida está tu frente de laureles" [Your brow is encircled by laurels]), and her "name radiates honor"; she is compared to a star rising over a dawning day. Chacón's poem is ornate but not gaudy, admiring but not flattering, directly political but a velvet hammer rather than a clanging gong.

In contrast, in "Nocturno a . . ." Chacón leaves readers with the distinct sense that an unnamed political figure has not lived up to his responsibilities with regard to the nuevomexicano public. This anonymous individual, a native nuevomexicano,[6] did not serve the community with honor and grace, and Chacón makes sure readers know, writing from the perspective of the unnamed person:

Bien sabe Dios que en nada
    cifraba yo mi celo
Sino en LLENAR LAS BOLSAS
    en el fecundo suelo
Que me envolvió en pañales
    cuando me vió nacer.

[God only knows
    that my true zeal
Lay only in FILLING MY POCKETS
    in the fecund land
That wrapped me in diapers
    when I was born.]

This is not Chacón's only open critique of those who would govern in New Mexico. In other poems, Chacón offers firm exhortations and advice for New Mexico's leaders, as in "A los legisladores," which commemorates the first legislative session for the new state. Chacón advises the representatives on how they will be seen by future nuevomexicanos, offering opinions about how they should comport themselves so that they will be positively remembered through the long lens of history:

¿Queréis ser acreedores al respeto
Y admiración de la nación futura?
De vos mismo depende:
Pues ya sabéis lo que el deber exige
Y que en la vida quien lo cumple asciende,
Y en el orgullo de su prole rige.

[Do you want to be worthy of the respect
And admiration of the future nation?
This all depends on you.
You are aware of what this obligation demands
And know that in this life he who fulfills the promise
Rises up and the pride of his descendants will never die.]

Chacón both commemorates the moment when New Mexico's internal governance became that of a state and not a territory, and makes clear the responsibility incumbent on those leaders, made more acute by the frequent negative representations of nuevomexicanos in the English-language press.

"A Nuevo México: En su admisión como estado" provides an illustrative example of Chacón's skill in couching political commentary in verse. In this piece, patriotic sentiment is first amplified and then tempered. Chacón opens the poem with ebullience and effortless poetic style:

> Por fin habéis logrado, suelo mío
> De lauros coronar tu altiva frente,
> Alcanzando del cielo del estío
> Una estrella gloriosa y esplendente.
>
> [At last, land of mine, I have lived to see
> Your head rising to meet a summer sky
> Crowned with glory and with a
> Glorious and splendid star.]

"¡Que viva Nuevo México, el Estado!" [Long live the state of New Mexico!], the poem cries. This dizzying nationalist rhetoric makes Chacón's about-face a few verses later especially unexpected. He counters the previous patriotic enthusiasm by citing the years and years of prejudiced resistance to New Mexico's statehood:

> Luchaste contra del hado endurecido
> Batiendo del Congreso la injusticia
> Y con ella el insulto proferido
> Del prejuicio racial por la malicia.
>
> [But you battled against that hardened fate
> Challenging the injustice of Congress
> And the insults born of racial hate
> So often invoked against you.]

But Chacón's patriotic positioning also perpetuates anti-Indigenous tropes, calling out New Mexico's past "luchando con el indio ingobernable" [battling the indomitable Indian]. This is not the only instance of anti-Indigenous reference to New Mexico's Native communities in Chacón's poetry, although this disturbing practice conforms with similar narratives of the period. Indeed, Chacón's contemporaries María Amparo Ruiz de Burton (California) and Jovita González (Texas) used similarly troubling language and tropes in their writing.

This poem also acknowledges and lauds the creation of New Mexican history by its own people—that is, the project Benjamin Read and others accomplished: "Quiero ver tus archivos relucientes / De datos limpios que tu nombre ensanchen / A través de los siglos sucedentes" [I want to see your archives gleam / With resplendent accomplishments bearing your name / Into the centuries to come]. This overt reproach in a poem celebrating New Mexico's late admission as a state is by no means Chacón's most critical expression in the collection, but it is a concise example of the complexity of his literary and political game.

Chacón openly celebrates patriotic American pride, as in "Oda a los héroes," where he lauds the American Legion veterans of World War I, among them many nuevomexicanos. Calling them Devil Dogs (Perros del Demonio), a term the Germans used in reference to US Marines, Chacón recalls the battles nuevomexicano soldiers fought in Château-Thierry and San Miguel. Similarly, in "A la patria," the rhetoric of the poem spirals upward, praising the new "patria" [homeland] of the United States: "Mi patrio amor solícito brindarte / Que resistir no puede ni el cinismo / Las glorias sin igual de tu heroísmo" [I seek to offer you, my native homeland, love / As the unequaled glories of your heroism / Overpower even the cynic]. The poem goes on to extol the nation's founding fathers by name:

> Por el suelo rodó la tiranía
> Al oír de John Adams la elocuencia
> Precursora de aquel gloriosa día
> En que Jefferson, lleno de preciencia
> Trazó de su inmortal sabiduría
> La gran Declaración de Independencia.

> [Tyranny roamed the land,
> Upon hearing John Adams' eloquence
> The precursor for that glorious day
> In which Jefferson, full of prescience,
> Drew out of his immortal wisdom
> The great Declaration of Independence.]

In "A la patria," Chacón reinforces the idea of New Mexico's loyalty to the United States and the state's participation in US national history.

Spanish-Language Poetics in New Mexico

Chacón's political poetry should not obscure our understanding of him as a creative writer aware of literary trends in the Spanish-speaking world. Several characteristics of Chacón's poetry reference the modernista literary movement, the so-called first literary movement originating in Latin America, independent from Spain and its inherited traditions.[7] In the prologue to *Poesía y prosa*, Read cites a poetic manifesto by Venezuelan-Guyanese author Anita Acevedo entitled *El arte y la poesía* that echoes the artistic sentiment of the modernista movement. We do not know where or how Chacón learned of Acevedo's work, and Read offers little contextualization for the quotation, but its sensibility resonates throughout Chacón's poetry:

> Y la poesía, la poesía es la más hermosa flor del lirico jardín del arte; la poesía es la flor de todos los tiempos y todas las razas, flor que crece fulgente y regla, lo mismo bajo los abrasadores rayos del sol del trópico, que bajo el frío glacial del polo; es la mariposa que ha derramado sobre el manto de todos los tiempos el polvo de oro de sus brillantes alas; es el pájaro mágico de blancas plumas.

> [And poetry, poetry is the most beautiful flower in the garden of lyric art; poetry is the flower of all times and all races, a flower that grows dazzlingly and nobly, as much under the burning rays of the tropical sun as under the glacial cold of the poles; it is the butterfly that has scattered upon the mantle of the ages the gold dust of its brilliant wings; it is the magic bird of white feathers.]

This explanation of poetry as "la más hermosa flor del lirico jardín del arte" and the transcendent view of art comprise aspects of the modernista view of poetry's value.

Modernista aesthetic is defined by several characteristic qualities. One of these is the use of sensorial language (colors, smells, textures) in which one sense is often paired with other senses, producing a synesthetic effect. In *Poesía y prosa*, Chacón makes use of sensorial descriptors in nearly every poem, from the "terciopelo radiante / radiant velvet," "cristalina fuente / crystalline spring," and "floripondios floridos / extravagant blooms of flowers" of "La creación" to the "cunita de plumón mullida / little cradle of soft feathers" where his daughter Julieta slept ("A mi hija, Julieta"). Chacón also implements the occasional near-synesthetic combination, such as "nectáreo verjel / nectar-filled garden" ("La vida"), "pecho deprimido / heavy chest" ("In memoriam"), or "cáliz doloroso / painful chalice" ("Devoción").

Modernista verse frequently utilizes exotic and cultured terms, examples of which abound in *Poesía y prosa*, as in "Al explorador del oeste":

> Por ésto la moderna arquitectura
> Hoy ostenta en sus dombos arrogantes
> Cincelada tu mágica figura
> Y en sus frisos y frescos deleitantes;
> Y así como la eterna cinosura
> Su ser presenta en célicos brillantes.

> [Today this modern architecture
> Flaunts itself in its haughty cupolas
> Its magical figures chiseled
> In delightful friezes and frescoes;
> And thus as with the eternal cynosure
> Your being is listed among brilliant heavenly figures.]

In certain poems, Chacón amplifies this sophisticated effect by addressing the poetic audience using the *vosotros* verb form, as in "A los legisladores":

> Guardáos de la malévola impostura
> De tiranuelos de anteriores años
> Que quisieran con blanda donosura
> Y al móvil de sus típicos amaños
> Haceros instrumentos de sus fines.

> [Be on guard against the evil designs
> Of petty tyrants of yore
> Who with false gentility
> Sought with vulgar deception
> To make you pawns in their designs.]

The use of "vosotros" should be seen not as a peninsularization, a mimicry of Castilian Spanish, but rather as a way to accentuate the *cultismos* that Chacón uses. A mixture of poetic and everyday language threads through the collection, but Chacón's use of elevated terminology draws his work into closer conversation with his Latin American modernista colleagues.

Thematically, modernistas elaborate topics relating to dreams and visions, and often incorporate the idea of disillusion or deception, properties held over from Latin American Romanticism. In *Poesía y prosa*, Chacón delves into all of these topics, from poems specifically about disillusion (*desengaño*), such as "Desengaños," "La vida," and "Una ilusión," to those more materially or politically focused on deception, like "Paradoja" or "El ingrato." The theme of dreams and visions recurs, as in "Anita," and is unmistakable in the poems Chacón wrote to his children.

In "A mi hijo, Felipe," Chacón's narrative "yo" dreams a vision heralding his son's birth, in which nymphs follow him to a flowery field where a bee moves from violet to violet, sipping nectar. The nymphs draw close to Chacón:

Un panal de rico almíbar
En mis manos me pusieron
Y cantando me dijeron,
"Las flores os dán la miel."
Por un momento, pasmado,
Ante cuadro tan curioso,
Perdíme en lo misterioso
Y en seguida desperté.

[A honeycomb of rich syrup
They placed in my hands
And, singing, told me:
"Flowers provide you with this honey."
For a moment, I was stunned,
Witnessing such a curious scene,
I was lost in the mystery
And then immediately, I awoke.]

The poetic Chacón realizes then that the garden was his home, and the bee led him to his destiny: the birth of his son Felipe.

In a similar vein, he writes of a vision of his daughter Josefina, whom he compares to a jasmine blossom. When he smells the blossom, his dream clouds over:

Y yo con éxtasis aspiraba
La suave aroma que dél manaba,
Soñando en sueños de la ilusión.

   Estando en ésto muy destraído
Ví que el espacio se oscureció,
Y yo en la sombra quedé inmersido,
Sentí mi pecho de pena hendido
Y do mí todo pasó... pasó...

[And I inhaled in ecstasy
The pleasant aroma that emanated from it,
Dreaming dreams of hope.

   Distracted by this
I saw that the space darkened,
And I remained immersed in the shadows,
I felt my chest split with sadness
And everything left me... left me...]

The shadow that appears over Chacón's fragrant vision foretells Josefina's death in childhood and the loss Chacón will experience. Visions and dreams such as these appear throughout the collection.

Like the modernista master poet Rubén Darío, celebrated for his archetypal poem "El cisne," Chacón incorporates numerous references to classical Greek and Roman mythology. His poems invoke Neptune, Jupiter, Athena, Pericles, Achilles, Erebus, Ceres, Venus Citerea, the Muses, and other mythological figures from the Greek and Roman pantheon. Real-life places are compared to Olympian heights or to the peace of the Elysian fields. Innumerable brows are crowned with Apollo's laurels, and oreads (wood nymphs) populate the landscape. Chacón thoroughly understands and knows how to strategically deploy these figures in the context of his poems, exposing and educating his readers in modernista and Romantic poetic styles. Chacón's personal inclination toward classical references is perhaps best represented in "A la patria":

> Quisiera yo la prodigiosa lira
> Que ha labrádole a Homero eterna gloria
> Para cantaros lo que al genio inspira
> Ese nimbo brillante de tu historia;
> Elaborarte cuánto mi alma admira
> De tus grandes hazañas la memoria,,
> Y en una Iliada hermosa, proficiente,
> Darte en mi trova lo que mi alma siente.

> [I wish that I had that splendid lyre
> Which gave Homer eternal glory,
> To sing to you that which inspires genius,
> The brilliant nimbus of your history;
> To paint you with the fire of he who admires
> The laurels encircling your memory,
> And in a beautiful and skillful Iliad,
> Give to you in my ballad that which touches my soul.]

Chacón also manifests his knowledge of peninsular Spanish literature, in particular its foundational works. In "A los legisladores," for example, Chacón admonishes the new nuevomexicano legislators to do well by the people of the state, reminding them that they are the "Hijos libres de aquellos capitanes / Que surcaron indómitos los mares / De la tierra del Cid y los Guzmanes" [They are the free sons of those sea captains / From the land of El Cid and Guzmán / Who sailed the untamed seas]. Chacón here invokes the medieval epic poem telling the story of Spain's national hero, *El cantar del mío Cid*, and seems to allude to medieval Spanish *reconquista* figure Alonso Pérez de Guzmán, known as Guzmán el Bueno. Later references to don Quijote de la Mancha, el Caballero de la Triste Figura, and Dulcinea del Toboso (all in the short story "Eustacio y Carlota") and Sancho Panza ("Nocturno a . . . ") reveal

Chacón's familiarity with the timeless early modern novel *Don Quijote de la Mancha* by Miguel de Cervantes. Although the references to Spanish literature are not nearly as numerous as the classical allusions, they suggest Chacón's awareness of and orientation to works representative of a globally acclaimed Hispanophone literature.

The Interior Sound of Poetry

The aesthetic impact of Chacón's poetry is not, of course, limited to its connection to other literary traditions; the lyricism of *Poesía y prosa* generates its own distinct effects. Chacón's ear for sound emerges in several poems at the more colloquial end of his wide poetic range, distinguishing them from the sound play sometimes found in *modernista* poetry. The humorous theme in "Caso singular"—an elder advising a chronically inebriated young man to avoid alcohol—is secondary to how the poem sounds, to how the words bounce off each other within the verses as Chacón amplifies their effect:

> Pero el súbdito de Baco,
>   bamboleándose repone:
> —No le atina usted, don Paco,
>   la manera en que a Climaco
>   el traguito le indispone:
>
> Mis crápulas sempiternas
>   las sigo desde muchacho,
>   y el néctar de las tabernas
>   no me causa más empacho
>   que hacerme agüadas las piernas.
>
> [But the drunkard, a slave to Bacchus,
>   staggers and responds:
>   "Mister Paco, you just don't get it
>   the way an itsy bitsy drink,
>   stirs up Climaco.

My debaucheries are all but divine,
>   I have been at them since I was a boy
>   and the taverns' sweet juice
>   causes me no greater ill
>   than to turn my legs to jelly."]

Chacón achieves a similar playful sonic effect in "Alternados," in which the spirited internal repetition of vowel sounds complements the joking topic of a deaf woman who tells everyone "sí" (and whose husband advises more "no" in the future), as well as in the tangled verses of "Asunto enredado."

Humor

Another delightful aspect of Chacón's poetry is his wit and humor, an expression of the *feliz ingenio neomexicano* [lively New Mexican intellect] Read hints at in the prologue. This is evident not only in how he pokes fun at particular political and public figures ("Un republicano real"), depicts characters (Melitón in "Eustacio y Carlota"), or lampoons a would-be suitor who admires his beloved's *ojos negros* [dark eyes] and ends up with a pair of *ojos negros* [shiners] himself, but also in wordplay. Chacón's pun-like jokes in several of the poems bring a chuckle because of their lighthearted approach and play on words.

"Caso Florido," for example, plays on how a woman's name changes in the Spanish tradition when she marries: Soila Corona marries a man with the last name Flores and becomes Soila Corona de Flores, which sounds like "soy la corona de flores" [I am the crown of flowers]. The marriage is, as Chacón shows, quite the "flowery affair." Something similar happens in "Caso Doloroso," where Dolores (named for the Virgin of Sorrows) Fuertes marries Gonzalo Ijar, becoming Dolores Fuertes de Ijar, or "a strong pain in the flank."

In "Asunto enredado," Chacón humorously comments on the circular reasoning of illness and cure as a young man with a poor memory is advised to take a prescription to improve it, but he cannot remember to do so. A similar quiet jest is in place with the couple in "Alternados." In "Una agudeza," Chacón shows a brother and sister parrying with their wits. First, the sister sings a verse to her brother that compares her face to the expensive pitchers she carries: "Qué jaras tan caras vendo" [What expensive pitchers I sell]. In return, her brother—"Más que Juanito era Juan / Y más que Juan era truhán" [Was more of a Juan than a Juanito, / And more than a Juan a rascal]—uses wordplay to make it sound as though her face is tired and worn: "Qué cara ajada estoy viendo" [What a tired face I see].

Chacón's humor also emerges in the fiction pieces "Un baile de caretas" and "Eustacio y Carlota" that close *Poesía y prosa*. In the first story, a masked ball takes place in a Colorado town in 1898. Pancho, a young man known for his indiscriminate interest in the town's women, is tricked into seducing someone who he thinks is a young woman, but who in fact is a masked member of a group of his young male friends. Pancho is described as a cad: "pulido y presuntuoso hasta ridículo extremo, y amante de las muchachas hasta la pared de enfrente, que éstas les hacía mil dengues, guiños y agasajos para granjear su cariño" [neat but vain in the extreme. He loved all the girls as they came through the door. He flirted with them in a thousand ways, using winks and caresses, trying to win their affection]. Chacón's description of the lothario's ardor for the supposed young woman cannot help but elicit a chuckle from the reader, as much for Pancho's over-the-top expressions of love as for the narrator's rolling commentary. The story abruptly ends with Pancho's abundant curses for his friends as he leaves town on the morning train, but he is met years later by the narrator: "Por fin recobró sus facultades normales, hasta el punto de desembuchar varias indecibles imprecaciones: sapos, y culebras, con algunas víboras entremezcladas por añadidura") [Finally, he recovered his senses, and he began to spew forth some unrepeatable damnations: toads and snakes, with some serpents mixed in for effect].

The majority of the novelette "Eustacio y Carlota," a story Chacón claims was taken from newspaper headlines, is tragic and somewhat sensational. The two eponymous siblings, who were separated as children, meet, fall in love, and marry, but before consummating their marriage they realize their shared history and end the affair. The most memorable and amusing element of the story is the character Melitón, who is described by Chacón with a tongue-in-cheek flourish. Melitón's manner of drawing his friend Orlando away from the doldrums of his rejected love for Carlota (who was renamed Amanda by her adoptive family) is to mock Orlando's wallowing, love itself, and the institution of marriage with great aplomb and to compose a pair of poems that echo Chacón's humorous verse, one of which is directed to the rejecting lover, Amanda:

Amanda:—
Quiero decirte
    Que yo no dejo de amarte;
    Que quisiera convertirte
    En diosa para, adorarte,
    Y con avidez asirte
    Y para siempre lazarte . . .
    Mas si al leer éste ensarte,
    Vas de mi amor a reírte,
    De plano quiero advertirte,
    Que muy lejos de olvidarte,
    Me voy al monte a gemirte,
    ¡A ver si un rayo me parte!
Tuyo, Melitón

[*Amanda:*
I wish to tell you
    that I never stop loving you;
    that I'd like to make you a goddess
    and adore you
    and seize you avidly
    and bind you forever . . .
    but if you should laugh
    at my love
    when you read this line,
    let me make it clear to you,
    that far from forgetting you,
    I'll go to the mountains
    and moan my loss,
    hoping that a flash
    of lightning might strike me!
Yours, Melitón.]

Orlando breaks into laugher at Melitón's caricature of Orlando's own mawkish verses dedicated to his love, Amanda, and that humor reaffirms their friendship.

Melitón's advice to his friend and his bantering verse remind the reader of the *carrilla* [joking disrespect] that many nuevomexicanos share with intimate friends and family.

Reflections and Religion

As Benjamin Read comments in the prologue, "En su carácter personal, 'El Cantor Neomexicano' es de índole filosófico" [As far as his personal character goes, "The Neomexicano Poet" is philosophically inclined], and this perspective is reflected in many of the poems. Some are thematic meditations: on the fleeting nature of childhood ("A la niñez"); on deception or a lack of reciprocity ("Desengaños," "Desencanto," "El ingrato," "Es el amor," "Paradoja"); on the transience of life and its fleeting beauty ("Una ilusión," "In memoriam," "Sueños y realidades," "Devoción," "Se aleja y se vá," "Otoñal"); or on the absurdity of self-importance—which he no doubt witnessed personally in the political sphere—in "Indiferente":

¡Pobrecitos, ridículos pigmeos,
Más dignos de piedad que de censura,
Que se creen insignes corifeos,
De bajo servilismo en la llenura!

Mas yo gozo mirando al sapo inflarse,
Que quería del buey las dimensiones,
Y en su empeño acabó por reventarse
Y murieron con él sus ilusiones.

[Poor little ridiculous pygmies!
More deserving of pity than censure,
Who think themselves distinguished coryphaeus,
Full of themselves if only by their lowly servility.

Yet I revel in the little frog puffing himself up,
Stretching to be the size of an ox,
Who through his efforts ends up bursting,
His dreams dying with him.]

Chacón's ruminations on other topics are equally evocative. Nature, as in "A mayo," is one of his primary muses and subjects:

Mes bendito en que las flores,
Con sus múltiples colores,
Vienen todo a matizar,
Es tu bálsamo el que inspira
Los acentos de mi lira
Para poderte cantar.

[Blessed month in which the flowers
With their many colors,
Unfurl and tinge everything,
Yours is the sweet balsam
That stirs my lyre
Its strains to sing to you.]

Throughout the collection, Catholic imagery and beliefs intersect with classical mythological figures and tropes. Poems that treat death (such as those dedicated to Chacón's deceased children) refer to Catholic faith traditions, while other poems, like "El angel de la guarda," invoke specific beliefs or understandings. Three poems are particularly expressive of how religion emerges in *Poesía y prosa*: "A María ante su altar," "El ateo y la verdad," and "La creación."

In "A María ante su altar," Chacón sets the scene of a supplicant kneeling before the Virgin Mary's altar. He incorporates many references to Marian beliefs and theology ("Fuiste tú por el Verbo proclamada / Para madre del Hijo que viniera" [You were proclaimed by the Divine Word / To be the mother of a Child sent to earth]), but the religious sentiment is intertwined with a modernista sensibility. It is a poem about the poetic voice's unworthiness before the Virgin Mary—a common theme in religious lyric poetry—but this subject is expressed through modernista tropes. The Virgin Mary is a "blanca azucena" [white lily], a "Bello broche de augusto crisantema / Que al abrirse desplega su hermosura" [Beautiful brooch of an august chrysanthemum / That displays its beauty as it unfolds its petals]. While modernista works are often secular in nature—the poems of writers such as Amado Nervo being the exception—Chacón here creates a modernista aesthetic in a Marian devotional work. As the poem pleads for the grace of the Virgin Mary's guidance, Chacón garbs her in the lyric of high poetry:

> Tú a quien ciñe magnífica diadema
> De estrellas con el sol por vestidura,
> Ilumina mi senda tenebrosa
> Con tu luz celestial esplendorosa. [. . .]
>
> Por eso, dulce madre, aquí rendido
> Ante el florido altar de tu santuario,
> En férvida plegaria yo te pido,
> Por tus penas atroces del Calvario,
> No me ciegue el engaño ni me espante
> La lucha que depárase delante.
>
> [You, crowned by a magnificent diadem
> Made from the stars and clothed by the sun,
> I implore you to light my treacherous path
> With your splendid celestial light. [. . .]
>
> I ask in fervent supplication
> that by the horrible sorrows you lived at the foot of the cross
> I will not be blinded and fooled,
> Nor my resolve weaken before the battle that
> Lies ahead and to which you have enjoined us.]

In "El ateo y la verdad," Chacón lays claim to a belief in God and the metaphysical realm through oppositionality. The poem contrasts what are presented as misguided atheist precepts with belief in a supreme deity. Although Chacón does not assert specifically Catholic beliefs, he refutes what he frames as a vacuity embodied by atheism, a subject of popular debate in the United States at that time. Chacón progresses through a series of arguments that outline from the perspective of the believer the fallacies of atheistic rationale. More than convincing someone who does not believe in God in a divine presence, the cascade of stanzas makes patent what seem to be Chacón's faith and religious convictions:

Aquí es do la razón ya se rebela
Y ofrece vigorosa su protesta,
Y la conciencia que en el alma apela,
Con sobrada razón nos amonesta.

Porque, si todo acaba con la muerte,
Si no hay un porvenir en ultratumba,
¿Qué importa el bien o el mal para tal suerte
Si en ella la Justicia se derrumba! . . .

¿Qué puede el pobre, insuficiente humano?
No alcanza aún ni a comprenderse él mismo,
Cuánto menos medir todo un Arcano
Con razones que rayan en cinismo.

[Here, then, reason must recoil
And bring forth a strong rebuke,
With the soul's conscience contesting
And with justifiable reason inspiring us.

If all were to end in death,
If there is no life beyond the grave,
Of what consequence is good or evil
If in this, our fate, Justice is overthrown?

What would be the fate of the wretched, imperfect human being?
A being who does not even understand his very nature
Nor is able to apprehend this grand Mystery
If his thinking redounds in cynicism.]

While the specificity of religious creed that appears in other poems is here absent, "El ateo y la verdad" asserts Chacón's conviction that a lack of belief in a higher power is fundamentally flawed and cannot help but lead to a lack of purpose and ethics in the lived world: "¿Qué importa el bien o el mal para tal suerte / Si en ella la Justicia se derrumba!" [Of what consequence is good or evil, / If in this, our fate, Justice is overthrown?].

The crowning work in *Poesía y prosa* is "La creación," a sustained imaginative and artistic effort built on Genesis, the first book of the Bible, and the story of the creation of the universe in seven days. "La creación" unfolds with a Baroque sensibility, similar to that superbly expressed by early modern poets Luis de Góngora and Sor Juana Inés de la Cruz and later interpreted by modernista poets. This style demands that readers take in furled or inverted lines and stanzas and reassemble their components to create meaning.

Chacón interlaces the well-known narrative of the creation of the universe with figures and ideas from classical mythology, creating a fascinating fusion. "'¡Y adelante, hasta la cima!' / dijo entonces el Señor" [The Lord then said, / "Onward! To the summit!"] is interlaced with references to the god of the seas, Neptune ("Que trocábase la tierra / en un imperio linfal / Do gobernaba Neptuno" [That the earth would be traded / for an inherited empire / Where Neptune would govern]) and allusions to the goddess of the harvest and growth, Ceres:

> Y los valles expansivos
>   de colores resaltaron;
> De Ceres en el dominio
>   nacieron aljofaradas
> Por las gotas del rocío
>   las mieses aprisionadas.
>
> [And the expansive valleys
>   shone their colors;
> At Ceres' hand
>   cornfields were born
> Trapped
>   by drops of dew.]

The prehuman space is filled with Aeolic lullabies, oreades, the Muses, Phoebus's light, Apollo, and many more such references. Chacón not only displays a broad grasp of this mythology and its symbolic logic in poetry, he seamlessly integrates them into a poem that is thematically Judeo-Christian. One fascinating complexity emerges as Chacón describes God's creation of the (female) earth, again using a classical metaphor:

> Aquí tenéis la tierra transformada
> Y en un elíseo campo convertida;
> Virgen que fue, la veo inmaculada,
> Su pecho lleno de inocente vida,
> Bañada por la límpida cascada
> O al lado de la fuente cual nereída
> Que se deleita con las notas de ella
> Dándole en cambio halagos de doncella...

> [Here thou hast transformed the earth
> Changed it into an Elysian field;
> Virgin that she was, immaculate,
> Her breast full of innocent life,
> Bathed by the limpid cascade
> Of a fountain where a Nereid,
> Delighting in its music,
> Exchanges maidenly flattery with her...]

Shortly thereafter, Chacón describes the creation of humankind in Adam, who is formed from the female earth:

> Tomando barro del bendito seno
> De esta doncella hizo Dios al hombre,
> Y de su aliento prodigioso, ameno,
> Le dió un alma inmortal al casto cieno,
> Y "Adán," le dijo, "tomarás por nombre."

> [Taking mud from the blessed breast
> Of that young maid, God made man,
> And with his prodigious, pleasant breath,
> He gave immortal soul to that pure mud,
> "Adam," he told it, "shall be your name."]

By using metaphor in this manner, Chacón paradoxically narrates a story of creation in which humankind is made from a woman, not from a man, a complexity resulting from the intersection between two origin narratives. In concluding, Chacón describes the emergence of Eve:

> Tiene formas de Venus Citerea,
> Tiene el alma de niño al nacer,
> Y sus ojos rasgados recrea
> Muy gozosa por todo el Edén.

> [She has the form of Venus Citerea,
> The soul of an innocent child,
> And her almond-shaped eyes
> Gaze gladly over all Eden.]

Through to the end, the knowledgeable Chacón interweaves classical references and modernista aesthetic sensibilities into a poem about the creation of the universe.

Poemas de familia

As Gonzales-Berry, Meléndez, and Meyer have noted, Chacón includes a number of poems dedicated to his family in "Cantos del hogar," the second section of *Poesía y prosa*. Sculpted with great craftsmanship and beauty, these poems fall into three general categories: poems to his immediate family, poems directed to his godchildren (affective family), and elegies for his children who died in childhood. There are also two poems dedicated to Chacón's mother, Lucía: one by Felipe Chacón and one by his uncle Pedro Chacón.

Chacón's poems to his family members are particularly winning, showcasing his lyrical skill as he writes with pride about his children in an endearing manner. For his daughter Herminia, Chacón commemorates her third birthday:

> El lapso de tres años
>   se cumple en pocos días
> Desde que tú viniste
>   la dicha a despertar;
> En mi alma estimulaste
>   las esperanzas mías,

Mi corazón colmaste
   de goces y alegrías
Y en un Edén tornaste
   tu natalicio lar.

[In a few days it will be
   three years that you have been with us,
A gift inspiring
   new hope in my soul.
You have filled my heart
   with happiness and joy
And with your presence you
   have turned our home into an Edenic paradise.]

Here, Chacón expresses tender love for his daughter, his "obra magna / de celestial creación" [master work / of heavenly creation]. Chacón writes in a similar vein to his other children, addressing Felipe, whose birth is foreshadowed by a vision of water-loving nymphs, and Julieta, on whom he calls down blessings from heaven: "Invocamos al Dios de tu destino / Que [. . .] / Derrame sobro [*sic*] ti sus bendiciones" [We call on God for your destiny / That beautiful gifts shower upon your soul from on high]. He sees the virtues of his daughter Elvira reflected in himself in the closing verses of a poem directed to her:

   Si acaso mi alma anhela excelsitudes
O en mi árida ventura hay flor amena
La que alguna virtud a mi alma inspira,

   Es fruto celestial de tus virtudes,
Es bálsamo que libo en la azucena
De tu alma angelical, mi tierna Elvira.

   [If my soul has sought greatness,
Or if I find a gentle flower in this arduous life—
The fruit of some virtue that aids my soul—

> It is but the heavenly manna rained down by your virtues,
> The comforting balm I take from the lily
> That is your angelic soul, my dear Elvira.]

In these poems, his affection for his children is spun into skillfully crafted verses, the words and metaphors noble, gentle, suggestive, and enduring.

In another poem to Elvira, an impish side to Chacón's poetic persona emerges. He opens the piece with a comparison of his daughter's eyes to two "stunning suns"—"un par fulgurante de soles"—that guide him along life's rocky path: "En mi senda de rudos peñoles, / Son la luz en mi oscura jornada" [On my path of rough peaks, / They are the light on my dark journey]. If Chacón's life is a field of fragrant blooms, yielding their "ricos fulgores" [rich brilliance] to the god Phoebus, he declares it is all the doing of "esas dos estrellitas" [those two little stars]. But the poem does not end with sweet modernist compliments for his dear daughter; rather, her eyes are

> [. . .] destellos vivaces,
> Juguetones que ríen perspicaces
> Cuando a darme una broma conspira,
> Ese cielo do brillan audaces
> ¡Esos ojos de luz de mi Elvira!

> [. . . the lively, spirited
> Sparks that cleverly laugh
> When they conspire to tease me;
> That heaven where doth audaciously twinkle
> My Elvira's light-filled eyes!]

Chacón turns the last stanza of a charming but somewhat staid poem on its head, revealing that his daughter's eyes laugh and joke and that she is audaciously her own person. Chacón closes the poem with this image, replacing the predictable representation of a demure girl with one that is self-possessed and confident in her interactions with her father.

Chacón's emotional complexity is channeled into beautiful elegies for his offspring who died in childhood. These poems reveal the sublimation of trauma and loss into verse, echoing the sentiment expressed in the prologue, in which Read quotes Chacón describing his life experiences:

> He sufrido rudos golpes de la suerte en varias distintas épocas de mi vida-dice él-pero no conozco pena que no haya podido conquistar. He sabido afrontar infortunios, acerbas tribulaciones, nutriendo el sentir de que hubieran podido ser peores aun, y así he podido triunfar de la adversidad. Es tan inútil como falto de sensatez el apenarse uno por lo que no tiene remedio. Con eso uno sólo agrava la situación. Hay que vencer las penas de la vida para poder vivir muchos años y ser feliz.

> [I have suffered cruel and harsh blows of fate at several points in my life—he says—but I know of no grief that I could not overcome. I have known how to face down misfortune, bitter tribulations, sustained in the idea that things could have been worse still, and thus I have triumphed over adversity. It is useless to the point of foolishness for one to grieve over what has no remedy. In doing so, one only exacerbates the situation. One must defeat life's misfortunes in order to live for many years and be happy.]

When Chacón writes about his deceased children, it is with a tone of acceptance of the pain, looking through metaphor and faith to explain trauma and loss. His poem to his son Buenaventura expresses this tension succinctly:

> Eras todo nuestro encanto,
> Luz de sol en nuestra vida,
> La que hoy vemos extinguida
> Por las lágrimas del llanto...
>
> Pero el alma halla consuelo
> Cuando en ésto yo me fijo:
> ¡Dimos en el mundo un hijo
> Por un ángel en el Cielo!

> [You had been our delight,
> The light of our days,
> A sun we now see extinguished
> By waves of tears of anguish.

> But my soul is comforted
> When I consider
> That while we gave the world a son
> We sent an angel into Heaven.]

Chacón likewise describes his daughter Melba's death, explaining that an angel such as her found no permanent home on earth:

> No estaba en propio local
> De esta vida en el vaivén,
> Por que un ángel no está bien
> En la vida temporal.
>
> [This little one did not find her place
> In this world's coming and going,
> Because an angel has no place
> In this earthly life.]

The untimely passing of Josefina, who died at the age of two, is explained with a vision: the poetic Chacón sees a jasmine blossom explode with fragrance and then a shadow comes over it; he feels dread and then the clouds lift. The poetic unfolding of his daughter's short life echoes the vision: she who was the "Jazmín precioso, luz de mi hogar!" [Precious jasmine, light of my home!] and described in modernist metaphor as having "labios de grana / Blondos cabellos, un ideal . . ." [pomegranate red lips, / Blonde hair, the ideal of beauty . . .] returns to heaven as a child: "¡Así tan pura como nació!" [As pure as she was born!]. This poem, echoing the tropes of dreams and prognostication that weave throughout the collection, affects the reader deeply. In these elegies, Chacón commemorates his lost children with tender and concise language, his images aligning for the reader, who can empathize with the pain expressed. Unlike the poems dedicated to other individuals, which were intended as gifts to their recipients, these poems are for Chacón, his wife, and their family, who mourned the deaths of beloved children.

Chacón offers a window into his affective family in two poems dedicated to his godchildren, Rosa Córdova and Jacobo Aragón. In both poems, Chacón compliments their accomplishments, praising the paths they have undertaken while at the same time invoking their parents' great care and effort in cultivating their progress. Chacón emphasizes the parents' love and pride in the poem to Rosa Córdova:

> Por eso es que palpitan
> Al impulso de tiernas emociones,
> De tus padres los dignos corazones,
> Y en ancho piélago de amor se agitan.
>
> [This is why
> The noble hearts of your parents
> Race and beat, urged on by tender emotions
> Stirring within the deep sea of their love.]

Chacón intermingles his praise with firm directives to both Rosa and Jacobo. In this sense, the poems themselves act out the role of *padrino* [godfather]: a parent-like figure from outside the immediate family who guides and provides resources for their *ahijados* [godchildren]. To Jacobo, for example, he advises devoted fealty to his parents, who have sacrificed much for their beloved son:

> Deja que sea tan sublime afecto
> De tu recíproca lealtad criterio,
> Y dales de la vida en el trayecto
> Completa gratitud y refrigerio.
>
> Habrás con ésto tu deber cumplido,
> Y ellos por eso vivirán dichosos:
> Será la realidad tu ser querido,
> Que adornaron sus sueños más hermosos . . .
>
> [Pledge that your sublime affection for them
> Will always be your loyal, shared principle.
> Ensure that over the course of your life
> You offer them full gratitude and sustenance.

With this, your duty will be complete
And for this, they will live blessed:
Your beloved being will be the fulfillment
Of that with which they adorned their most beautiful dreams . . .]

Chacón enacts the fulfillment of a padrino's responsibility through affectionate admonishments in these poems, revealing an important facet of family life in early twentieth-century New Mexico. Godparents are not symbols, but rather loving, authoritative figures in the lives of their ahijados, the children of family and friends who are shared with them as if they were their own. Included in the section "Cantos del hogar," these poems reinforce the social contract of *comadrazgo/compadrazgo*, the chosen bonds that transform friend to family (through co-mothering/co-fathering) common in New Mexico then and now.

Chacón includes two poems dedicated to his mother, doña Lucía Ward, Viuda de Chacón. The verses offer a dual view of Lucía Chacón and insight into the long literary legacy of the Chacón family. "A mi amada hermanita, Lucía," written for Lucía Chacón by her brother-in-law Pedro Chacón (Felipe's uncle), is framed by Felipe M. Chacón's introduction to the work, which states that his uncle was a prolific poet, though few of his works survived: "Mi tío Pedro fue un poeta inspirado; escribió numerosas poesías de gran mérito y delicado gusto, que murieron con él: no fueron conservados los manuscritos. Esta es la única poesía suya que he podido encontrar, que fue conservada por mi madre misma" [My uncle Pedro was an inspired poet: he wrote a number of poems of great merit and fine taste, most of which died with him, as the manuscripts were not preserved. This is the only poem of his that I have been able to find, as it was saved by my mother]. Chacón ensures that readers are aware of his uncle's poetic abilities, "de gran mérito y delicado gusto," and includes Pedro Chacón's poem in a place of honor in his own book. Aside from revealing how important the personal poems were to their subjects (Lucía Chacón kept this poem for years before Felipe M. Chacón printed it), the poem offers a glimpse into familial relationships in New Mexico in the late nineteenth century. Pedro Chacón thanks his *cuñada* [sister-in-law], whom he would later call *hermanita* [little sister], shifting a legal relationship to a blood relation in response to her bringing him into her home after the death of his parents:

Al mirar la grandeza de tu alma
Se llena mi existir de sentimiento,
Y me elevo hasta el mismo firmamento
Proclamándote mi ángel redentor. [. . .]

Dios sólo puede compensar tus hechos
Tan heróicos, tan nobles, tan piadosos;
En la gloria laureles honorosos
Coronarán sin duda tu virtud.

[Upon seeing the greatness of your soul
My being is filled with emotion,
And I rise up to the heavens
To proclaim you my redeeming angel. [. . .]

Only God can reward your deeds
So heroic, so noble, so faithful;
Your virtue will surely be crowned with laurels
In the sweet hereafter.]

Pedro Chacón's existential dismay at the beginning of the poem is assuaged by the generosity and kindness of his sister-in-law, and she is uplifted with the language of heroes.

But the picture Felipe M. Chacón paints of his widowed mother starkly contrasts with the vision of his uncle's poem. Chacón's father, Urbano Chacón, passed away when Felipe was thirteen, and his early departure profoundly affected Chacón and his siblings, as well as his mother, who would later remarry. Chacón employs the poetic "yo" in "Al enviudar mi madre" to express the perspective of his mother, as Gonzales-Berry noted (192). Although the title implies talk *about* his mother, Lucía Chacón speaks directly in the poem itself, as Chacón imagines his mother's interior life:

Traspasada de mil tribulaciones,
Sola, sola lloré,
Y al tenderme la noche sus crespones,
Mi llanto con suspiros agoté.

    Y sus arrullos de dolor nutridos,
El aquilón dejando
En estridores lúgubres fundidos,
Me perdí entre las sombras . . . suspirando . . .

    [Pierced by a thousand sorrows,
Alone, all alone, I cried
And as the night hung its dark curtain about me,
I was overcome by sobs and sighs.

    Its lullabies of pain thus fed,
The north wind departs
Its dismal intensity diminished,
And I am given to the shadows, sighing.]

Not only is the keen appreciation for his mother's emotional state apparent, the verse makes clear through language choice just how intensely loneliness weighed down Lucía Chacón: "sola, sola lloré." That unwanted solitude is exactly what she had sought to assuage for her cuñado Pedro years before.

Historical and Social Poems

Shifting from the familial to the historical and social, Chacón circles outward from New Mexico to engage national and global social questions. The poems "El obrero" and "Al explorador del oeste" reveal Chacón's lyric ruminations in Spanish on workers and on the idea of "the West" popularly promulgated elsewhere. "El obrero" resembles a contemporary commentary on labor, a laud for the worker. Chacón lists feat after feat carried out by laborers: building roads, excavating mountains, manufacturing textiles, building skyscrapers ("rascanubes," as Chacón calls them), and defending the country from foreign enemies. All of these manmade accomplishments are the laborers' handiwork:

    Florece la industria
        De modos diversos
    Con mil bendiciones,
        Favor al obrero.

[Industry flourishes
   In a variety of ways
And with a thousand blessings,
   Thanks to the worker.]

Lacking context regarding the poem's creation, we cannot say with certainty if Chacón was responding to a specific paradigm through this poem, but the alignment of "El obrero" with the working man, and not the upper classes of society, is in keeping with Chacón's poems that critique those who enrich themselves through others' labor and money.

"Al explorador del oeste" is an unusual entry in *Poesía y prosa*. The poem is a glorification of explorers who came to "the West"—that is, Anglo travelers who made their way to what formerly had been Mexican and Spanish territories and beyond. Perhaps in keeping with Chacón's works that praise the United States, this poem buys into the idea of the brave and noble traveler who risks life and limb and leaves behind dear family members to enter the unknown of what, at least for nuevomexicanos, had long been familiar. This strange triangulation—approval for manifest destiny expansionism written from the perspective of a nuevomexicano in Spanish for a Spanish-speaking audience—is clearly rooted in US history, with references to American Revolutionary War sites Lexington and Concord:

   ¡Valiente explorador, cuánto os admiro!
   Vos os legásteis en perenne gloria
   La página brillante en que hoy os miro
   Del güaldo Oeste rubricar la historia,
   Historia escrita en eternal papiro,
   Por Lexington y Concord principiada
   Y en los grandes patriotas perpetuada.

   [Brave explorer, how we admire thee!
   You arrived in enduring glory
   On the shining pages of the West's history,
   Yellowed by time,
   Its history inscribed on eternal papyrus,

Begun in Lexington and Concord
And carried on by great patriots.]

The poem maintains this tone throughout, replicating the trope of the industrious Anglo westerner—"Enérgico tu empeño laborioso" [your energetic, laborious effort]—that was so often disparagingly contrasted with nuevomexicanos' supposed lack of industry or progressivism in the nineteenth century. This raises the question: how was the imagined audience intended to react to this poem?

Nuevo México

In contrast to Chacón's concise focus on the politics of New Mexico and its people, there are fewer examples of linguistic nuevomexicanismos and allusions to specific people and places in his writings. Regional lexicon occasionally emerges as do references to New Mexico–specific historical figures, whom Chacón calls up as fluidly as he does Thomas Jefferson, George Custer, and John Adams.

Chacón's translation of "Un sabio" includes nuevomexicano vocabulary: he does not render the wise owl as *búho* (a peninsular term) but rather uses the Nahuatl-origin *tecolote*, a word that has a specific meaning—screech owl—but is also the general term for "owl" in New Mexican dialect. In a similar manner, Chacón's tecolote is wise because he does not spread *mitote* [gossip], another term commonly used in New Mexico. Thus, "todos aquellos que alzan mitote, / tomen ejemplo del tecolote" [All who blunder, who then murmur and backstab / Should learn the ways of the screech owl]. Chacón successfully captures the vernacular sense of the original poem, conveying it to his readers in terms with which they are familiar. As Chacón demonstrates elsewhere in the collection, his word selection is never a result of a lack of knowledge of other dialects or registers; he here deploys a mestizo prosody (Nogar 348) with full awareness of its effect. A similarly quiet nuevomexicano echo can be heard in "A la Srta. Adela Cruz," in which the verse uses regional conjugation practice in the preterit tense: "Do alcanzastes un éxito glorioso" [For earning great success].

Chacón draws the reader to the local again in the points of reference he employs in some of his poems. "A Santa Fe" and "A Nuevo México" clearly address nuevomexicano place and history. In other instances, Chacón's quick mind echoes the works of his cousin Eusebio Chacón, who in his *Tras la tormenta, la calma* simply placed his novelette in New Mexico and Santa Fe without any particular fanfare. In the same way that Chacón casually references figures from both US history and Spanish letters, he invokes significant figures from New Mexico's centuries-long history, placing them on an even playing field with national or international personae. In "Nocturno a...," Chacón incorporates the narrative of Juan de Oñate, who led New Mexico's settlement expedition in 1598:

>   Que en lápida mortuoria
>   mis fátuas fechorías
>   Sellaron para siempre
>   de Oñate el porvenir.

>   [My foolish exploits
>   inscribed on my headstone
>   Sealed Oñate's fate
>   forevermore.]

Such nuevomexicano markers are more frequent in his short stories.

"Don Julio Berlanga," with its depiction of a nuevomexicano shepherd returning to Las Vegas, New Mexico, from Rolin (Rawlins), Guayuma (Wyoming), resonates with details specific to New Mexico. Chacón's description of this sober, hardworking man and his attendance at a local *baile* is on the nose in reference to New Mexico. But beyond the description of don Julio, his occupation of shepherding outside of New Mexico, specifically in the sheep-heavy country of Idaho and Wyoming, is representative of a seasonal work route frequently traveled by nuevomexicanos and southern Coloradans of the epoch.

In "Eustacio y Carlota," reference to New Mexico is more evocative than concrete; the only specifically nuevomexicano character in the story is Melitón González (Eustacio and Carlota Quintanilla, the novelette's protagonists, are from a "pobre familia española" [poor Spanish family] in the eastern United States). Melitón's distinction of having fought with the Rough Riders in San Juan, Cuba, could have led readers to connect the distinctive character with Maximiliano Luna, Chacón's contemporary, the son of a prominent nuevomexicano family who died while fighting in the Philippines in 1899.

Conclusion

Chacón's poetry and prose reveal the mind of a brilliant thinker who was socially active and politically engaged. *Poesía y prosa* is a work of art manifesting the *literatura nacional* that many nuevomexicanos strived to produce. Authors, including Felipe M. Chacón, sought to create a body of literature not only for the sake of pleasure—one that "alcanza a servir de solaz y recreo, para hacer amenas las horas que se dediquen a su lectura" [manages to provide solace and recreation, and to make the hours dedicated to its reading pleasant]—but also as a demonstration of nuevomexicano intellect in the face of xenophobic criticism and political marginalization based in part on the use of the Spanish language.

Chacón created this literature in the hours between his paying jobs, spinning art out of that limited time and space. Indeed, we wonder if there are more nuevomexicano examples yet to be found. Read says, "Muchas de las poesías que Chacón ha escrito durante su vida, no verán jamás la luz de la publicidad: 'Se han perdido en el naufragio de la desidia,' como él mismo lo dice" [Many of the poems that Chacón has written during his life will never see the light of day as published works: "They have been lost drowning in indolence," as he himself says]. If *Poesía y prosa* is what remains of Chacón's much larger body of literary writing, the tip of the iceberg of his larger literary production, what might be recovered from other nuevomexicanos of his epoch, writing in Spanish or bilingually? We wonder which writers of his generation, laboring quietly in Spanish, might have abandoned their writing or, lacking a legacy such as that provided by doña Herminia, produced works that have soundlessly languished.

We agree with Benjamin Read that "este libro [*Poesía y prosa*] sin presumir yo virtudes de profeta, está destinado a labrar una memoria imperecedera para este hijo privilegiado del gran estado de Nuevo México" [without attributing to myself the virtues of a prophet, [*Poesía y prosa*] is destined to carve out an everlasting memory for this favored son of the great state of New Mexico]. With this volume, we make the works of "el feliz ingenio neomexicano," Felipe M. Chacón, available to present-day readers, and in doing so, we acknowledge his literary and historical complexity.

Notes

1. Though research on Chacón has been relatively quiet since the 1990s, earlier studies brought to light important facets of his biography and historical significance. Doris Meyer (1977) considered Chacón a Chicano movement precursor, highlighting his bilingualism and choice of genre in *Poesía y prosa*, and provided analyses of several of his poems. Erlinda Gonzales-Berry (1989) weighed the unique sociopolitical dynamic at play in Chacón's writings, posited categories for their analysis, and read his work alongside that of the contemporaneous nuevomexicano Vicente Bernal. In *So All Is Not Lost* (1997), Meléndez provided the most detailed treatment of Chacón's biography, articulating his role in Spanish-language nuevomexicano newspapers and the literary movement of the day, noting how the publication of *Poesía y prosa* was seen as a triumph and culmination of that movement. This scholarship provides a point of departure for further study of Felipe M. Chacón's writing, in particular *Poesía y prosa*, and establishes Chacón among those early nuevomexicano writers in need of literary recovery and critical examination.

2. All quotations are as they appear in the present volume. Readers can easily locate the page number of the complete poem or prose piece by consulting the alphabetical list at the front of the book.

3. Gonzales-Berry (191–92) noted that modernista tropes and techniques emerge in Chacón's poetry.

4. As Meyer observed, *Poesía y prosa* carries a Mexican copyright: "Queda hecho el depósito que ordena la ley, para la protección de esta obra, en la República de México" [The appropriate steps, as ordered by the law, have been taken to protect the rights to this work in the Republic of Mexico]. Chacón offers no explanation for this legal declaration but perhaps, cognizant of his bilingual and Hispanophone readership, he envisioned a US-Mexico cross-border audience the likes of which had flourished in New Mexico in the nineteenth century.

5. An August 15, 1908, article from *La Voz del Pueblo* reported on Chacón's reading of "Mi escogido y mis razones" to the Club Larrazolo (also called the Sociedad Larrazolo). The same article published a portion of the poem, reported that it was met with great applause, and pledged to republish it later in its entirety.

6. Gonzales-Berry (192) suggested that the unnamed figure is territorial governor Miguel Otero.

7. Latin American *modernismo* is often linked with the founding of the Mexican literary magazine *Revista Azul* in 1894, which flourished from the late nineteenth century through the early twentieth in the works of writers Rubén Darío, Manuel Gutiérrez Nájera, José Martí, and many others.

Works Cited

Chacón, Felipe Maximiliano. *Obras de Felipe Maximiliano Chacón, "el cantor neomexicano": Poesía y prosa*. Albuquerque, NM, 1924.

Gonzales-Berry, Erlinda. "Vicente Bernal and Felipe M. Chacón: Bridging Two Cultures." In *Pasó por aquí: Critical Essays on the New Mexican Literary Tradition, 1542–1988*, ed. Erlinda Gonzales-Berry. Albuquerque: University of New Mexico Press, 1989, 185–98.

Meléndez, A. Gabriel. "Nuevo México by Any Other Name: Creating a State from an Ancestral Homeland." In *The Contested Homeland: A Chicano History of New Mexico*, ed. David Maciel and Erlinda Gonzales-Berry. Albuquerque: University of New Mexico Press, 2000, 143–68.

———. *So All Is Not Lost: The Poetics of Print in Nuevomexicano Communities, 1834–1958*. Albuquerque: University of New Mexico Press, 1997.

Meyer, Doris. "Felipe Maximiliano Chacón: A Forgotten Mexican-American Author." *New Scholar* 6 (1977): 111–26.

Nieto-Phillips, John M. *The Language of Blood: The Making of Spanish-American Identity in New Mexico, 1880s–1930s*. Albuquerque: University of New Mexico Press, 2004.

Nogar, Anna M. "Navigating a Fine Bilingual Line in Early Twentieth-Century New Mexico: *El cantor neomexicano* Felipe M. Chacón." In *Writing/Righting History: 25 Years of Recovering the U.S. Hispanic Literary Heritage*, vol. 10, ed. Antonia Castañeda and Clara Lomas. Houston, TX: Arte Público Press, 2020, 337–49.

Read, Benjamin. "Prologue." In *Obras de Felipe Maximiliano Chacón, "el cantor neomexicano": Poesía y prosa*. Albuquerque, NM, 1924, 5–14.

ANNA M. NOGAR AND A. GABRIEL MELÉNDEZ

Notes to the Spanish and English Editions of Poesía y prosa

For each translation to English of Chacón's poems, we have included an estimation of the type of poetic form of the Spanish original. We have done this to highlight Chacón's craft in creating the originals, a poetic precision and rigor that is difficult to reproduce effectively as much because of the complexity of the act of translation as for the fact that certain poetic forms readily recognizable to a Spanish reader may be unfamiliar or unintelligible to an English reader. We wanted to make clear for English-only readers the extent to which the Spanish originals skillfully and meticulously conform to Spanish-language poetic forms, displaying Chacón's mastery of the language and his encyclopedic knowledge of literary styles.

Our translations render the sense and meaning of the originals, but they do not conform to the meter and rhyme of the verse forms from which they derive. Chacón goes well beyond common popular verse styles like the *romance* (source for the present-day corrido) to create new works using more obscure and intricate poetic forms (*octava real*, *quintilla*, *soneto*). We include both Chacón's original notes and our comments (labeled "Editors' note") in the notes.

In the Spanish transcription of *Poesía y prosa*, we have largely left Chacón's writing as he composed it. There are some non-normative spellings and typos from the original that we have chosen to conserve to represent his style; we revised others for clarity. Poetry was Chacón's passion, but not his trade, and these works are the product of an author for whom writing poetry was an activity constrained to fleeting moments of leisure.

We have not attempted to make this new publication a precise facsimile of the original 1924 book. The formatting, style, and some punctuation have been updated to make the work more accessible to contemporary readers. In the original

Poesía y prosa, there are inconsistencies between the titles as listed in the index and the actual titles of the works; in addition, some of Read's quotations of the poems do not match the lines in the poems themselves. He may have misquoted or may have cited a different version. We have decided to retain these original discrepancies. The accurate titles of the poems and short stories are found in the alphabetical list at the front of this volume. Finally, since Chacón made use of ellipses in his writing, in the discussions where we quote truncated lines of poetry, we have added square brackets around any inserted ellipses.

For Chacón's renderings of other authors' English-language poems into Spanish, we have included transcriptions of the originals with the set of translations to English. With the exception of "Un sabio," for which he did not indicate an author, Chacón left good clues to find the original poems. We have found evidence of published versions of them that Chacón could have feasibly accessed, and we indicate these sources in the notes.

Spanish Transcription of Poesía y prosa

ÍNDICE

Prefacio
Prólogo
Oda a los héroes
A la patria
A Santa Fe
Alternados
Fragmentos
Celos y amor (Canción)
A María ante su altar
Caso florido
Ayer y hoy
El obrero
Desengaños
A la Señora Adelina Otero-Warren
Filosofando
Otoñal
A mayo
El ingrato
A Nuevo México
La vida (Soneto)
Al explorador del oeste
A la niñez
Una ilusión
Caso singular
La navidad
Desencanto
Asunto enredado
A los legisladores

Nocturno a . . .
Es el amor
Una agudeza
Paradoja
In memoriam
Sueños y realidades
Complacencia
Devoción
Indiferente
Mi escogido y mis razones
Caso doloroso
Se aleja y se vá
El ateo y la verdad
El angel de la guarda
Axiomas
Anita
Al enviudar mi madre
A la Srta. Adela Cruz
La creación
A mi hija, Herminia
A mi hijo, Felipe
A mi hija, Josefina
A mi hija, Julieta
A mi hija, Elvira
A mi Elvira
A mi hijito, Buenaventura
A mi hijita, Melba
A mi ahijada, Rosa Córdova

A mi ahijado, Jacobo Aragón, hijo
A mi amada hermanita, Lucía (por Pedro C. Chacón)
Salmo de la vida (Longfellow) Traducción
La fénix (Dryden)
Un sabio
Un bello ideal (Sam Wallis [sic] Foss)
La visión de Baltasar (Byron)
En la muerte de una joven (Byron)
María Estuardo y su doliente (E. Bulwer Lytton)
Un republicano real (Saetas políticas)
Un baile de caretas
Don Julio Berlanga
Eustacio y Carlota (Novelita)

OBRAS DE
FELIPE MAXIMILIANO CHACÓN,
"EL CANTOR NEOMEXICANO"

Poesía y prosa

Con un Prólogo por el Hon. Benjamin M. Read,
Autor de "Illustrated History of New Mexico," "
Sidelights on New Mexico History," etc., etc.

Publicado por F. M. Chacón,
Albuquerque, N. Mex.
EE. UU. de A.

© 1924 by F. M. Chacón

La propiedad de esta obra está protegida por ley y el Autor se reserva el exclusivo derecho de conceder o no, su reproducción.

Queda hecho el depósito que ordena la ley, para la protección de esta obra, en la República de México.

Prefacio

Al presentar este libro a los que lo leyeren, lo hago libre de presunciones de vanidad, que son tan chocantes en las personas.

Estoy por admitir que las obras de que se compone adolecen de imperfecciones, que podrían palparse al sujetarse a restricciones fundamentales. Por lo tanto, las ofrezco únicamente como una simple contribución a la Lectura Recreativa, para las masas populares de los pueblos, con debidas apologías a Teólogos, Filósofos, Retóricos y Lógicos.

Con estas breves aclaraciones, espero que mi libro sea acogido con el mismo espíritu en que lo ofrezco; y si el mismo alcanza a servir de solaz y recreo, para hacer amenas las horas que se dediquen a su lectura, dentro de sus admitidas limitaciones, quedará ampliamente remunerado el modesto esfuerzo de El Autor.

FELIPE MAXIMILIANO CHACÓN

Prólogo

El autor de este libro muy acertadamente ha dicho, al presentar al público cierto periódico, por medio de un artículo de fondo de su brillante pluma, lo que sigue: "Al paso que los años desenvuelven su curso en los confines del tiempo, van dejando como huella distintas épocas que caracterizan, de un modo especial, las contínuas sucesiones del progreso humano."

Comentando yo lo mismo, no hallo duda de que, en curso de esta evolución del tiempo, las obras literarias de Felipe Maximiliano Chacón están destinadas a dejar como huella una época distinta en la historia literaria de los Estados Unidos de América.

Digo una época distinta, por haber producido un genio netamente americano, el primero que diera lustre a su Patria en el bello idioma de Cervantes.

El poeta Chacón no debe ninguna apología por haber escogido la lengua castellana para dar forma a las brillantes producciones de su talento. En sus "Cantos patrios" Chacón ha querido manifestar que las alabanzas y loores de los héroes que ha producido el pueblo americano, al cual él pertenece, no se limitan a nuestro propio idioma, idioma que tanto amamos, el inglés, sino que lo mismo se cantan, con lujo de belleza, en otros idiomas del mundo civilizado, que los hijos de América han alcanzado a cultivar en curso de sus numerosas conquistas.

Nació Chacón en la población de Santa Fe, capital del estado de Nuevo México, el día 6 de diciembre de 1873, por lo tanto, he tenido yo el gusto de conocerle desde su muy tierna niñez, y en curso de los largos años he acostumbrado llamarle simplemente, "Felipe." Era su padre el finado don Urbano Chacón, uno de los primeros exploradores en el campo del periodismo en la parte sur del estado de Colorado, y la parte norte del entonces territorio de Nuevo México.

Don Urbano publicó "El Explorador," en Trinidad, Colorado, durante los últimos años del '60, y "El Espejo," en Taos, N.M., en los primeros años del '70. Este último periódico don Urbano después trasladó a Bernalillo, N.M., viniendo a ser una singular coincidencia que Felipe estableciera y dirigiera otro periódico en el mismo lugar, "El Faro del Río Grande," exactamente 30 años después. El padre del autor de este libro, don Urbano, publicó también "La Aurora," en Santa Fe, durante los primeros años del '80, y por fin murió a fines de 1886, cuando servía su segundo término de Superintendente de Escuelas del condado de Santa Fe, quedando Felipe huérfano de padre a la tierna edad de 13 años.

La madre de Felipe es la Sra. Da. Lucía Ward Vda. de Chacón, quien actualmente reside en Albuquerque.

El autor de este libro recibió su educación elemental en las escuelas publicas de Santa Fe, y su instrucción más avanzada en el Colegio de San Miguel, que los Hermanos Cristianos de la Orden de San Juan Bautista de la Salle aun dirigen en Santa Fe.

Felipe siempre fue de suyo muy estudioso, dedicando todo el tiempo que sus ocupaciones le permitían, al estudio o lectura de buenos libros. Una prueba de lo bien que nuestro poeta ha sabido aprovechar su tiempo, es la manera en que ha alcanzado aprender y cultivar la lengua castellana, sin ninguna ayuda superior, en un país cuyo idioma es el inglés, y donde hay pocas o ningunas oportunidades de aprender el castellano con propiedad.

El que este escribe siempre ha sentido que Felipe no se dedicara más exclusivamente a la literatura, habiendo dado ya la mayor parte de su vida al comercio. Esto habrá sido, tal vez, obra del Destina más bien que de su inclinación natural, pues, como él mismo dice en una de sus estrofas:

> El Destino es un sordo que no escucha
> La voz del sufrimiento que le invoca,
> Y no hay bicho que estando ya en la lucha,
> Se escape de la suerte que le toca.

Una de las cosas que todos los que le conocemos admiramos, es la facilidad con que escribe lo mismo el castellano que el inglés, lo mismo en poesía que en prosa. Felipe ha escrito muchas poesías en inglés, serias, festivas y de amor, y para dar una idea de su feliz ingenio en el particular, no me parece fuera de lugar el reproducir, como muestra de lo mismo, las siguientes tres composiciones en el dicho orden, respectivamente:

PARTING

Not dead but living whilst they be,
To me my loved ones die,
And one by one they pass from me
With but my last good-bye.
Yet feel disheartened? I refuse!
My haughty spirit soars on high,
And with each knock and slap and bruise
Unmoved I give my last good-bye.

IN MEXICO

We met: for me 'twas love at first sight,
She was divine;
I prayed her then my soul delight.
Asked her to make my future bright,
To be but mine,
Said she: "No entiendo!"

I love you more than tongue can tell,
I yield supine;
Without thee life, in sadness' spell,
Is but a winter's barren dell,
Won't you be mine?
Said she: "No sabe."

Unbounded wealth at your command,
Rich, superfine,
All at your feet, belle of this land,
You'll find anon as you demand,
If you'll be mine,
Cried she: "¡Ay Dios!"

Diamonds, gold, all to surprise,
A treasure's thine;

I'll give you, love, a paradise,
A home that queens may long for twice,
Won't you be mine?
Said she: "Oh! Yes me quiere."

Estos versos deben tomarse en el espíritu que el autor los intentó: como una ocurrencia de buen humor, y bajo ningún concepto, en sentido ofensivo. Entre sus composiciones en amor se encuentra el siguiente soneto:

WOULDST THOU?

Sad I long as in life I stroll
For the days of the past to return;
Not the time but its pleasures I mourn
In the folly so plain in the scroll
Of the woes I now sadly enroll;
Yet I see them but giving in turn
Recollections I willingly spurn
For another new hope in my soul.
Couldst thou only perceive in my heart
But to fathom my deepest regret,
Couldst thou only perceive ere we part
How it beats all alone for you yet,
Wouldst thou know why we drifted apart,
Then perchance you'd forgive and forget.

Como traductor del inglés al castellano, y vice versa, sólo tenemos que referirnos a las traducciones de obras de grandes poetas de habla inglesa, que aparecen en este libro, para palpar la pericia del autor; sus íntimos conocimientos de ambos idiomas.

Las obritas que constituyen este libro, han sido escritas al impulso de condiciones aisladas, y son mas bien fruto accidental, que intencional, del autor: no las escribió con el intento de publicarlas en forma de libro, lo cual queda probado con el solo hecho de que las mismas cubran tan extenso número de años, pues Felipe escribió la poesía titulada "Una ilusión," que aparece en este libro, cuando sólo contaba 17 años. Escribió también versos de carácter político, cuando sólo tenia 14 años de edad, los cuales a la sazón fueron extensamente celebrados en Nuevo México.

En su carácter personal, "El Cantor Neomexicano" es de índole filosófico. Esto se puede fácilmente palpar de su conversación misma: "He sufrido rudos golpes de la suerte en varias distintas épocas de mi vida-dice él-pero no conozco pena que no haya podido conquistar. He sabido afrontar infortunios, acerbas tribulaciones, nutriendo el sentir de que hubieran podido ser peores aun, y así he podido triunfar de la adversidad. Es tan inútil como falto de sensatez el apenarse uno por lo que no tiene remedio. Con eso uno sólo agrava la situación. Hay que vencer las penas de la vida para poder vivir muchos años y ser feliz."

Otro característico de Chacón es su aversión a la publicidad, su aborrecimiento de aparecer notorio. Su hermoso poema titulado "Oda a los héroes," que escribió al impulso de justos sentimientos patrios, que le inspirara la victoria de los Aliados en la Guerra Mundial, jamás la publicó antes de que apareciera en este libro. El Autor no quería hacer el papel del que buscarse notorio por cosas triviales, no porque considerase trivial el triunfo de las armas de su Patria, sino por su falta de aprecio de tan hermoso esfuerzo de parte suya. Chacón es un genio, y como todos los genios, no se sabe estimar a sí mismo.

Cierta escritora, que responde al nombre de Anita Acevedo, bajo el tema de "El Arte y la Poesía," ha dicho:

> El arte es un sol esplendente, sin ocaso, que deslumbra todas las pupilas, hacia cuyo llameante y fragoso incendio tienden su titánico y luminoso vuelo los gigantes cóndores de las aspiraciones legítimas; es un piélago inmenso sin orillas, sobre cuya límpida y sonora superficie se deslizan los blancos cisnes de los anhelos castos, desgranando las rosas líricas canciones entre el rumor de las alas y el beso de las espumas; es un luminoso y dilatado arco iris tendido sobre la azul diafanidad de un cielo y hacia cuyos vívidos colores baten sus poderosas alas las mariposas de los supremos deseos: es la radiante estrella que ilumina el amplio derrotero que conduce hacia la cumbre excelsa de la gloria y bajo cuyos vibrantes ósculos de oro abren sus broches los adorantes lirios de los sueños. Y la poesía, la poesía es la más hermosa flor del lirico jardín del arte; la poesía es la flor de todos los tiempos y todas las razas, flor que crece fulgente y regla, lo mismo bajo los abrasadores rayos del sol del trópico, que bajo el frío glacial del polo; es la mariposa que ha derramado

sobre el manto de todos los tiempos el polvo de oro de sus brillantes alas; es el pájaro mágico de blancas plumas, que en dulce lenguaje de los trinos ha revelado a todas las generaciones la secreta pasión de Romeo, el ósculo de Paolo, las promesas de Abelardo, la pasión de Otelo, ciego de locura, y armado de puñal; la agonía de Desdémona, y el viaje triunfal de Dante al Paraíso, en la amable compañía de Beatriz.

Poniendo estas apreciaciones al lado de las obras de Chacón, no puede uno menos que ver la Poesía íntimamente relacionada con el Arte. Los bellísimos cuadros de la fantasía que Felipe hace resaltar en sus versos son una viva inspiración para las artes del pincel y del cincel. Tómense por ejemplo aquellas estrofas de "La creación," que nos dan escenas típicas de épica hermosura, ubérrimos paisajes de pintoresca naturalidad, hablando del efecto del nacimiento del sol, entre ramajes y flores y aguas:

> Deslumbrante cayó del quieto lago
> Cual ornato en las aguas cristalinas,
> Do el ramaje teñido de su halago
> Daba júbilo en torno a las ondinas.
>
> Floripondios floridos destacaban
> Contrastado blancor al verde campo,
> Do felices oréadas entonaban
> Gratos loores al beso de su lampo.
>
> Y del campo bellísimos brocados
> Que formaban palmeras y abedules,
> Aspiraban sonrientes y extasiados
> Creciente vida en matizados tules.

¿Quién puede leer estas estrofas sin ver en ellas magnífico alimento para el ingenio del Arte?

Ha dedicado Felipe siete años de su vida al periodismo: fué editor asociado de "La Voz del Pueblo," de Las Vegas, N.M, desde el otoño de 1911 hasta la primavera de 1914; fundó y dirigió "El Faro del Río Grande," en Bernalillo, N.M., en 1914, y en la primavera de 1915 trasladó este semanario a Albuquerque.

Corto tiempo después vendió su interés en este periódico y se fue otra vez para Las Vegas, en donde tomó cargo de "El Independiente" como editor y gerente. También tuvo a su cargo y dirección, "El Eco del Norte," de Mora, N.M., en 1918, pero a fines del mismo año se retiró del periodismo y de nuevo se dedicó al comercio. En noviembre de 1922, sin embargo, por fin volvió al campo del periodismo, tomando cargo de "La Bandera Americana," semanario que se publica en Albuquerque, N.M., del cual es actualmente editor y gerente.

En mi humilde concepto, el pueblo de los Estados Unidos debe sentirse orgulloso de haber producido uno de sus conciudadanos, que diera lustre a su Patria con las producciones de su talento en la lengua de aquellos reyes, los reyes Católicos, que tan señaladamente contribuyeron al descubrimiento de América, el continente que habitamos.

Por otra parte, los pueblos de habla española, lo mismo americanos que europeos e insulares, deben dar la mas generosa acogida a las obras de Chacón, obras de uno que, desde extranjero suelo ha sabido hacer honra al dulce idioma de España: lengua de sus propios países, hecho que de suyo reviste méritos acreedores a profundo aprecio.

Muchas de las poesías que Chacón ha escrito durante su vida no verán jamás la luz de la publicidad: "Se han perdido en el naufragio de la desidia," como él mismo lo dice, indicando que nuestro poeta no se ha preocupado mucho que digamos de los méritos de sus obras en lo pasado; no las ha apreciado suficiente para conservar los manuscritos y darles publicidad en alguna forma, por algún medio, aparte de las que componen este libro, el cual, sin presumir yo virtudes de profeta, está destinado a labrar una memoria imperecedera para este hijo privilegiado del gran estado de Nuevo México.

En conclusión, deseo advertir que este Prólogo ha sido vertido al castellano por El Autor mismo de este libro, aprobando yo, implícitamente, su versión de mis conceptos y sentir en el particular.

Benjamín M. Read
Santa Fe, Nuevo México,
a 18 de febrero de 1924

PRIMERA PARTE

Cantos patrios y misceláneos

A mi madre, Da. Lucía Ward Vda. de Chacón,
dedico estas páginas

—El Autor

ODA A LOS HÉROES

A la legión americana

1.

Con el alma de orgullo rebosando,
En medio del placer de la victoria,
Quiero expresar, vuestro valor cantando,
Mi admiración de la perenne gloria
Que allá en los campos del lionor luchando
Vuestra proeza incorporó en la Historia,
Su lealtad demostrando consistente
El Estado del Sol Resplandeciente.[1]

El mundo retorcíase angustioso
Al ímpetu atrevido del tirano
Que arrasaba la tierra proceloso;
Que saciaba sus furias el prusiano
En los templos y hogares del hermoso
Suelo de Bélgica y de Francia, en vano,
Hasta que al mundo horrorizó Germania
En la hecatombe cruel del Lusitania

Y pasmado de horror el Universo
Vé de sangre inocente enrojecidas
Las aras de Neptuno, y al anverso,
Las manos del teutón empedernidas
Lievando al colmo su maligno esfuerzo:
Verdugos del hogar, de hijas queridas,
Madres y esposas, que en bestial fiereza
Hacían carnaval de la Pureza.

Y desde el fondo de la mar nutridos
Lamentos de dolor el alma hendieron;
La Civilización estremecidos
Vió sus cimientos y a la vez se oyeron
De mil Brenos los "¡Ay, de los vencidos!"
Que amenazantes de furor rugieron,
Queriendo anonadar con loca audacia
¡La causa misma de la Democracia!

Así pasaron días y semanas
Y los meses en años se trocaron
Y en lides submarinas inhumanas
Las infamias teutonas aumentaron;
Y a grado tal sus correrías insanas
Los derechos de América violaron,
Que Usona[2] expide su inmortal proclama
De "¡Armas al hombro, que la Patria os llama!"

II.

Ahí fue do vosotros respondísteis
Con denuedo y valor de americanos,
Ahí donde ofrecisteis
Pelear por los derechos soberanos
Del hombre, hasta, morir por rescatarlos;
Y al dejar a la esposa y a los hijos,
Y a los padres queridos al dejarlos,
Cori vuestros ojos fijos
En el hogar risueño
Que guardara en amor vuestros amores,
"Adios" dijísteis vos, y con el ceño
Del espartano izando los colores
De la Patria querida,
"¡Presente!" respondísteis,
Tiñendo en el honor la despedida.

Y marchando allá vas, hueste gloriosa,
Al toque del clarín que el alma inflama;
Ya tu antorcha encendiste
De la Justicia en la suprema causa
Y el Orbe con sus vítores te aclama;
Ya no habrá espera, ni cuartel, ni pausa,
Hoy que dejaste de la Industria el arte
Y por la libertad de las naciones
El culto de los dioses diste a Marte
Tornando al enemigo tus cañones.

Y marchando allá vas, hueste gloriosa,
Hasta cruzar indómita los mares
Donde te espera Francia jubilosa
En medio de sus múltiples pesares.

Mas densos nubarrones obscurecen
De nuevo el horizonte,
Mientras las hordas enemigas crecen
En formidable avance por el monte,
Gritando "¡Hasta Paris!" en voz de lema;
Y Francia entristecida y agobiada
Escucha sin temor el anatema
Tocando a sus guerreros retirada.

Pero la escena cambia repentina
Y el sol de la mañana
Como antorcha divina
Sale vertiendo rayos de esperanza

Cual nuncio de victoria en lontananza.
Es primero de junio
Y avanzando a lo lejos
¿Qué voces cantan con marcial acento
Sus místicos festejos?...

Y las hordas germánicas vacilan
Y en las alas del viento
Vuelan más claras las ingentes notas;
La furia del embate se detiene
Y de tierras indígenas remotas,
Con el tropel de sus camiones viene
Un ejército audaz desconocido,
Viene cantando, "¡Hasta acabar con ellos
Que no volvemos hasta haber vencido!"

Y suben más arriba los destellos
De aquel orbe encendido
Que vísteis bendecir en Monte Belleau
Vuestra marcha magnífica, estratégica,
Do al rugir del cañón, con patrio celo,
¡Os cubrísteis de gloria, hijos de América!
Y el reino de Plutón en lid horrenda
Se oye estallar cual huracán rugiente
De vuestro acero en la triunfal contienda;
Y la sombra de Wáshington ingente,
Impávida y tremenda,
Que allí aparece entre su regia prole,
Terror infunde al luchador germano
Que vá en retreta con su inícua mole.
Y fue tal en la lid vuestra bravura
Que el huno mismo os diera en patrimonio,
Por título de honor en su pavura,
El encomio de "Perros del Demonio."

Pero altivos seguís, neomexicanos,
En Chateau Thierry y San Miguel luchando,
Y en alianza de hermanos
Laureles de victoria conquistando.
Y volvían de nuevo los destellos
De aquel orbe encendido,

A ver de vuestras armas los descuellos
Y oíros el solemne prometido
De no cesar hasta acabar con ellos,
De no dar treguas hasta haber vencido . . .

Cada golpe que daban vuestras armas
Hendían los teutónicos salientes
Llevando al enemigo las alarmas
De contínuas derrotas contundentes.
Y el trono del Imperio se mecía
Con el odio del mundo en la balumba;
Mas llega de noviembre
El undécimo día
Y en abyecta derrota se derrumba . . .
La nación altanera del prusiano
Vé rodar por el fango su corona
Y al Kaiser con Nerón y Diocleciano
Burlado en el desprecio de Belona;
Le vé también en vergonzosa fuga
Perderse el bemol de un de profundis
Que se arrastra en el cieno de la oruga
Suspirando "Sic tránsit gloria mundis" . . .

Está ya la conquista consumada,
Vuestra santa misión está cumplida;
¡Mirad vuestra victoria coronada
Y en gloriosa epopeya convertida!

Cuan hermosos ondean los colores
Del pendón estrellado,
Mientras os canta universales loores
En éxtasis el mundo rescatado.
Y en vosotros, los hijos de este suelo,
En vos, neomexicanos,
Que en formidable duelo

Vencisteis con valor de americanos,
El mismo eterno Olimpo que os aclama
En un coro de vítores creciente,
¡Un torrente de gloria en vos derrama!

Notes

1. Nuevo México.
2. Voz compuesta de las letras iniciales de United States of North America, con las misma significación. —El Autor.

A LA PATRIA

Cuatro de julio, 1776–1918

Permíteme pulsar !oh, Patria mía!
Mi lira deficiente para darte
De sus férvidas notas la armonía,
Y empuñando felice tu estandarte,
Pletórico mi pecho do alegría,
Mi patrio amor solícito brindarte,
Que resistir no puede ni el cinismo
Las glorias sin igual de tu heroísmo.

Contemplo en tus anales esplendentes
De Napoleón bizarro la proeza
Que pudo conmover los continentes;
La contemplo teñida en la nobleza
De las almas de aquellos insurgentes
Altivos que fundaron tu grandeza,
Y un templo libre alzaron para el hombre,
Do cantara alabanzas en tu nombre.

Por el suelo rodó la tiranía
Al oír de John Adams la elocuencia
Precursora de aquel gloriosa día
En que Jefferson, lleno de preciencia,
Trazó de su inmortal sabiduría
La gran Declaración de Independencia,
¡Madre bendita do los patrios lares
Donde hoy alza mi musa sus cantares!

Quisiera yo la esplendorsa lira
Que ha labrádole a Homero eterna gloria
Para cantaros lo que al alma inspira
Ese nimbo brillante de tu historia;

Pintaros con el fuego del que admira,
Los lauros que circundan tu memoria,
Y en una Iliada hermosa, proficiente,
Darte en mi trova lo que mi alma siente.

Mas al pensar bendigo yo la estrella
Que dirige en la tierra mi destino,
Y que guía mis pasos con su huella
De cívica igualdad por el camino,
Bajo el pendón augusto que descuella
Sobre tu altar cual símbolo divino,
Do Wáshington trazó con letras de oro
"La Libertad," el sin igual tesoro.

Recibe, por lo tanto, Patria mía,
Las notas de mi ardiente patriotismo
En este aniversario de aquel día
En que al suelo rodó el imperialismo,
Con su yugo fatal de tiranía
Y el mísero baldón de su cinismo,
Y nació como el sol de la mañana
¡La eterna Independencia Americana!

A SANTA FE

Suelo bendito de la antigua villa,
Histórico verjel donde las flores
Abren gustosas ante el sol que brilla
Sus broches de perfumes y colores;
Allí donde florecen de tu arcilla
Frutas y mieses, entre mil amores,
Bajo tu azul repleto de fragancia
Se ha macido la cuna de mi infancia.

Bendito es para mí tu suelo hermoso
Como es bella la flor de tus pensiles,
Bendito por el ósculo afectuoso
Que ha brindado a mis labios infantiles,
El amor maternal que cariñoso
Mi ser alimentó en otros abriles,
Que allí sufrió sobre amoroso lecho
Por darme vida de su noble pecho;

Bendito porque abrigas en tu seno
Del autor de mi tiempo la ceniza,
Y porque tú eres relicario ameno
De hermanos que la muerte arrojadiza
Arrebató, como la voz del trueno
Arrebata la calma; y tu inverniza
Escarcha ya mi madre ha bendecido
Con lágrimas que viuda allí ha vertido

Y aunque tristes memorias aparecen
Cuando van mis recuerdos al pasado
Y forman una escena en que me ofrecen
Mil dolores que mi alma han penetrado,
Al mirar tus espinas que adolecen

También miro el arbusto perfumado
De la rosa halagueña del cariño
Que me dieron mis padres cuando niño.

Nunca olvido esos toques peregrinos
Que manan de tus regios campanarios
Ni de tus aves los vibrantes trinos
Que anuncian dulces tus albores diarios;
Lo mismo tus arrullos vespertinos,
Susurro de tus árboles agrarios
Que me arrebatan con deseo ardiente
Una vez mas de respirar tu ambiente.

Mas si la suerte inevitable mía
Quiere llevar a mi bajel bogando
Lejos de tí con gélida apatía.
Y nunca llegan a tu ambiente blando
Los tristes ecos de mi nostalgía,
Mira en el éter y verás brillando
De mis recuerdos la constante estrella,
Que tú entre halagos estarás con ella . . .

ALTERNADOS

Una vieja de Orizaba
Tan sorda que nada oía,
Cuando alguien la interrogaba
Tan sólo "sí" respondía.

Una vez mortificado,
Mas con calma, su marido
Le dijo, —Si te han hablado,
Como ahorita ha sucedido . . .

Toma consejo de mí,
Que bien te aconsejo yo,
Una vez diles que "sí"
Y otra vez diles que "no."

FRAGMENTOS

No critiquéis desdeñoso
Lo que viéreis a otro hacer,
Que no todo es malicioso
Lo que suele parecer.

Hay cosas inofensivas,
Hijas de buena intención,
Que las convierte en nocivas
La mala interpretación.

Y alegrías que son penas
Bajo lo superficial,
Y cosas que siendo buenas,
Por encima se ven mal.

Juzgar a primer partida,
A la calumnia equivale,
Que en las cosas de la vida
La intención es lo que vale.

CELOS Y AMOR

Canción

Me celan las mariposas
    que vuelan en tu jardín,
    porque ellas buscan las flores:
    en él te buscan a tí;
    me celan los petirrojos
    que alegres vienen y ván,
    porque ellos conmigo buscan
    los balcones de tu hogar.

CORO

Porque yo niña, voy suspirando,
    siempre buscando con ansia voy,
    cual mariposas y petirrojos,
    ¡ay! de tus ojos cándido amor;
    porque tus ojos son expresivos,
    cual dos misivos del alma son,
    yo veo en ellos con esperanza,
    la venturanza que anhelo yo.

Quisiera yo ser abeja,
    y en el carmín y azahar
    de tu nectárea boquita,
    ¡un mar de dicha libar!
    Que si fuera golondrina,
    buscaría con afán,
    el arrayán de tu seno
    dichoso para nidar.

CORO

Porque yo niña voy suspirando . . .

Me dicen niña que el cielo
 es paraíso eternal,
 y galardón de los buenos,
 ¿lo podré, niña, alcanzar?
 Tú sabes, porque a tu lado
 surge de dicha un Edén,
 y yo en tu amor !todo un cielo
 alcanzara a poseer!

CORO

Por eso, niña, voy suspirando . . .

A MARÍA ANTE SU ALTAR

¡Criatura sin igual! ¡Blanca azucena!
Fulgente aurora que introduce el dia,
Disipando las horas de la pena,
Llenando de esperanza el alma mía,
A tí mi acento férvido levanto
Y festejo tus glorias con mi canto.

Apenas niña en el mundano suelo
Era tu alteza ya tan encumbrada,
Que mediante un arcángel, desde el cielo
Fuiste tú por el Verbo proclamada
Para madre del Hijo que viniera
Y al hombre con su sangre redimiera.

¡Bello broche de augusto crisantema
Que al abrirse desplega su hermosura!
Tú a quien ciñe magnífica diadema
De estrellas con el sol por vestidura,
Ilumina mi senda tenebrosa
Con tu luz celestial esplendorosa.

Comprendo que es muy grande mi flaqueza,
Y que tres enemigos peligrosos,
Con suave, lisonjera sutileza,
Me persiguen con dardos ponzoñosos,
Y yo de sus hechizos fascinado
Temo al báratro eterno ir arrastrado.

Por eso, dulce madre, aquí rendido
Ante el florido altar de tu santuario,
En férvida plegaria yo te pido,
Por tus penas atroces del Calvario,
No me ciegue el engaño ni me espante
La lucha que depárase delante.

¡Oh, madre sacratísima y piadosa!
Cuando llegue yo al fin de mi sendero
No permitas que sea mi alma odiosa
A la vista de tu Hijo justiciero:
Sí que un solio de célicos querubes
La eleven hasta él en blancas nubes.

Entonces yo sus glorias ensalzando,
A tí, llena de gracia y de ternura,
En júbilo mis ojos elevando,
Te confiese que debo mi ventura,
Acogiendo benigna tú, entretanto,
El homenaje de mi pobre canto.

CASO FLORIDO

Era Soila hija querida
De un tal Anselmo Corona,
Y era atractiva persona
De unos veinte años de vida.

Por fin la solicitó,
Jurándole sus amores,
Un joven, Jacinto Flores,
Y con éste se casó.

Aquí resulta en primores
El nombre de nuestra dama,
Pues veréis que ahora so llama
"Soila Corona de Flores."

AYER Y HOY

Flor del campo Purpurina,
Casta como la pureza
    de la niñez,
Miré tu aurora divina
Velada por la belleza,
    tan sólo ayer.

Llegó tu vestal mañana
Y te adornó con su armiño,
    la doncellez,
Y a la mariposa ufana
Diste halagos de cariño,
    tan sólo ayer.

Pues eras niña inocente
Que por el campo corrías
    en el vaivén
De este mundo inconsistente
Que tú aun no conocías
    tan sólo ayer...

Pero temprano en tu día
Llegó el invierno escarchado
    que marchitó
Las flores que poseía
El arbusto seco, ajado,
    que tú eres hoy...

EL OBRERO

Hundido en las rocas
    Estalla el barreno
Hendiendo peñoles,
    Montañas abriendo;
Y el pico y la pala
    Con gran movimiento
Nivelan la ruta
    Por monte y desierto,
Y en cambio aparecen,
    Las vías de acero
Cortando distancias
    En menos que medio;
Florece la industria
    De modos diversos
Con mil bendiciones,
    Favor al obrero.

Las ruedas fabiles
    Que giran al vuelo
De rica labranza
    Forjando el apero,
O materias primas
    Así convirtiendo
En útiles telas
    Que viste el labriego,
O luce en festines
    El rico banquero,
Dios hizo posibles
    Favor al obrero.

Dibuja sus planos
    Perito ingeniero,
Los que desarrolla
    Cualquier arquitecto;
Se cavan y fundan
    Los firmes cimientos,
Los muros grandiosos
    Armados de acero,
Y altivos levantan
    Hacia el firmamento
Los mil rascanubes,
    Colegios y templos
Sus picos y espiras
    Y cúpulas regios,
Y todo se alcanza
    Favor al obrero.

Si altivos tiranos
    De exótico suelo
La Patria amenazan
    Con tono altanero;
Si acaso en millones
    Recluta el Gobierno
Para defenderse
    Con firme denuedo,
Esos que trabajan
    Responden con celo
Que el de cualesquiera
    Patriotas no menos;
Y cuando ya exhala
    Clarín halagüeño
Toque de victoria
    Tras combate fiero,
La sangre de aquestos,
    Que fluye a riachuelos,
Escribe gloriosa,
    "¡Que viva el obrero!"

DESENGAÑOS

Cuando joven aun y muy hermosa
Há tiempo yo te ví
Y te pedí tu mano, desdeñosa
Me la negaste a mí.

Y quitaste de un mundo muy risueño
El néctar y la flor,
Dejándome el acíbar de tu empeño
En cambio de mi amor.

Mas pasaron tus días y llegaste
Al desengaño cruel,
Do el cáliz de dulzura en que soñaste
Se convertía en hiel.

Y hoy que el mundo nocivo tan temprano
Tu armiño ya empañó,
Ninguno como amigo os dá su mano,
¡Ningúno, sólo yo!

A LA SEÑORA ADELINA OTERO-WARREN

Candidata republicana para el Congreso, 1922

Ceñida está tu frente de laureles,
Y tu nombre de honores irradía;
Hoy se asoma tu estrella en los dinteles
De la aurora triunfal de un nuevo día.

El mundo avanza con la idea humana
Y nacen nuevas cosas en la vida;
Hoy refleja la luz de la mañana
En otra esfera la mujer nacida.

Nacida en el sufragio igual al hombre,
Pero en lo espiritual, más elevada;
En pureza moral labra su nombre
Y la tierra va bien en su jornada.

Aquesta evolución tan meritoria,
Marcando el alto paso del Progreso,
Cubrirá Nuevo México de gloria
Poniendo una mujer en el Congreso:

Habilidosa, competente, honrada,
De alma gentil, de corazón sincero,
¡Héla ahí, la del pueblo proclamada,
La dama típica, Adelina Otero!

Vástago noble de español linaje,
Y más aún, americana pura,
Pero ¡qué importa el exterior ropaje
Del que amerita distinguida altura!

No es exclusiva la grandeza humana,
Que no limita con nación ninguna;
Del alto cielo su poder dimana
Y a quien le place su belleza aduna.

Mas no es esta lisonja que motiva
El servil interés del egoísmo,
Que sólo encierra mi intención altiva
Teñir en la Justicia un idealismo.

Salud! Salud! Un brindis de alegría,
Placer del progresivo ciudadano,
Os manda junto con la trova mía,
¡El saludo de un pueblo soberano!

FILOSOFANDO

Mientras Sofía estudiaba
    Libros de filosofía.
Zenón, su esposo, afilaba
    Un cuchillo que tenía.

Llamando ésto su atención,
    Preguntó ella lo que hacía,
Y le respondió Zenón;
    "Poco más filo, Sofía."

OTOÑAL

Hojas que el viento arrebata:
Se ven doquier arrolladas,
Marchitas, secas, ajadas,
Cual quiso la suerte ingrata.

Antes de regia verdura
Frondosos bosques formaron
Y el horizonte pintaron
Deslumbrante de hermosura.

Y con ellas los cantores
Jilgueros en el follaje,
Rindieron en homenaje
Sus matinales loores.

Y en torno de ellas surgía
Suave, aromado el ambiente
Que aspiraban do aliciente
Palpitando de alegría.

Pero esos días pasaron
Con los goces que trajeron
Y en cambio sólo nos dieron
Los recuerdos que dejaron.

Hoy por incierto camino
Al ir la vida cursando,
Van como yo, suspirando,
Al impulso del Destino.

Pues donde todo remata,
Ellas son del hombre iguales,
Que al fin somos los mortales
¡Hojas que el viento arrebata!

A MAYO

Mes bendito en que las flores,
Con sus múltiples colores,
Vienen todo a matizar,
Es tu bálsamo el que inspira
Los acentos de mi lira
Para poderte cantar.

De verde se viste el monte,
Polícromo el horizonte
Destaca rico esplendor,
Y entre vivientes alfombras
Cantan dulce las alondras,
Canta alegre el ruiseñor.

Nútrese de aroma ingente
Y de elixir el ambiente
Que respira, todo ser,
Y en tí la vida renace,
Vivifica, satisface,
Todo es dicha por doquier.

Ceres con magia fecunda
En pródigo mar inunda
De riqueza sin igual,
Los huertos y los sembrados
Que respiran extasiados
Tu néctar primaveral.

Canta el líquido fluyente
De la cristalina fuente
Alabanzas a tus pies,
Y llega a mí su murmullo
Como celestial arrullo
De mi ventana al través.

Mes bendito en que las flores
Con sus múltiples colores
Inspiran gozo y placer,
Tú que traes la nueva vida
¡Deja que en mi alma entumida
Vuelva Dios a renacer!

EL INGRATO

Si has tenido en la vida desengaños,
Habrás sido también casual testigo
Do algún ingrato que creíste amigo,
Andaba desvalido en los antaños;

Pisando abrojos mil en sus peldaños,
Y tú le diste, como un padre, abrigo.
¿Tú le ayudaste cuando fué mendigo?
Aguarda, pues, los venideros años:

Si algún día el destino le enaltece
Y a tí te abruma suerte malhadada,
El que de humano corazón carece,

Ni verte a tí, su bienhechor, le agrada,
Mas si el mundo a pedradas te adolece
¡Con el mundo él te arroja su pedrada!

A NUEVO MÉXICO

En su admisión como estado

Por fin habéis logrado, suelo mío,
De lauros coronar tu altiva frente,
Alcanzando del cielo del estío
Una estrella gloriosa y esplendente;

Estrella cuyos lámpos matinales
Os proclaman Estado soberano,
Que brille de la Patria en los anales
¡Eterno en el pendón americano!

Honor para tus hijos, que han sufrido
Contigo numerosos desengaños
Y con ellos tan sólo conseguido
El injusto baldón de muchos años;

No obstante la lealtad indisputable
Que a la Patria tus hijos ofrecieran,
Luchando con el indio ingobernable
Y contra los del Sur que secedieran;

No obstante que valientes se lanzaran
A batir a sus étnicos hermanos
Y con sangre que en Cuba derramaran
Probaran ser del todo americanos.

Cuántas veces recuerdo os encontrara
Buscando en el espacio nebuloso
Un destello de luz que os animara
De nuevo en el sendero fatigoso.

Y ¿lo viste? Lo viste en lontananza
Perderse de la niebla en la espesura
Y perdiste con eso la esperanza
Y exhalaste suspiros de amargura.

Luchaste contra del hado endurecido
Batiendo del Congreso la injusticia
Y con ella el insulto proferido
Del prejuicio racial por la malicia.

Mas sufriendo contigo si sufrías
Yo seguí de tus pasos tras la huella . . .
Hasta que al fin, en claras lejanías,
Presentóse bellísima tu estrella,

Nacida entre arreboles orientales:
Y gustoso tomándola el Destino
Hoy te dá sus fulgores celestiales
Inundando de gloria tu camino . . .

Ahora yo quiero, mi querido suelo,
Que digno de esa gloria, tu gobierno
Tienda sus alas por el ancho cielo
Y sepulte en el golfo de lo eterno

Leyes injustas que tu nombre manchen;
Quiero ver tus archivos relucientes
De datos limpios que tu nombre ensanchen
A través de los siglos sucedentes.

Ver que el honor para tu historia escriba
Con luz de su pincel inmaculado,
Hechos que lleven la mirada arriba
Y te hagan de la Unión feliz dechado.

Entretanto, tus hijos hoy elevan
De yítores un coro entusiasmado,
Cuyos ecos de júbilo resuenan . . .
"¡Que viva Nuevo México, el Estado!"

LA VIDA

Soneto

Errática vagaba por doquiera,
Con vario giro de incesante vuelo,
Palomita ambiciosa cuyo anhelo
Un nectáreo verjel tan sólo era.

Y continuando unfana su carrera,
Vino la noche y la metió en desvelo,
Y ya en mi casa, en su ambición y celo,
Tomó el candil por flor en primavera.

Y sus alitas rápidas girando,
Ansiosa por lograr su prometida,
Se fue a la llama del candil volando;

Y en fragmentos quemados convertida
La ví después, y suspiré exclamando:
¡Es un dolo de engaños ésta vida!

AL EXPLORADOR DEL OESTE

¡Valiente explorador, cuánto os admiro!
Vos os legásteis en perenne gloria
La página brillante en que hoy os miro
Del güaldo Oeste rubricar la historia,
Historia escrita en eternal papiro,
Por Lexington y Concord principiada
Y en los grandes patriotas perpetuada.

Tenías el hogar, sus, bendiciones,
Los tiernos hijos, la querida esposa,
Todos aquellos temporales dones
En que la vida plácida reposa;
Pero tenías más, tus convicciones
Y la resolución siempre afanosa
De acometer inciertas prospectivas
Y hacerlas realidades positivas.

Mas al pensar imaginar bien puedo
Tu corazón titánico oprimido,
Con un suspiro penetral y quedo
Responder el adiós enternecido
Del hogar que dejabas por tu credo,
Credo tal vez de inspiración nacido
Al resplandor de algún florido sueño
Que os diera sus colores halagüeño.

Y como el Mago en rumbo a la Judea,
Por una estrella guiado en su camino,
Seguiste el incentivo de una idea;
Y de Colón cursando con el tino
Del Astro Rey la luminosa tea,
Llegaste felizmente a tu destino,
Y con proeza indómita tu hueste
Buscóse las riquezas del Oeste.

Tu camino rugoso y escarpado
Intrépido cursaste y decidido,
Y sufriste en el monte, desolado,
Sus rigores enfermo y entumido,
Expuesto del salvaje encarnizado
Al golpe desalmado, embrutecido,
Que ha logrado en terrífica matanza
Darle a Custer eterna remembranza.

En mil formas la muerte desafiaste
Travesando los montes y espesuras,
Y las áridas pampas do iniciaste
Todo ese panorama en que hoy figuras
Cual móvil prototipo de un contraste:
Uniste las oceánicas honduras
Y sembraste por medio continente
Del progreso la magia floreciente.

Esa marcha contínua de dolores
Conduciste resuelto y valeroso,
Hallando penas en lugar de amores,
Cuidado por doméstico reposo.
Mas de todo ese mar de sinsabores,
Enérgico tu empeño laborioso
Pudo, elevando tu inmortal estrella,
Marcarle al mundo provechosa huella.

Ya de Webster el cuadro se deshizo,
Que al Oeste le dió calamidades,
Perpétuas nieves por eterno piso...
Hoy tus rústicas chozas son ciudades
Y las pampas fecundo paraíso,
Y ya les diste a las posteridades
Aquel tesoro de valor magnífico
Excavado a la costa del Pacífico.

Quisiera yo la prodigiosa lira
Que ha labrádole a Homero eterna gloria,
Para cantaros lo que al genio inspira
Ese nimbo brillante de tu historia;
Elaborarte cuánto mi alma admira
De tus grandes hazañas la memoria,
Y en una Iliada hermosa, proficiente,
Darte en mi trova lo que mi alma siente.

Torvo, severo, inculto, denodado,
Espíritu en esfera distinguida,
Titán por los peligros indomado,
Vencedor en batalla endurecida;
Hoy tiene vuestro nombre asegurado
Su puesto en los anales de la vida,
Esculpido en valor y sufrimiento,
Y alzado en perdurable monumento.

Por ésto la moderna arquitectura
Hoy ostenta en sus dombos arrogantes
Cincelada tu mágica figura
Y en sus frisos y frescos deleitantes;
Y así como la eterna cinosura
Su ser presenta en célicos brillantes,
¡Hoy luce, continente a continente,
El gran explorador del Occidente!

A LA NIÑEZ

Eres tú la edad bendita
De inocentes ilusiones,
En que el corazón se agita
Contento porque palpita
Do no existen aflicciones.

Cruzan por límpida mente
Blancas palomas volando;
Notas de un alma inocente
Que vibran por el ambiente
Como del cielo bajando.

Es tu pena momentánea,
Cosa que en placer se funde,
Que tu lágrima espontánea
Sólo es risa simultánea
Que con ella se confunde.

Tus penas no son abrojos,
Sino hijas de la ilusión
Sencilla de tus antojos;
¡Son lágrimas de los ojos
Y no las del corazón!

Tierna emoción jubilosa
Nace en el alma del niño
Cuando vé a la mariposa
Nutriendo sobre la rosa
Los brocados de su aliño.

¡Vuela! Allá vá en pos de ella,
Lleno de inmensa delicia
De flor en flor tras la huella,
Y del mundo en la querella
Esa es toda su codicia.

¡Dulces horas matinales,
Sin pesares ni desvelos,
En que gozan los mortales
Dicha plena entre timbales,
Carritos y caramelos!

Y siendo tú tan preciosa,
Nada vale mi cariño:
¡Qué diera, niñez hermosa,
En la vida borrascosa,
Yo por volver a ser niño?

Todo era flores ¡ay! flores
Que sin espinas nacieron
De la la vida en los albores,
Mas su fragancia y colores
En el capullo murieron...

Mas eres la edad bendita
De inocentes ilusiones,
En que el corazón se agita
Contento porque palpita
Do no existen aflicciones.

UNA ILUSIÓN

¿Porqué me llena de encanto la sonrisa
Que vierten de tu hechizo los fulgores,
Tan suave como el beso de la brisa
Que nace del perfume de las flores?

¿Es, acáso, una gloria trascendente
El suelo que te vió nacer un día,
O porqué es tu mirada tan ingente
Y tu acento celeste melodía?

¿Serás la Venus de divina alteza
Que en otra edad idolatró el pagano,
Y así, favor a tu ideal belleza,
Amor infundes al tender la mano?

Miro yo de tus ojos la hermosura,
Con su rayo de luz fascinadora,
Cual prodigio que torna mi ventura
En un caos de pasión abrasadora.

Miro tu imagen de castaños rizos:
Ondina, tierna de pasiva calma,
Que velada de mágicos hechizos
Me arrebata con éxtasis el alma.

Tienes tú magnetismo sobrehumano,
Y aunque te estudio, deslumbrado quedo,
Eres mujer y por lo tanto arcano
Que yo, como hombre, comprender no puedo.

Mas si eres diosa que adoró el romano
Cuando sólo eras ilusorio mito,
¡Con gusto haré mi corazón pagano
Y elevaré tu ser a lo infinito!...

　　Perdone el Cielo el loco devaneo
Que a mi cerebro causa tu hermosura:
El Cielo te hizo de esplendor febeo
Y obra del Cielo causa mi locura.

　　Mas ¡ay! en vano el corazón se agita
Cuando miro tu imagen prepotente,
Y ese túrgido seno que palpita
Y el candor que fulgura de tu frente...

　　Es mejor consignarte a lo futuro
Como sueño ilusivo del pasado,
Que de la noche bajo el manto oscuro
Nació tan sólo para ser soñado.

　　Así es que ¡adios! te dice mi existencia,
Quiero truncar la flor en el botón,
Quiero borrar tu imagen con mi ausencia
Y que el tiempo se lleve... ¡una ilusión!

CASO SINGULAR

Un anciano aconsejaba
   a un borracho habitual,
   contrario al vicio del cual,
   de éste modo se expresaba
   con acento paternal:

—El ser humano embrutece
   con ese jugo infernal,
   que la razón entorpece,
   y la cabeza enloquece,
   y al hombre vuelve animal...

Pero el súbdito de Baco,
   bamboleándose repone:
   —No le atina usted, don Paco,
   la manera en que a Climaco
   el traguito le indispone:

Mis crápulas sempiternas
   las sigo desde muchacho,
   y el néctar de las tabernas
   no me causa más empacho
   que hacerme agüadas las piernas.

LA NAVIDAD

Era la noche de calma plena,
mostraba el cielo su claridad,
y a media noche, de gloria llena
dábase al hombre la enhorabuena
por ser del Cristo la Navidad.

Baja del cielo, diáfano, hermoso,
vertiendo un ángel gloriosa luz,
y a los pastores, con alborozo
dice les traigo nuevas de gozo,
¡que hoy en Judea nace Jesús!

Canta en seguida del cielo un coro
su dulce antífona celestial,
¡GLORIA IN EXCELSIS...! eco sonoro
que se difunde con notas de oro
por todo el ámbito terrenal...

Llenos de dicha, fe y esperanza
van los pastores hasta Belén,
y allí postrados en alabanza
píos contemplan su bienandanza
dando al Mesías el parabién.

César Augusto vése ignorado
y distinguido el casto pastor:
¡el que se exalta, se vé humillado
y el que se humilla se vé exaltado
por el heraldo del Redentor!

Vuelen las notas angelicales
de aquel mensaje de amor y paz,
a las naciones que hoy en fatales
lides derraman rojos raudales
de sangre y ruina con furia audaz.

Séales este glorioso día
fúlgido foco de inspiración;
¡truéquese la hórrida lid impía
en dulces cántigas de alegría
dignas de célica bendición!

En santo júbilo estimulemos
entre los hombres el buen humor;
nuestras rencillas hoy olvidemos
y con los ángeles prodiguemos
al desvalido bondad y amor.

DESENCANTO

En una noche del mes de junio
    un plenilunio
ví que se hundió,
De densas nieblas en la espesura
    do su hermosura
desvaneció...

Así la luna de mis amores,
    en interiores
días perdí,
Entre las nieblas del desencanto
    cuyo quebranto
bien merecí.

Pasión ardiente de mil ensueños,
    entre desdeños
ví que se hundió,
Pero con ella, frágil, inquieta,
    ¡una coqueta
despareció!...

ASUNTO ENREDADO

Un médico le decía,
En audiencia consultoria,
A un mancebo que tenía
Averiada la memoria:

—Tome usted esta receta,
Es un remedio eficaz,
Le costará una peseta
Y quedará usted en paz...

Unos tres días después
Volvió el mancebo afligido,
Dijo al doctor, —Mal me ha ido,
Salió la cosa al revés:
Porqué no me cura usted
Primero la enfermedad,
Que con memoria podré
Tomar con puntualidad
La medicina después,
Que hoy se me olvida tomar...

A LOS LEGISLADORES

Primer sesión legislativa de estado, del estado de Nuevo México

En el puesto estáis ya los escogidos
Del Cuerpo Soberano del Estado,
De laureles ceñidos.
A vosotros el pueblo ha consagrado
El honor de su fe, de su confianza,
De vuestra integridad ya convencido;
Os ha hecho su objeto de alabanza
Y al pináculo augusto
Do el gran Solón eternizó su nombre,
Os elevó con espontáneo gusto
A que os labrárais inmortal renombre.

¿Queréis gozar felices esa gloria,
Y que perdure inmaculada y pura
A través de los siglos de la Historia?
¿Queréis ser acreedores al respeto
Y admiración de la nación futura?
De vos mismo depende:
Pues ya sabéis lo que el deber exige
Y que en la vida quien lo cumple asciende,
Y en el orgullo de su prole rige.

Hoy los ojos del mundo,
Cual justiciera, veladora tea,
Fijos están con interés profundo
De vuestro cargo en la inicial tarea
Por lo tanto, atención a mis acentos,
Hispanoamericanos,
Hijos de padres nobles y valientes,
Bravíos, soberanos,
Que no han sabido doblegar sus frentes

Ni han conocido superior ninguno
Por muchos siglos ya retrocedentes;
Hijos libres de aquellos capitanes
Que surcaron indómitos los mares
De la tierra del Cid y los Guzmanes,
Y aquí en el continente americano
Os han legado los benditos lares
Que a sangre y sacrificio conquistaron
Bajo el nítido azul neomexicano.

   Guardáos de la malévola impostura
De tiranuelos de anteriores años,
Que quisieran con blanda donosura,
Y al móvil de sus típicos amaños,
Haceros instrumentos de sus fines;

   Recordad vuestro origen con orgullo
De cuerda discreción en los confines,
Y elevadlo dechado a lo infinito
Tan limpio como flor en el capullo,
Mas firme como roca de granito.
Sed vosotros el par de los modelos
Y no seáis por otros dirigidos,
Y alzaréis vuestros nombres a los cielos
Del óleo santo del honor ungidos,
Y vuestra gloria en el presente caso
Será la luz de una constante aurora,
Que irá brillando de la vida al paso,
¡Que en oriente nació deslumbradora
Para nunca ponerse en el ocaso!

NOCTURNO A . . .

Sátira política, adaptación del "Nocturno a Rosario," de Manuel Acuña

I.

Pues bien! yo necesito
  deciros que si lloro,
Hiriendo con mis quejas
  al frígido aquilón,
Tan sólo consideren
  que el Hado a mi desdoro
Me arranca de mi silla,
  me quita mi tesoro
Y paso yo al olvido
  cual rápida ilusión

II.

Quiero que el pueblo sepa
  que ya hace muchos días
Estoy atolondrado
  de tanto no dormir;
Que el diablo se ha llevado
  las esperanzas mías,
Que en lápida mortuoria
  mis fátuas fechorías
Sellaron para siempre
  de Oñate[1] el porvenir.

III.

De noche, cuando pongo
    mis sienes en la almohada,
Queriendo que Morfeo
    me calme el padecer,
Horrendas pesadillas
    perturban mi jornada,
Fantasmas enemigas
    me dán su carcajada
Y loco y aturdido
    Yo vuelvo amanecer.

IV.

Comprendo que la silla
    que dejo yo vacante,
Mis anchas posaderas
    jamás ocuparán...
Mas la amo, y al mirarla
    con otro tan distante,
Bendigo sus desdenes
    con alma sollozante
Y en vez de amarla menos,
    la quiero mucho más.

v.

A veces pienso en darle
    mi eterna despedida,
Borrar en mis recuerdos
    a toda esta región...
Mas si es en vano todo
    y el alma no se olvida
Del pueblo trasquilado
    que dejo a mi partida,
¡Qué quieren, pues, que yo haga
    con este corazón!

vi.

Y luego que ya estaba
    concluído mi santuario,
Y alzado yo a la dicha
    de un dios sobre su altar;
Mamando del Gobierno
    mi bien gordo salario,
Del pueblo con destreza
    talando el honorario
De todos los destinos
    que pude legislar...

VII.

¡Qué hermoso hubiera sido
    vivir bajo aquel techo,
Con Pancho y don Jacinto
    que hoy gimen de mi azar!
Los dos previlegiados,
    yo siempre satisfecho,
Los tres una sola alma
    (un tercio en cada pecho),
¡Y yo de sus lisonjas
    an medio como un zar!

VIII.

¡Figúrense que hermosas
    las horas de esa vida!
¡Qué dulce y bello el viaje
    por un tierra así!
Mas viendo ya en la huesa
    mi santa prometida,
¡Quisiera que estallara
    de nieble estremecida
Centella fulminante
    por mí, no más por mí!

IX.

Bien sabe Dios que ese era
　　el insular desvelo
Que como a Sancho Panza
　　me pudo mantener...
Bien sabe Dios que en nada
　　cifraba yo mi celo
Sino en LLENAR LAS BOLSAS
　　en el fecundo suelo
Que me envolvió en pañales
　　cuando me vió nacer.

X.

Esa era mi esperanza...
　　mas ya que a sus fulgores
Se opone "Teddy" Roosevelt
　　de allá de Washingtón,
¡Adiós, por la vez última,
　　halagos y rencores,
Mi gloria de cacique,
　　mis tachas y mis flores,
Mi garra ejecutiva
　　a mi poder, adiós!

Note

　1. Nombres ficticios han sido sustituídos por los verdaderos, en debido respeto a las personas a que pertenecen, exceptuando el de Roosevelt, que sólo se menciona incidentalmente. —El Autor.

ES EL AMOR

    Calentura de lágrimas y risa;
Causa de insomnia que a demencia tira;
Dulce placer, dolor que martiriza
Cuando a su impulso el corazón delira;
Es una comezón que se desliza
Del ojo al alma y en el alma gira
Sin poderse rascar; fuente de errores;
Lecho de espinas que parecen flores.

UNA AGUDEZA

Una jara en cada mano
Josefita, y ella en medio,
Fue a confundir a su hermano
Para quebrantar el tedio.

—Oye, Juanito, repite
Lo que te voy a ir diciendo,
Pero tal como lo oíste:

—De Guadalajara vengo,
Jaras traigo, jaras vendo,
A medio doy cada jara,
¡Qué jaras tan caras vendo!...

Como el hermano Juanito,
Más que Juanito era Juan,
Y más que Juan era truhán,
Así respondió diciendo:

—De Guadalajara vengo,
Jaras traigo, jaras vendo,
Y en medio de jara y jara
¡Qué cara ajada estoy viendo!

PARADOJA

    Con frecuencia común y lamentada,
Cuando tú hayas palpado de la vida
La dura realidad en tu jornada,
Hallarás, en verdad que desagrada,
La gratitud del hombre desmentida:

    Sin pensar en el perro agradecido,
Creerás hallar la gratitud, sin yerro,
En el hombre que tú has favorecido,
Pero hallarás tu error esclarecido:
Humano más que el hombre lo es el perro.

IN MEMORIAM

Nada extraño el mirarte ahí tendido,
Convertido en materia inanimada;
El lapso de tu vida ya vencido,
Está ya tu misión desempeñada;
Por la noche tu lámpara ha vertido
Varia luz que le fue predestinada,
Y hoy al verla sin luz en su peana
Comprendo que ha llegado la mañana.

Pero siento mi pecho deprimido;
El alma de dolor arrebatada;
¿Quién no siente al partir un ser querido
Que se vá para siempre en su jornada!
Sé también que con labio enternecido,
Al dejar esta mísera morada,
Un "adios" a mi nombre tu alma unía
Cuando el último aliento se perdía.

Ausente estaba yo; ni en tí pensaba
En aquel trance de inefable pena
En que la muerte prematura entraba
Ya de tu vida en la final escena,
Ni cuando tu ceniza ya ofertaba
A la tierra en final la enhorabuena,
Pero hasta el cielo elevaré un sudario
Que te valga ante el Cristo del Calvario . . .

De nobles sentimientos adornada
Cruzó tu alma la efímera existencia,
Y a través de tu vida infortunada
Brillaba extraordinaria inteligencia;
Fue tu pecho sensible la morada
De cándida lealtad a la conciencia,
Y asilo fue tu corazón sincero
A dolor de tu humano compañero.

En vista de tan bellas cualidades,
Que adornan una fase de tu historia,
Contemplo que del tiempo en las edades
Cada estrella lucífera cursoria
Que compone de pléyades miríades,
Ha tenido una sombra transitoria:
Se ha trocado en capuz la luz del día
Y el plenilunio en abismal umbría.

Ví la joya en el fango que rodaba
Mancillar sus primores diamantinos,
Mientras mi alma tus yerros deploraba;
Ví la linfa en hervores cristalinos
Que túrbidos el cieno los trocaba,
Y entendí que Quien traza los destinos,
Como práctico ejemplo contra el vicio
Le dió al mundo tu ser en sacrificio.

¡En ésto ha sido tu misión sublime!
¡Grande es quien vive para bien del hombre!
Que tu vida en sus páginas imprime,
Sin letras, sin alarde, sin renombre,
Un volumen de máximas que anime
A odiar los yerros y a elevar el nombre;
Es un faro que alumbra el arrecife
Do se chocara el navegante esquife.

¡Duerme feliz! El llanto que han vertido
Concha y René,[1] amargo y doloroso,
El Cielo calmará cornpadecido;
Bajará del consuelo el sol piadoso
De ellas en torno al suelo humedecido,
Y de ese suelo elevará vahoso
Blanco dosel para la triste fosa
Do tu cadáver en la paz reposa.

Note

1. Esposa e hija, respectivamente.

SUEÑOS Y REALIDADES

I.

 Es el Destino aquel monarca ingente
Que dijo al hombre en su primer mañana:
"Levántate y camina"...
El hombre levantóse y caminando
De aquel impulso prepotente al móvil,
Fue cursando del tiempo las edades
Sin más luz que alumbrara su sendero,
Acerca del futuro a que camina,
Que aquella gran verdad que dijo Iriarte
Con certeza que todo lo ilumina,
Que la muerte por fin "con pies iguales
mide la choza pajiza y los palacios reales."

 Así quiso el Destino caprichoso
Levantar de los hombres en la vida
Al César poderso;
Ese altivo titán que rivaliza
Con el genio de Aníbal en la guerra
Y el del gran Cicerón en el Estado,
Sobrepuja a Alejandro en la conquista
Y a los Pompeyo los derrota en Munda;
Ese mílite audaz que se ha lanzado
Contra el fiero simún de los desiertos
Y la tromba temible de los mares,
Y en su lucha febril ha penetrado
Del enemigo en los pomposos lares
Y todo el Universo conquistado.
Mas después de sus múltiples victorias,
Ya de eternos laureles coronado,
Le halla el fin terminante de sus glorias
Transido de dolor, decepcionado...

Son los idus de Marzo: ya es el tiempo,
Y la escena, el Senado:
Los trágicos actores se preparan
Con seguro puñal bajo la toga
Para inmolar la víctima del drama.
Entra el César incauto en el proscenio
Y encuentra a sus amigos:
De cada amigo espera una sonrisa,
La sonrisa bendita de un hermano,
Pero llega la ráfaga inverniza
Y arrebata las flores del capullo
Y marchita sus hojas de esmeralda,
Dejando sólo en su lugar espinas,
Y todo desvanécese en la nada . . .

Las heridas primeras las resiste
Con su típica audacia,
Pero al sentir la del querido Bruto
Más profunda en el alma que en el cuerpo,
Exclama con la voz del sentimiento,
Y el alma rebosando de amargura,
"¡Tambien tú, caro Bruto, me condenas?
Entónces, ¡muera el César!" y perdida
Su voz en la emoción de su quebranto,
Cae al suelo sin quejas y sin vida:
¡Ruedan glorias, grandeza y todo aquello
A los pies de la estatua de Pompeyo!

Así dá ese monarca sus decretos,
Del todo indiferente,
Y ¿a qué fuera el llamarlos indiscretos?
El Destino es un sordo que no escucha
La voz del sufrimiento que le invoca,
Y no hay bicho que entrando ya en la lucha
Se escape de la suerte que le toca.

II.

Siendo la dama Natura
De virtudes rica fuente
Ha brotado a su vertiente
A raudales la hermosura.

　Ella le ha prestado al día,
Del Astro Rey los fulgores,
Al iris bellos colores
Y a las aves melodía;

　Al páramo le dió arenas,
Al prado extensa, llanura
Y a los montes la verdura
Con sus aromas amenas;

　Celajes al firmamento,
Su resplandor a la luna,
Y es del Universo cuna
Desde su primer momento.

　Al despuntar los albores
Serenos de una mañana,
Andaba Natura ufana
Entre perfumes y flores;

　Ván los primeros destellos
Hasta el riachuelo sonoro,
Y se vé brillar el oro
Entre sus blondos cabellos;

　Y sus formas peregrinas
Su blanca tez desplegando,
Se veía contemplando
En las aguas cristalinas.

Ángelo y Rafael tiñeron
En bellezas de aquel día,
La gloria que hoy irradía
Do sus nombres so inscribieron...

Perdido de arróbamiento
Y encendido de pasión,
Puso el Destino al momento
En ella su admiración...

III.

Y los dos por el Cielo vinculados,
Desde aquel día hermoso en que se vieron,
Acompañan al hombre.
Y lo mismo al pastor en su cabaña
Que al magnate perdido en sus riquezas,
Del tiempo en la carrera transitoria
Ella a todos les brinda sus bellezas
Y él traza los eventos de su historia.

COMPLACENCIA

Un galán que pasaba por el parque,
Con paso muy elástico y veloz,
Encontróse una dama que al instante,
Saludó tan gracioso cual precoz:

—¡Cuánto admiro, mujer, esos tus ojos,
Que el Dios de las bellezas te donó,
Su mirada mitiga mis abrojos
Por ser la de OJOS NEGROS que amo yo.

Muy lejos de brindarle una sonrisa,
La dama al galán se dirigió,
Y empuñando su mano arrojadiza,
¡Dos grandes OJOS NEGROS le plantó!

DEVOCIÓN

Soneto

Hay en el mundo un jardincito hermoso
Que yo cultivo con amor y esmero,
Y ni el mundo, su lujo y su dinero
Son para mí tesoro tan precioso.

Pero es también un cáliz doloroso
Que yo en el alma con pavor venero,
Y to bendice el corazón sincero
Con lágrimas que nutren mi sollozo.

¡Oh, cielo, qué tesoro me ha costado
Ese albergue de un polvo tan querido,
Ese sitio de flores nacarado!

Su cadáver precioso está dormido
Bajo esa bóveda que yo he regado
Con lágrimas del alma que he vertido.

INDIFERENTE

No me mueven los seres presuntuosos,
De su propia importancia alucinados,
Que como pavos reales vanidosos
Quisieran darme su desprecio inflados.

Porque yo no me presto para tanto:
Cébense bien en su vacío orgullo,
Que de la indiferencia bajo el manto
Triplicado desdén les retribuyo.

¡Pobrecitos, ridículos pigmeos,
Más dignos de piedad que de censura,
Que se creen insignes corifeos,
De bajo servilismo en la llenura!

Mas yo gozo mirando al sapo inflarse,
Que quería del buey las dimensiones,
Y en su empeño acabó por reventarse
Y murieron con él sus ilusiones.

Sigan, pues, adelante con empeño,
Murmuren hasta el colmo de su agrado,
Mas sepan que su inquina y su desdeño
A mi ser no le llegan ni a cuidado.

MI ESCOGIDO Y MIS RAZONES

Al Hon. Octaviano A. Larrazolo

Leída por el autor ante la "Sociedad Larrazolo,"
en Las Vegas, Nuevo México, en octubre de 1908.

    ¡Salve, ilustre campeón, sois bienvenido!
Si oís el eco de la voz que os llama
Proclamando que sois el escogido,
Sabed que no es el eco de un Partido
Unicamente el eco que os aclama
De nuevo el candidato enaltecido
Para su delegado en el Congreso;
Que si bien el demócrata ha querido
Alzar tu nombre en su estandarte impreso,
Es el amor universal que grita,
"¡Que viva Larrazolo y el Progreso!"
Y de orgullo entusiástico se agita;
¡Es la unánime voz del pueblo egrégico
Del histórico y culto Nuevo México!

    Dos años há que nominado fuiste
Contrario a la facción predominante,
Y en lucha subsiguiente conseguiste
De esa misma facción salir avante.
Mas favor al pillaje organizado
De villanos que impulsa el egoísmo,
Del villano el sirviente está sentado
En tu silla con gélido cinismo;
El sufragio del pueblo despreciado,
Ha triunfado el apóstol del cohecho,
De bajo servilismo propagado,
Y el gusto popular está deshecho.

Mas hoy de nuevo a la batalla vienes
Armado cual Minerva la instructora,
De Júpiter nacida de las sienes
Con su lanza y broquel de vencedora;
Hoy el cetro empuñado firme tienes
De Palas la de Atenas fundadora,
Y como Aquiles su favor obtienes;
Hoy vienes cual reflejo de la aurora
Que sube al claro azul de la esperanza,
¡El ídolo del nuevomexicano
Que si bien es adverso a la venganza
Su amor a la justicia es soberano!

¿Cuánto más elevado en el concepto
De todo concienzudo americano
Fuera de Andrews el grato retrospecto;
Cuánto más encumbrado
En los pechos de un pueblo agradecido,
Si hubiera sus deseos acatado
Y el tritinfo a Larrazolo concedido;
Si hubiera renunciado,
Accediendo a la voz de la conciencia,
La victoria ficticia que le dieron
Los crímenes de Colfax y Valencia?

Cuando esos fraudes a la luz salieron,
Como rasgo manchado de la Historia,
Si hubiera entónces con viril nobleza
Su falsa mayoría repudiado,
Y dando voz del alma a la grandeza,
De este modo exclamado:
"¡No soy yo quien abriga esos delitos,
Que son hijos de espíritus mengüados
En el Honor y en la Moral proscritos!
¡No soy yo quien burlados

Quiere dejar del pueblo los deseos
Por ver sus propios fines realizados!
Aprobarme yo electo delegado
Por medio de un sistema deshonroso,
Trocaría un honor muy encumbrado
En fruto de un origen vergonzoso.
¡Tóme el cargo del pueblo el preferido,
La voz del pueblo es ley, y la respeto,
Y sin bien en mi contra ha decidido
Yo sincero bendigo su decreto!"
¡Oh, cuánta admiración hoy circundara,
Con su nimbo de gloria,
El recuerdo que fúlgido brillara
De "Bull" Andrews ornando la memoria!

Pero una acción magnánima como esa
Procede de un espíritu gigante,
Noble y viril en toda su entereza;
Que abarca en sí los atributos bellos,
Andrews, que tú ni por encima ensayas,
Y de esta clara luz a los destellos
¿Puédes ver, por ventura, dónde te hallas?...

¿Qué pierde el cuyo triunfo le es robado?
¿Qué gana la victoria mal habida?
¿Olvida el mundo el genovés honrado
Que dió a España la tierra apetecida;
Que desafió la furia de los mares
Por mirar conseguida
Esa gloria de glorias singulares,
Porque Vespucio arrebatarle quiso
La diadema inmortal que hoy irradía
Del templo de Colón en los altares?
Hoy los hechos cual sol arrojadizo
Lanzan sus rayos al eterno día,

Mas su luz imparcial y justiciera
Pone aquel en las sombras de la Historia,
De Colón elevando la lumbrera
Al pináculo augusto de la gloria.

   Así a tí, Larrazolo, ya encendida
La sangre que circula por las venas,
En el orgullo ibérico teñida
Del nuevomexicano, las cadenas
Rómpense ya de la opresión temida
Que al libre los tiranos depararon,
Por vindicar la ofensa cometida
Cuando a tí la victoria te frustraron.
Y al fin de la carrera ya emprendida,
Cual Corebus de olímpicos honores
Tu altiva frente de laurel ceñida,
Con Temis justiciero en su dictamen,
Cumplido el gusto popular expreso,
Entrarás con tu enseña enaltecida,
Irradiante de honores al Congreso.

   Que el sol de junio al despuntar apenas
Sus rayos en el límpido horizonte,
En tí ha dado un Pericles, cual de Atenas,
Que el enemigo sin temor afronte;
Nos ha dado tu lógica elocuencia,
Bello don del "nativo" predilecto,
Para destruir la despreciable creencia
Del que tacha al latinoamericano
De inferior al sajón por intelecto.
Pues como el cóndor que arrogante sube
A la cúspide altiva de los Andes,
Tú elevas al "nativo" hasta la nube
Con esos timbres de tu mente grandes.
Y hoy que fogosa la campaña avanza

Tienes al pueblo por tu fiel escudo,
Y la voz de ese pueblo en alabanza
Que te brinda su férvido saludo:

   ¡Salve, ilustre campeón, sois bienvenido!
Si oís el eco de la voz que os llama,
Proclamando que sois el escogido,
Sabed que no es el eco de un Partido
Unicamente el eco que os aclama
De nuevo el candidato enaltecido
Para su delegado en el Congreso;
Que si bien el demócrata ha querido
Alzar tu nombre en su estandarte impreso,
Es el amor universal que grita,
"¡Que viva Larrazolo y el Progreso!"
Y de orgullo entusiástico se agita;
¡Es la unánime voz del pueblo egrégico
Del histórico y culto Nuevo México!

CASO DOLOROSO

Doloritas, hija amada
    de don José Armando Fuertes,
    casó, pero mal no aciertes,
    con persona respetada.

Gonzalo Ijar, licenciado,
    hijo del mismo lugar,
    con ella se ha desposado,
    y así su nombre ha quedado
    "Dolores Fuertes de Ijar."

SE ALEJA Y SE VÁ

La vida es un iris de inestables colores,
Los varios primores de un prisma trivial;
Efímero ensueño de llanto y de risa,
Y así se desliza, se aleja y se vá...

Tan sólo es mirage que el ojo fascina
De aquel que camina sediento detrás;
Vapor que transita por el firmamento,
Y en breve momento se aleja y se vá...

Es sueño ilusorio, florido y dorado,
Que no han realizado los hombres jamás;
Escena confusa de luchas preñada,
Que a poco a la nada se aleja y se vá...

Pero hablo del hombre que deja esa vida
Pasar consumida por la ociosidad:
Su vana existencia, volátil historia,
Con breve memoria se aleja y se vá...

Porque sólo el hombre que lucha cada hora,
Y en eso mejora la posteridad,
Transmite su nombre perenne a la Historia,
¡Jamás su memoria se aleja y se vá!...

EL ATEO Y LA VERDAD

—Mentira el más allá, dice el ateo,
Erguiéndose con tono de profundo,
Y con ese falace balbuceo
Quiere tan sólo convencer al mundo.

Así colmado de ilusión que ciega,
De orgullo audaz y vanidad maldita,
De Aquel que le hizo la existencia niega
Y la esperanza al porvenir le quita.

Alimentando con insano empeño
Los devaneos de su mente loca,
No vé que dá a lo Eterno su desdeño
Y la Justicia Divinal derroca.

La causa de los justos anonada;
El premio de los buenos lo destruye,
Y al bueno y al injusto hunde en la nada,
Sin premio y sin castigo, pero arguye:

—¿De dónde vino Dios? ¿Qué le produjo?
¿Hay acaso otro ser más poderso,
Que le dió ser al Ser que nos condujo
A soñar en un mundo pesaroso?

Titulan ese Dios justo y benigno:
Sin embargo creó un mundo de inocentes
Que destinó a sufrir todo lo indigno
De un semejante al Dios de los creyentes.

¿Pudiéra un ser piadoso destinarnos
A sufrir los dolores de este mundo,
Y después, siendo justo, condenarnos
Al tormento de un Érebo profundo?

Absurdo! La feraz naturaleza
Es la potencia que nos dá la vida;
Es la madre de toda la grandeza
Que está en el Universo comprendida.

Y cuando ésta se agota desvalida,
Con todos los vigores de su esencia,
¡Adiós las ilusiones de otra vida,
Que todo se acabó con la existencia!...

Así nutre tan sólo una quimera:
La insostenible, insubstancial doctrina
Que la materia mísera quisiera
Darnos por fuente de Creación Divina.

En tal concepto es acreedora ella
Al desplego de Gran Sabiduría
Que dá en legiones la brillante estrella,
La míes que nutre el luminar del día.

Así pues, son poderes naturales
Los que al hombre le dán inteligencia,
Sublimes creaciones, ideales,
Y en su pecho la voz de la conciencia...

Aquí es do la razón ya se rebela
Y ofrece vigorosa su protesta,
Y la conciencia que en el alma apela,
Con sobrada razón nos amonesta.

Porque, si todo acaba con la muerte,
Si no hay un porvenir en ultratumba,
¿Qué importa el bien o el mal para tal suerte
Si en ella la Justicia se derrumba!...

¿Qué puede el pobre, insuficiente humano?
No alcanza aún ni a comprenderse él mismo,
Cuánto menos medir todo un Arcano
Con razones que rayan en cinismo.

Grande es el hombre que a medir alcanza
La grande pequeñez que le adolece,
Y al medir le dá al Cielo su alabanza
Y por ello en el Cielo se enaltece.

Encuéntrase razón muy bien certera
El que sabe apreciarse en lo finito,
Que en todo caso lo imposible fuera
El medir con lo humano lo infinito.

Aquí ha llegado la verdad que alumbra
Y vemos ésto en claridad patente:
Dios es luz tan brillante que deslumbra
Los pobres juicios de la humana mente.

EL ANGEL DE LA GUARDA

En una tarde plácida y serena,
Por cierta calle popular pasaba
Una joven viniendo de la escuela,
De un convento de Hermanas.

Sus graciosos y púdicos gracejos,
Con sus labios angélicos de grana
Y el endrino esplendor de sus cabellos,
Encendían el alma . . .

¿Cuántos hay en el mundo depravado
Que presas de la gula se proscriben!
¿Que talaran por un deseo insano
La virtud de una virgen! . . .

Pero a esta joven atrayente, amable,
Otro ser al hogar la acompañaba;
Era tan sólo su bendita madre;
¡El angel de la guarda!

AXIOMAS

Nunca de sabio te alabes:
Tén presente a todas horas,
Que aun si es mucho lo que sabes,
Es mucho más lo que ignoras.

No te infle lo que te viene
De mera casualidad;
Más vale lo que se obtiene
De fiel laboriosidad.

Se engaña en su propia vista
Quien, irrisorio a porrillo,
Se presume ser legista
Porque huele a tinterillo.

Ninguna gloria conquista
Quien a los grandes remeda,
Que "aunque la mona se vista
de seda . . . mona se queda."

ANITA

Ví una virgen hermosa, inmaculada,
En un cuadro magnífico pintada:
Obra de algún pincel
Como el de Rafael:
Y en su faz exquisita,
Con sus ojos radiantes de belleza,
Ví un reflejo de mística pureza:
¡Ví tu retrato, Anita!

AL ENVIUDAR MI MADRE

    En mis días pasados yo veía
Sin nieblas el azul,
En que mi sol esplendoroso ardía
Cual bella antorcha en zafirino tul;

    Suave el ambiente que me circundaba
De dicha sin igual,
Con aquel ser querido que yo amaba
Como quiere la flor al manantial . . .

    Pero se trueca en ráfaga el ambiente
Que surge a mi redor,
Y sólo deja el huracán rugiente
Cabe una tumba, una marchita flor.

    Invadió la penumbra el firmamento
Con su negro capuz,
Y ominosas, mi triste sufrimiento,
Me daba sombras en lugar de luz.

    Traspasada de mil tribulaciones,
Sola, sola lloré,
Y al tenderme la noche sus crespones,
Mi llanto con suspiros agoté.

    Y sus arrullos de dolor nutridos,
El aquilón dejando
En estridores lúgubres fundidos,
Me perdí entre las sombras . . . suspirando . . .

A LA SRTA. ADELA CRUZ

En el día de su graduación de la escuela superior

Allí estás de laureles coronada
De Minerva en el templo luminoso,
De tus padres y amigos admirada
Do alcanzastes un éxito glorioso.

Allí estás como límpida azucena
Que abriera su capullo en la alborada,
Tu tierna vida de esperanza llena,
Y un feliz porvenir en tu jornada.

Hoy dieciseis abriles han pasado
Desde que al seno del hogar viniste,
Y es tan grande el honor que has conquistado
Como el orgullo que a tus padres diste.

Así eres a la vez nítida emblema,
Que simboliza el paternal cariño,
Que guió tus pasos y labró el diadema
Que hoy ciñe de tu frente el albo armiño.

Has sido diligente en tus estudios
Y hoy te son tus laureles escolares,
Presagio de la vida en los preludios
De un viaje hermoso en los mundanos mares.

Mas no olvides, Adela, en tu alegría,
Al mirar tus esfuerzos coronados,
Que tus padres velaron noche y día
Tus pasos con tan bellos resultados.

Que hoy reposan en tí sus esperanzas,
Rebosando de amor sus corazones,
Sé digna de sus tiernas alabanzas
Y en la vida tendrás más galardones.

Sigue así como vás: flor que perdura
De la intemperie en el jardín ilesa,
Conquista admiración con su hermosura:
Nectáreo dulce de sin par pureza.

Y tú eres una flor: flor delicada
Que en la dulzura y el honor se mece,
Y debes mantenerte inmaculada
Do la virtud en su blancor florece.

Yo a tus padres y a tí los felicito,
Rogando que en el libro del destino
Tengas en letras de diamante escrito,
Un mar de venturanza en tu camino.

LA CREACIÓN

I.

    Fijó el Señor su divinal mirada
De la tierra en el átomo perdido:
Una masa sin formas, escarpada,
Un aborto en tinieblas inmersido
Que nació de la nada.
Todo era oscuridad en aquel seno,
Salvo el destello de la chispa ardiente
Que Júpiter mandaba con el trueno
De su voz estridente,
Y el fogonazo del volcán rugiente . . .

    Mas al ver en su mente retratados
Los fulgores sin fin de la Hermosura,
Dios de siete colores combinados
Produjo la criatura
Que trocó aquel abismo tenebroso
En ámbito de luz esplendoroso.

    Entonces vino ya el segundo día
En claridad suavísima inundado,
Y el perfil de la tierra se veía
Sobre diáfano fondo dibujado.

    Y todo estaba bien: Dios complacido
Siguió por el camino del Progreso,
Y allá en la inmensidad dejó tendido
El manto que circunda el Universo;

Ese manto de azul tan delicado
Que desplega su bóveda en altura,
De innumerables soles tachonado
Y de celajes de sin par blancura.

Con esto el beso de la blanda brisa,
Como influjo de virgen seductora,
De tierno halago, de vestal sonrisa,
Nos dió divina la siguiente aurora...

II.

"¡Y adelante, hasta la cima!"
   dijo entonces el Señor,
Con el éxtasis que nace
   de los mares al rumor,
Que trocábase la tierra
   en un imperio linfal
Do gobernaba Neptuno
   cual monarca universal.
Pero estos vastos dominios
   quiso el Señor dividir,
Para que también la tierra
   comenzara a producir.
Concentráronse las aguas
   en un lugar separado
Y nació el prado anchuroso
   de rica esmeralda ornado;
Flores de gran hermosura
   bellos jardines formaron
Y los valles expansivos
   de colores resaltaron;
De Ceres en el dominio
   nacieron aljofaradas

Por las gotas del rocío
    las mieses aprisionadas;
Las colinas tapizadas,
    las montañas primitivas
Imponentes levantaron
    sus regias crestas altivas,
Y por doquier ostentaron
    rica estera sin igual
De terciopelo radiante
    de belleza vegetal.

Se oyó el sonoro murmullo
    de la cristalina fuente
Que gustosa alimentaba
    las flores a su vertiente;
Aparecieron los lagos
    y los mares ondulantes,
Do refleja el firmamento
    focos de luz rutilantes;
La inmensidad del océano
    apareció majestuosa,
Cual fantástico idealismo
    de potencia misteriosa.
En tanto el blando susurro
    del follage cipresino,
Sus eólicos arrullos
    tocando en laúd divino,
Entre uno y otro horizonte
    de verdor sin paralelo,
Describían sin palabras
    la omnipotencia del Cielo . . .

III.

   Al cuarto día el astro más fulgente
Apareció en el éter incrustado,
Y al ver el rayo de su luz ardiente
Su mismo Autor quedó maravillado:

   Se concibe un espléndido retrato,
E impulsando su inmenso poderío,
Ordena, que cediendo a su mandato
Nazca el bello Monarca del Estío.

   Y del campo bellísimos brocados
Que formaron palmeras y abedules,
Aspiraban sonrientes y extasiados
Creciente vida en matizados tules.

   Y las rosas sus pétalos de grana,
Y los lirios sus broches purpurinos,
Bañaban a la luz de la mañana
En medio de cristales diamantinos.

   Deslumbrante cayó del quieto lago,
Cual ornato en las aguas cristalinas,
Do el ramage [sic] teñido de su halago
Daba júbilo en torno a las ondinas.

   Floripondios floridos destacaban
Contrastado blancor al verde campo,
Do felices oréades entonaban
Gratos loores al beso de su lampo.

   Del mar inmenso en las rizadas ondas,
Cayó brillante su fulgor naciente,
Allende brizos de espigares blondas,
Formando un cuadro de belleza ingente.

Después en el crepúsculo se hundía,
Y ocultando sus últimos reflejos,
Una visión grandiosa aparecía
Decorando la bóveda a lo lejos.

Con su rápida luz mi fantasía
Cruzó los siglos que abarcó el pasado,
Para ver las bellezas de aquel día,
Que en medio de ellas medité pasmado:

—¿Podrán ser una lluvia de diamantes
Caída de regiones ignoradas,
O por acaso de placer brillantes
Lágrimas tiernas de inocentes hadas?

—¿Podrán ser el horóscopo que indica
De los seres humanos el destino;
Que en signos misteriosos pronostica
La suerte individual del peregrino?

—¿Reflejos de esperanza, los que animan
Del ingenio el arranque repentino,
O las chispas brillantes que iluminan
De las Musas el ámbito divino?...

No sé lo que serán: que pobre humano,
No alcanzo a comprenderme ni a mí mismo,
¿Cuánto menos medir todo un Arcano
Con el mismo criterio en que me abismo!

Paréceme risible más que serio
El mortal en mil modos circunscrito,
Que pretende sondear aquel Misterio
Que se ensancha y se pierde en lo infinito.

Grande es el hombre que a medir alcanza
La grande pequeñez que le adolece,
Y al medir le dá al Cielo su alabanza
Y por ello en el Cielo se enaltece.

Nace la luna do refleja hermosa
La luz febea que a lo lejos gira,
Y con semblante de beldad piadosa
El gran axioma del Creador inspira . . .

IV.

La luna y las estrellas
   que fúlgidas nacieron,
Y bellas adornaron
   su campo de zafir,
Al irse la penumbra
   por fin palidecieron,
Del sol a los destellos
   de súbito se hundieron
Pasando a las antípodes
   su luz a difundir.

El sol blandió de nuevo
   sus lampos orgulloso,
Y el mundo presentaba
   riquísimo esplendor;
Acuátiles criaturas
   en número cuantioso,
Poblaron de su especie
   el piélago anchuroso,
Naciendo entre las aguas
   del mundo al rededor.

La délfica Polimnia,
    de Apolo la inspirada,
Nos dió los dulces trinos
    de alígero cantor,
Que Dios de la armonía
    el arte tan preciada,
Dispensación divina
    de todos admirada,
Ha creado en los gorjeos
    que vierte el ruiseñor.

El pavo con su pluma
    de galas ofuscante,
Del cisne en la laguna
    el ampo encantador;
Jugando la pantera
    con la gacela errante,
Las tímidas palomas
    en cúspide arrogante,
Recíprocos afectos
    brindaban al condor.

Los tigres y leones
    vivían lado a lado;
Lamían al cordero
    de instinto fraternal;
Era este un paraíso
    de amor ilimitado,
De vida confraterna
    bellísimo dechado,
Un vástago celeste
    trocado en terrenal . . .

V.

    Aquí tenéis la tierra transformada
Y en un elíseo campo convertida;
Virgen que fue, la veo inmaculada,
Su pecho lleno de inocente vida,
Bañada por la límpida cascada
O al lado de la fuente cual nereída
Que se deleita con las notas de ella
Dándole en cambio halagos de doncella . . .

VI.

    Tomando barro del bendito seno
De esta doncella hizo Dios al hombre,
Y de su aliento prodigioso, ameno,
Le dió un alma inmortal al casto cieno,
Y "Adán," le dijo, "tomarás por nombre."

    Le hizo a su imagen; sobre lo creado
Le dió dominio pleno y bienandanza;
Así que del Señor por el agrado,
Sus obras en el hombre han culminado,
Y es el hombre de Dios la semejanza.

    En el séptimo día descansaba
Lleno el Señor de tierno regocijo;
Después sus ojos al Olimpo alzaba
Y a todo aquel Edén do se recreaba,
Para el bien de los hombres lo bendijo

VII.

    Y todo el Universo complacido,
Aleluyas de júbilo entonando,
Por la mano del Cielo bendecido,
Y de múltiples galas revestido,
Ebrio de gozo continuó cantando...

VIII.

    Pero Dios no quedó complacido,
Aun poniendo a las plantas de Adán
Un Edén de bellezas henchido
Que pudiera feliz gobernar.

    Porque el hombre, ¡sublime criatura,
El aliento y la imagen de Dios,
Merecía en excelsa ventura,
Todavía más grande favor!...

    Baña el Cielo de luz esplendente
De aquel valle florido el matiz,
Y nos dá una mañana preingente,
Que no puédese bien describir;

    Surge suave, balsámica brisa,
Perfumada de nítida flor,
Y su halago de amor electriza
El ambiente que Adán respiró.

    Contribuye sonora fontana
Sus arrullos de suave rumor,
Y cediendo a tan linda mañana
En un sueño profundo se hundió.

Dios se acerca, le encuentra dormido,
Y resuelve hacer dél otro ser,
Para darle la esposa al marido,
Para darle una reina aquel rey.

Pero Adán entretanto soñaba
Que del cielo bajaba un querub,
Cuya diestra al tender señalaba
Dos estrellas en un cielo azul;

Que le dijo el querub suspendido
En el ampo de gasa etereal:
—Este cielo a dos astros unido
Trae consigo el destino de Adán...

A la dicha que el hombre sentía,
Contemplando tan grata visión,
Como en sueño infantil sonreía,
Cual sonríe ante el cielo la flor.

Mas de pronto una niebla ominosa,
Impelida de fuerte aquilón,
En su fuga llegó procelosa
Y aquel cielo brillante opacó.

En seguida un arcángel parece,
Ataviado de diáfano tul,
Y estallar en su mano parece
De una espada de fuego la luz;

Fulminante tronó sucedida
De vulcánico estruendo fatal,
Y la tierra sintió estremecida
En su sueño pronóstico Adán.

Sin poder comprender lo que vía,
De aquel rayo estridente a la voz,
Despertó, y a su lado tenía
Más hermosa que célico sol,

A la madre primera en lo creado,
A la Eva que el Cielo le dió,
Cuyos ojos en sueño inspirado
De dos astros tomaron fulgor.

Tiene formas de Venus Citerea,
Tiene el alma de niño al nacer,
Y sus ojos rasgados recrea
Muy gozosa por todo el Edén.

Los copiosos castaños cabellos
Que bañaban su tez de marfil,
Sus mejillas rosadas con ellos,
Y sus labios de rico carmín,

Rebosaban al hombre de agrado,
De contento, de dicha, de amor . . .
Ah! Las nieblas no habían llegado . . .
Muy felices quedaron los dos . . .

IX.

Y todo el Universo complacido,
Aleluyas de júbilo entonando,
Por la mano del Cielo bendecido
Y de múltiples galas revestido,
Ebrio de gozo continuó cantando . . .

FIN

SEGUNDA PARTE

Cantos del hogar y traducciones

A MI HIJA, HERMINIA

Perlita del océano
   incierto de mi vida,
Erótico trofeo
   del triunfo de mi amor;
Abriga en tí mi seno
   la joya más querida,
La marca de pureza,
   pureza, enriquecida
Por la inocencia casta
   de la niñez fulgor.

Esas miradas tiernas
   que nacen de tus ojos,
Radiantes de hermosura,
   brillantes como sol,
Prodíganle a mi vida
   placeres por abrojos,
Tornando en mi sendero
   del hado los despojos
En celestial delicia
   de paternal amor.

Herminia, ¡mi chatita!
   manjar de mil amores,
Auréola que circunda
   mi ardiente corazón;
Quisieran emularte
   del campo bellas flores,
Quisieran describirte
   mis débiles loores,
Mas eres obra magna
   de celestial creación . . .

El lapso de tres años
    se cumple en pocos días
Desde que tú viniste
    la dicha a despertar;
En mi alma estimulaste
    las esperanzas mías,
Mi corazón colmaste
    de goces y alegrías
Y en un Edén tornaste
    tu natalicio lar.

Felices desde entonces
    papá y mamá vivimos,
Contigo muy dichosos,
    los días pasan bien,
Limpióse el horizonte
    y despejado vimos
El sol de tus fulgores
    y tanto te quisimos
Que ya no sé ni como
    brindarte el parabién.

El cielo nos la preste
    con alma pura y bella,
Estímulo de dicha
    sin límite, ideal;
Que brillen sus virtudes
    constantes como estrella,
Que fluyan a raudales
    las venturanzas de ella,
Y Dios la guarde ilesa,
    ¡perlita angelical!

A MI HIJO, FELIPE

    A la sombra de un helecho
Que majestuoso se erguía,
A la margen do corría
Un caudaloso raudal,
Sobre el cesped yo sentado
Con mi vara y con mi anzuelo,
Esperaba con anhelo
De la pesca algún caudal.

    La tarde estaba serena,
Y aumentaba mi delicia
La placentera caricia
De la brisa ocasional.
Estando así destraído
Y al rumor de la vertiente,
Apareció de repente,
Cual visión espiritual,

    Un grupo de blancas ninfas
En ténues nubes flotando,
Que se venía acercando
Hacia mí, sin vacilar;
Conjeturé que serían,
Tal vez, ufanas ondinas
Que las aguas cristalinas
Venían a contemplar.

Mas luego cambió la escena:
Veía yo un arbolado
En un campo decorado
Por las flores de un verjel:
De las blancas azucenas
A las violetas pasaba
Una abeja, que libaba
De los nectáreos la miel.

　　Caminando entre las flores
Por doquiera la seguí
Esperando hallar así
El sitio de su taller.
Pero de nuevo aparecen,
En ténues nubes flotando,
Y vienen a mí volando
Lis ninfas que antes miré:

　　Un panal de rico almíbar
En mis manos me pusieron
Y cantando me dijeron,
"Las flores os dán la miel."
Por un momento, pasmado,
Ante cuadro tan curioso,
Perdíme en lo misterioso
Y en seguida desperté.

　　Desperté, nada veía,
Pero en vano fue mi empeño,
Quise explicarme aquel sueño
Pero no lo conseguí.
Mas hoy que vén mis recuerdos
Lo que pasó en aquel día,
Conjeturo que seria
Esto lo que en él yo ví:

Era el jardín nuestro hogar:
Y todas aquellas flores,
Símbolo de dos amores
Que en el nuestro el cielo unió;
La abeja era mi destino
Que yo segíua en mi anhelo,
Cuando nos mandaba el cielo
Al hijo de nuestro amor.

　　Sí, el panal era sin duda,
Nuestro hijito idolatrado:
Miel que la vida ha endulzado,
Cera que luz vierte ya,
Luz que disipa las sombras
Que cruzan por nuestra senda,
Y del mundo on la contienda,
Nuestro impulso animará.

A MI HIJA, JOSEFINA

Era mañana de primavera,
Surgían auras del mes de abril,
Y yo esperaba que floreciera,
De tanta vida que renaciera,
Una maceta. de mi pensil.

Ví entre sus hojas que pendulaba
De un jazmincito blanco el botón,
Y yo con éxtasis aspiraba
La suave aroma que dél manaba,
Soñando en sueños de la ilusión.

Estando en ésto muy destraído
Ví que el espacio se oscureció,
Y yo en la sombra quedé inmersido,
Sentí mi pecho de pena hendido
Y do mí todo pasó... pasó...

Mas todo aquello pasó al instante,
Cual breve soplo del vendaval,
Y el sol de nuevo nació brillante,
De nueva vida reververante,
Típica vida primaveral.

Volví los ojos a la florera,
Como atraído por el amor,
Y ¿cómo explico lo que sintiera
Viendo en el acto que se volviera
Mi botoncito fragante flor!

Flor que me daba feliz llenura,
Dicha completa a mi bienestar,
¡Era mi Melba, mi hijita pura,
Mi Josefina, sol de hermosura,
Jazmín precioso, luz de mi hogar!

Dos años dista ya esa mañana,
De mil delicias fiel manantial:
Do ella recibe mi vida ufana,
Dulces gracejos, labios de grana,
Blondos cabellos, un ideal . . .

Logre mi anhelo ver concedido,
Del mismo Cielo quo me la dió,
Que tras de mucho de haber vivido,
Vuelva a su seno como ha venido,
¡Así tan pura como nació!

A MI HIJA, JULIETA

Soliloquio

Veo que estás sonriéndote dormida:
Duermes un sueño de inocente calma
En tu cunita de plumón mullida.

Sueñas tal vez, blanquísimas palomas,
Que cambian sus cucúes a tu lado,
En medio de un Edén rico de aromas;

Aromas que las dalias y las rosas
Ofrecen como incienso a tu sonrisa
En el sueño infantil en que reposas.

Hace tres meses que viniste al mundo,
Cual nuncio celestial de nuestra dicha,
Querub hermoso de mi amor profundo.

Y si un regio monarca me ofertara
Por tu ser sus riquezas y su trono,
¡Mi anatema a su insulto le arrojara!

Que tus deudos y yo cuando nos vemos
En esos tus ojitos perspicaces,
Y un mar de amor inmenso te ofrecemos,

En cambio recibimos, extasiados,
En triple recompensa, tu sonrisa,
¡Más preciosa que un mundo de reinados!

Hoy, dos almas que unidas forman una,
Y en una por tu dicha se desvelan,
Desde el lado halagüeño de tu cuna,

Invocamos al Dios de tu destino
Que en tu alma resplandezcan bellos dones,
Y doquiera que curses tu camino,
Derrame sobre tí sus bendiciones.

A MI HIJA, ELVIRA

Sonetos

I.

Cual diáfano celaje que circunda
La cúspide que altiva se levanta,
Y en ondas de blancura sacrosanta
La tosca formación toda se inunda;

Cual vierte su belleza en la rotunda,
Que en grietas de aspereza se quebranta,
Do el verdor de los pinos se levanta
Del sol ornado por la luz fecunda,

Así, mi bien, con plácida ternura,
Tu difundes la esencia de tus flores
Por el tosco sendero de mis días;

La cúspide soy yo, tú la hermosura
Que envuelve mi aspereza en sus fulgores
Y cubre mis abrojos de alegrías . . .

II.

Y al ósculo del hálito surgente
Que trajo repentino su frescura,
Se torna blanca niebla en gota pura
De líquido cristal; en prisma ingente.

Do nace un esplendor iridescente;
Y aspiran de su bálsamo la altura
Y el valle pintoresco que fulgura,
Un mar de bendiciones floreciente.

Si acaso mi alma anhela excelsitudes
O en mi árida ventura hay flor amena
La que alguna virtud a mi alma inspira,

Es fruto celestial de tus virtudes,
Es bálsamo que libo en la azucena
De tu alma angelical, mi tierna Elvira.

A MI ELVIRA

    Tengo yo un parecito de estrellas,
Cada día que brillan más bellas
En el cielo amoroso de mi alma;
Que le marcan el paso a mis huellas
Por un valle de goces y calma.

    Son un par fulgurante de soles,
En mi senda de rudos peñoles,
Son la luz en mi oscura jornada,
Y por ellos un mar de primores
Cada día me dá la alborada.

    Si mi hogar tiene un rasgo del cielo
En que cifro devoto mi anhelo
Encendido en doméstico encanto;
Si es la planta que en mi árido suelo
A mi vida le dá su amaranto;

    Si mis campos se visten de flores,
Y difunde sus ricos fulgores
En altura gratísimos Febo;
Si mi pecho rebosa de amores,
A esas dos estrellitas lo debo.

    Porque son los destellos vivaces,
Juguetones que ríen perspicaces
Cuando a darme una broma conspira,
Ese cielo do brillan audaces
¡Esos ojos de luz de mi Elvira!

A MI HIJITO, BUENAVENTURA

Volaste al cielo, ángel mío,
De alba pureza aureolado,
Y con tu ausencia ha quedado
El mundo opaco y sombrío.

Tus padres y tus abuelos
De dolor están transidos,
Porque al irte vén perdidos
Muchos floridos anhelos.

No olvidamos ni un momento,
Tus gracejos celestiales,
Tus miradas ideales
Y las notas de tu acento.

Eras todo nuestro encanto,
Luz de sol en nuestra vida,
La que hoy vemos extinguida
Por las lágrimas del llanto . . .

Pero el alma halla consuelo
Cuando en ésto yo me fijo:
¡Dimos en el mundo un hijo
Por un ángel en el Cielo!

A MI HIJITA, MELBA

Era una noche de otoño,
Que yo con pena y cuidado
Veía que un viento helado
Ajaba un tierno retoño.

Retoño que había nacido
En el jardín de mi amor,
Tan puro como la flor
Que dél hubiera crecido.

Unos cuantos días vivió
En este valle de duelos,
Cuando dichosa a los cielos
Sus blancas alas tendió.

Hoy su ceniza reposa
Al pie de una triste selva,
Pero el alma de mi Melba
Es una estrella gloriosa;

No estaba en propio local
De esta vida en el vaivén,
Por que un ángel no está bien
En la vida temporal.

A MI AHIJADA, ROSA CÓRDOVA

I.

 ¿Puédes tú comprender por qué palpitan,
Al impulso de tiernas emociones,
De tus padres los dignos corazones
Y en ancho piélago de amor se agitan?

 ¿Puédes tú comprender por qué para ellos
Tienen hechizos la sonriente aurora,
El beso de la brisa arrobadora,
Y del orbe del día los destellos?

 Es por tí, bella Rosa, que sus vidas
Son un sueño de blancas ilusiones,
Que unieron para tí sus corazones,
Formando un alma en cuyo amor anidas...

II.

 ¿No vés los campos y los jardines,
Cuyos jazmines te dán su amor?
¿Y que te ofrece de los pinares
Dulces cantares el ruiseñor?

 Más que las flores es tu hermosura,
Cosa más pura es tu candor,
Oí tu acento, místico, santo,
¡No tiene canto ya el ruiseñor!

Sigue la ruta ya comenzada,
Rosa aromada, bella ilusión,
Y del que te ama serás orgullo
Que en el capullo del corazón,
Ya floreció . . .

Por eso es que palpitan
Al impulso de tiernas emociones,
De tus padres los dignos corazones,
Y en ancho piélago de amor se agitan.

A MI AHIJADO, JACOBO ARAGÓN, HIJO

Es grande el regocijo, caro ahijado,
Que siento palpitar dentro mi seno,
Al ver en tu niñez pronosticado
Un porvenir de venturanza lleno.

Muy grato es ver en tu misión temprana
Ya florecer la doctrinal semilla
De la enseñanza provechosa y sana
Que hoy ejemplar en tu conducta brilla.

Ella es el fruto, que con mucho esmero,
Tus padres en tu ser han cultivado,
Cual ricas flores del amor sincero,
Que reflejan su esfuerzo coronado.

Por eso, ahijado, sugerirte quiero,
Hoy que pisas tus prístinos peldaños,
Cómo cumplir con tu deber primero
Para con ellos en futuros años.

Sabe que aquellos que tu ser te dieron,
Llenos de fe, de amor y de confianza,
Desde la cuna do tu ser mecieron
Han cifrado en tu vida su esperanza.

El deseo más hondo que han guardado
Es ver a su Jacobo ya crecido,
En medio de los hombres admirado,
De bellísimos dotes distinguido.

En tu dicha la suya se comprende:
Mira el amor con que tus pasos velan,
Y nunca olvides que de tí depende
Que ellos realicen lo que tanto anhelan.

Deja que sea tan sublime afecto
De tu recíproca lealtad criterio,
Y dales de la vida en el trayecto
Completa gratitud y refrigerio.

Habrás con ésto tu deber cumplido,
Y ellos por eso vivirán dichosos:
Será la realidad tu ser querido,
Que adornaron sus sueños más hermosos . . .

Nació la aurora, y al nacer el prado
Se vió de flores y de vida lleno,
Y el sol de la mañana despejado
Temprano el día lo anunció sereno.

Por eso yo en seguridad preveo,
Sin abrojos futuros tu camino,
Y por eso al brindarte mi deseo
¡El orgullo eres ya de tu padrino!

A MI AMADA HERMANITA, LUCÍA

Poesía que yo aprecio mucho por haberla escrito mi querido tío, el finado Sr. D. Pedro C. Chacón, en obsequio a mi madre, a quien él cariñosamente llamaba "mi hermanita." Mi tío Pedro fue un poeta inspirado; escribió numerosas poesías de gran mérito y delicado gusto, que murieron con él: no fueron conservados los manuscritos. Esta es la única poesía suya que he podido encontrar, que fue conservada por mi madre misma. —El Autor

   Levanta, hermana, tu divina frente,
Escucha atenta a mi quejoso canto,
Quiero expresarte con amor ardiente
Lo que ocultaba del silencio el manto;

   El sentimiento puro que concentro,
Que recóndito estuvo luengamente,
Y son ecos que salen de mi centro,
Escúchalos, hermana dignamente:

   Vino el hado vestido de furores
En un tiempo de dicha lisonjera,
Rebatóme, ¡desgracia lastimera!
Mi ventura, mi paz, y mi placer.

   Vino ese hado feroz, inexorable,
Mató el alma de un ser a quien yo adoro,
De la madre que estimo sobre el oro,
De ese ser a quien debo yo mi ser.

   No fue todo, que mientras yo esperaba
Que cambiase la suerte de mi vida,
Vino la parca intrépida, homicida,
Y . . . ¡a mi padre adorado asesinó!

Dardo mortal entónces a mi pecho
Dióle aquel lúgubre y fatal evento...
¡Ay que triste pesar y qué tormento
Cuando ví que mi gloria terminó!

Y al verme solo, pobre, abandonado,
Todo era triste en el contorno mío:
Era mi suerte un áustero sombrío,
Que irritado bramaba en tempestad.

Y en medio de esta ponderosa bruma
Yacía el alma sin ningún asilo...
Mas vino un ángel de mirar tranquilo,
Vino a calmar la bruma pertinaz.

Tú fuiste ese ángel, mi amorosa hermana:
El iris tú que en la región del duelo
Levantóse, cual seña de consuelo,
A volver a mi cielo su turquí.

Tú al ver mi vida en tan penoso estado,
Movida de piedad y de ternura,
Me dijistes en tono de dulzura:
"Pobre ser, a mi lado has de vivir."

Oí tú voz dulcísima, hechicera,
Y hacia tu amparo recurrí anheloso:
En tí encontré, feliz y venturoso,
Una madre de amor y de piedad...

Sí, tú has sido mi madre, hermana mía:
Tú has mimado mi vida pesarosa;
Mi marchita pupila lacrimosa
La ha enjugado tu célica bondad.

Autora has sido de mi nueva historia:
Tú me has vuelto la paz que era perdida,
Feliz miro la gloria de mi vida
Al mirarme a tu lado con placer.

Y el recuerdo fatídico y funesto
De mi gloria perdida de otro día,
Se convierte de pronto en alegría
A tu presencia, angelical mujer...

Alma heróica, benigna, incomparable,
¿Quién eres tú, que mi angustiosa pena.
Adivinaste, y de piedades llena
Escuchaste la voz del corazón?

Al mirar la grandeza de tu alma
Se llena mi existir de sentimiento,
Y me elevo hasta el mismo firmamento
Proclamándote mi ángel redentor.

Y aunque no puedo en mi ardoroso anhelo
Compensar tu bondad como mereces,
Mi ardiente pecho palpitó mil veces
Inundado en tu amor y en gratitud.

Dios sólo puede compensar tus hechos
Tan heróicos, tan nobles, tan piadosos;
En la gloria laureles honorosos
Coronarán sin duda tu virtud.

—Pedro C. Chacón

SALMO DE LA VIDA

Traducido del inglés

No digáis con acento dolorido
   Que la vida es un sueño sin valer;
Muerto estáis en el alma si dormido,
   Y las cosas no son su parecer.

La vida es cosa real, cosa tangible,
   Y en la tumba no cumple su misión;
"Polvo eres, en polvo convertible,"
   Para el alma no tuvo aplicación.

Ni el dolor, ni tampoco la alegría,
   Es la meta mundana del mortal,
Sino obrar con el fin que cada día
   Nos ayude en la vida a progresar.

El arte es lento, pero el tiempo vuela,
   Y aunque fuerte y bizarro el corazón,
Palpita como lánguida vihuela
   De marcha funeraria al triste son.

Del mundo borrascoso en la contienda,
   Al estar de la vida en el vivaque,
¡No viváis como reses en hacienda,
   Sed héroes activos y al ataque!

No confíeis del tiempo venidero;
   Dejad lo que ha pasado, do pasó;
Obrad en lo presente por entero
   Con el Cielo por guía y con valor.

Las grandes vidas todas, muestran ellas
    Cómo hacer de la nuestra un ideal,
Y dejar al partir eternas huellas
    Impresas en la arena temporal;

Huellas sí, que algún otro ser humano,
    De la vida cursoria en la alta mar;
Algún náufrago triste, algún hermano,
    Al mirarlas se pueda reanimar.

Por lo tanto ¡adelante con denuedo,
    Todo obstáculo y suerte hasta vencer!
Conquistad en el bien, seguid sin miedo;
    Trabajando alcanzad a merecer.

    —Henry Wadsworth Longfellow

LA FÉNIX

Traducida del inglés

Al darse al vuelo por la vez primera
La prodigiosa Fénix al nacer,
Sus plumíferos súbditos la adoran
Y aclaman por su reina en su querer;
Al dirigir su vuelo hacia el oriente,
Sus números mayores se levantan,
Y los poetas del aire jubilosos
Sus glorias en el éxtasis le cantan.
Y al brindarle sus áereos festejos
Las huestes numerosas que la sigan,
Rodeándola así en festal concurso,
Con las alas aplausos le prodigan.

—John Dryden

UN SABIO

Traducción liberal

Discreto en la encina donde moraba
un tecolote todo observaba;
quieto y callado todo él oía,
pero en silencio permancía;
yerros ajenos de tantos cuyos.
él apreciaba que no eran suyos;
todos aquellos que alzan mitote,
tomen ejemplo del tecolote.

—Desconocido

UN BELLO IDEAL

Traducción

Dejadme vivir donde pasa el camino
Que la suerte a los hombres trazó:
Son buenos, son malos, son débiles, fuertes,
Sensatos o sandios, lo mismo que yo;
Y siendo cual yo, ¿por qué desdeñarlos,
O arrojar del cinismo el baldón? . . .

Dejadme vivir donde pasa el camino
Que la suerte a los hombres trazó:
Vivir sin fijarme ni en raza ni en nombre,
Amigo de todos los hijos de Dios.

—Sam Walter Foss[1]

Note

1. [Editors' note: Chacón erroneously identified this author as Sam Wallis Foss and translated only a portion of the original poem.]

LA VISIÓN DE BALTASAR[1]

Traducida del inglés

El rey, del trono en la silla,
Sátrapas llenan la sala,
Y un millar de luces brilla
En aquel festín de gala;
Mil cálices de oro en mano,
Vasos del culto divino,
El sacrílego pagano
Profanaba con el vino.

Pero así al estar gozando,
Van los dedos de una mano
Sobre la pared trazando
Las palabras de un arcano;
Era mano de varón
Que solitaria escribiera,
Y en mística ondulación
Las figuras recorriera.

La vió el monarca temblando,
Pidió que el festín cesara,
Y con voz trémula hablando,
Blanca de terror la cara,
Dijo, "Vengan sabios seres
Y magos de esta región,
Y expongan los caracteres
Que causan mi turbación."

Y los magos de Caldea
Acudieron en llenura,
Pero ninguno sondea
La misteriosa, escritura;
La consternación reinaba.
Entre los hombres de ciencia,
Mas muda, ignota quedaba
La aterradora, sentencia . . .

Pero un cautivo[2] se hallaba
En la tierra de Babel,
Y por éste el rey mandaba,
Y viene el joven doncel;
Viene, lee la profecía
Y descifra su entidad,
Y al amanecer el día
Vé cumplida su verdad:

"Llega el fin de Baltasar,
Termina aquí su reinado;
La balanza al computar
Falto le ha manifestado;
Su mortaja, el manto real,
Y sus culpas sin abono,
El medo está en su portal
Y el persa sube a su trono."

—Lord Byron

Notes

1. Ultimo rey de Babilonia, cuya ruina fue anunciada en un suntuoso convite, con las palabras "Mane, Thecel," Phare, 538 ant. de J. C. —El Autor
2. El Profeta Daniel.

EN LA MUERTE DE UNA JOVEN

Traducción del inglés

Callados están los vientos,
Silencia a obscuridad;
Ni un céfiro exhala alientos
Del bosque en la soledad;
Mientras yo en su tumba helada
Flores vengo a tributar
A Margarita,[1] mi amada.

En esta estrecha celda su ceniza,
Que antes con tanta animación brillara,
Es presa de la Parca arrojadiza;
Ni valer, ni hermosura que integrara,
Pudieron redimir por fin la vida
Que el Rey de los Terrores arrancara.

Oh! si tan sólo compasión sintiera
Ese Rey, o decretos tan terribles
El Cielo a derogar condescendiera,
Aquí el doliente, en términos sensibles,
Su fúnebre dolor no revelara,
Ni triste esas virtudes relatara.

Pero, ¿porqué gemir? Su alma se eleva
Allende donde el orbe cotidiano
Sus fulgores espléndidos releva,
Y los ángeles la guían de la mano
A donde con placeres inmortales
Se retribuyen las virtudes reales.

¿O dében los mortales presuntuosos,
Locos, la Providencia reprochar?
Ah! no, que esos impulsos vanidosos
Vuelen lejos de mí con su tentar;
Jamás en estos trances angustiosos
Mi sumisión a Dios quiero esquivar.

Pero el recuerdo para mí es precioso
De sus virtudes y su hermosa faz,
Que mueven a mi afecto lacrimoso
Y adueñan en mi pecho amor feraz.

—Lord Byron

Note

1. Margaret Parker, hija del almirante Parker, y de quien Byron estaba enamorado, en 1802, cuando el autor (Byron) tenía solamente 14 años.

MARÍA ESTUARDO Y SU DOLIENTE

Traducida del inglés

María Estuardo, reina de Escocia, fue decapitada a la edad de 44 años, dos meses, por orden de su prima Isabel, a la sazón reina de Inglaterra (1523–1603). Sus criados, gimiendo rogaban que se les permitiese tomar cargo los restos y darles sepultura, pero se les negó esta solicitud. El cadáver fue cubierto con una tela de fieltro verde que fue arrancada apresuradamente de una mesa de billar, y dejado en completo abandono, salvo por un perrito faldero que no pudo ser inducido a que abandonara los restos de su ama. Este fiel animalito fue hallado muerto dos días después, al lado del cadáver, y el caso hizo tan honda impresión en el ánimo, aún del empedernido ministro de Isabel, que fue mencionado en los partes oficiales. —El Autor

Del hacha del verdugo
   la obra consumada,
El cuerpo abandonado
   sobre una mesa está;
La tierra de legiones
   de humanos habitada
Ninguno halló que fuera
   su polvo acompañar

La obra más hermosa
   de mano de Natura
Jamás que en forma humana
   espléndida brilló;
Un rayo matutino
   del sol de un alma pura
Que sobre un trono humano
   consume su fulgor.

La Venus de la tumba,[1]
    la muerte y el destino,
La voz de la sirena
    que un huracán cernió
Con cada melodía
    de su acento argentino,
Tal fue la que a la vida
    la intriga arrebató.

Tal fue la que la infamia
    dejaba en abandono
A corroerse aislada
    en lóbrego capuz...
¡Una estrella se hundía
    del mundo en el encono
Y no hay quien eche menos
    el rayo de su luz!

¡Austero Knox, escucha,
    que aquella triste escena
Una verdad más áspera
    Puede muda enseñar
A las pompas reales,
    que la ruda condena
Que a los pecados reales
    pudiste predicar!

¡Su labio ya no puede
    más víctimas captarse,
Su mano sediciosa
    cuán impotente está!
Oh, Dios! y ¿qué es un rey?
    ¿un ser al incrustarse
Corona en la cabeza?...
    ¡Fastosa nulidad!

El mundo que está lleno
    de vida, amor y afecto,
Sin duda que podía
    un ser proporcionar;
De sus millones UNO,
    en el local trayecto,
Que el polvo de una reina
    dignárase a velar.

Mas ni un sólo ojo humano
    se acerca a su ceniza...
Pero, mirad! ¿Qué agita
    de pronto el funeral?
¿Qué queja por la sala
    doliente se desliza,
Do no hay un ser humano
    que pise ni el umbral?

Ah! cerca de la forma
    que humanos no atendían
Un ser en el olvido
    vigila el polvo fiel;

Y más y más se apega
    al pecho do latían
Caricias ya pasadas,
    !pasadas, suerte cruel!

Y mira aquellos ojos
    glaseados que aun quiere;
Ansioso y anhelante
    su aliento espera oír;
No sabe que en la vida
    hasta el cariño muere,
Y el amor en la muerte
    concrétase a huír.

Halaga como en antes
    aquella mano helada;
Escucha de sus labios
    la voz que no habla más;
Ni pompa, ni descenso
    preocúpanle por nada,
La muerta era su reina,
    ¿qué importa lo demás?

Con ojos lacrimosos
    que el mismo horror no arredra,
Vigila el barro inerte
    con formas de mujer;
Y así sobre aquel seno
    exánime de piedra,
Vertió el postrer halago
    y aliento de su ser.

Y cuando los cerrojos
    discordes rechinaban
Y llegan ya los pasos
    que cruzan el dintel,
La compasión humana,
    que cínicos negaban,
Se encoge de vergüenza
    ante aquel ojo fiel;
Aquel ojo que mira
    cual si un reproche diera
A los que así pudieron
    matar y abandonar;
Y otra mirada tierna
    le dá a su compañera
Ansiando de aquel sueño
    poderla despertar.

Descubren el cadáver
    y tocan la ceniza;
Se oyó un quejido ténue...
    por fin duermen los dos:
El barro de aquella alma
    que el odio martiriza,
Lo mismo que la vida
    que amando se inmoló.

¡Semíramis de Albión,
    salud, el cielo estalla!
Guardado en ese crimen
    vuestro destino está;
Mas cuando vuestros ojos
    repasen la rondalla
Que viles escribientes
    se prestan a forjar;

Cuando en remordimiento
    tardío ya enterada
De aquel esclavo triste
    que al lado se encontró
De aquella forma inerte,
    sangrienta, inanimada,
Que tu implacable inquina
    voraz anonadó;

¿Acáso tu álma entónces,
    en lóbregos prospectos,
No preverá la hora
    postrera de tu fin?
¿Cuando esos que se inclinan
    a tu corona abyectos
Del trono tambaleante
    se aparten para huír?

¿Cuando tu grande pecho
    solloce de quebranto
Y en lágrimas tus ojos
    ansíen encontrar,
Buscando en el vacío,
    en vano, el eco santo
De un corazón amigo,
    y busquen . . . sin hallar? . . .

No importa que se agolpen
    el clero y la nobleza
Queriendo los dolores
    de tu altivez calmar;
Más vale aquella angustia
    que se agotó a entereza
Cabe la cruenta víctima
    de tu malicia audaz.

—E. Bulwer Lytton

Note

1. Libítina; diosa que presidía a los funerales.

TERCERA PARTE

Saetas políticas y prosa

UN REPUBLICANO REAL

1.

¡Pues bien! Es el caso
   que en época atrás,
Cuando hubo una guerra
   feroz sin igual,
Por dar a la Patria
   solidaridad,
Un republicano
   que dice que es "Real,"
Pieza de cuartilla
   o claco no más,
Diz que fue a la guerra . . .
   ¿sería a pelear? . . .
De espaldas al fuego,
   corriendo hacia atrás,
Los ojos abiertos,
   la boca aun más,
Temblando de susto
   por ver estallar
De horrísino embate
   metralla fatal;
Y en esa figura,
   ridícula asaz,
Densos nubarrones
   de humo y de gas,
Por todos los poros
   solióse tragar,
Dejando la guerra,
   volviendo al hogar,
Inflado de gases
   inmenso costal.

Hoy el veterano,
    en su ancianidad,
Delira que es poeta,
    porque delirar
Bien puede quien pudo
    la Patria salvar...
De espaldas al fuego,
    corriendo hacia atrás...

II.

De aquestos delirios
    doliente al estar
En días pasados
    nuestro militar,
Llególe noticia,
    del todo mendaz,
Que Guillermo, el Toro,
    ¡qué barbaridad!
Pensión venidera
    logróle aumentar,
Por la bizarría,
    que supo enseñar...
De espaldas al fuego,
    corriendo hacia atrás...

III.

Al leer la noticia
    nuestro militar,
Cabriolas al aire
    se puso a bailar,

Cantando y gritando
　　con júbilo tal,
Primero una jiga,
　　después el can can,
Que en estas y en otras
　　tropieza quizás,
Y al suelo cayendo
　　revienta el costal
¡Con un estallido
　　del mismo Satán!
Y dél escapándose
　　el denso caudal
Que marras en guerra
　　solióse tragar,
Con luengas estrofas
　　de humo y de gas.
¡Por Jestas, al Toro
　　se puso a encomiar!
Y a soplos y soplos
　　de gas y más gas,
Sin pensar siquiera
　　en la caridad
Debida a la Prensa
　　y a la humanidad,
¡Llenó una gaceta
　　de verbosidad,
Que parece el Cuento
　　de Nunca Acabar!
En fin, las estrofas
　　son veinte y dos más
De absurdo pleonasmo
　　que huele a corral;
Y en éstas afirma,
　　¡qué temeridad!

Que este mismo Toro
  ¡diz que es "la Verdad,"
La misma "Honradez"
  y la "Honestidad!"...
Pero esto no importa,
  señor militar,
El pueblo ya sabe
  del Toro incapaz
Los verdes tomates
  que sabe pelar,[1]
Y usted ¡ay! no puede
  el sol eclipsar
Con esas estrofas
  de humo y de gas,
No importa que fuera
  valiente a guerrear...
De espaldas al fuego,
  corriendo hacia atrás...

IV.

Dice que es el Toro,
  "sin exagerar,"
El Cid Campeador,
  ¡ahí pudo acertar!
El Cid ya sabemos
  que muerto está ya,
Y por estar muerto,
  yo admito en verdad,
Entre el Cid y el Toro
  simil entidad,
Y no le doy contra,
  señor militar.

Pero aquí ya vamos
    un punto a tocar,
Que es muy delicado,
    ¡cuidado al entrar!
Porque las mujeres
    usted al pintar
"Lloronas que saben
    tan sólo llorar,"
A tanto se expone
    por versificar
Que al fin las mujeres
    le van a linchar,
O al menos quitarle
    la ropa en un zas,
Untarle resina,
    y hacerle emplumar;
Y en esa figura,
    en marcha triunfal,
Por todas las calles
    sacarle a pasear:
Funesta deshonra,
    para un militar
Que pudo valiente
    la Patria salvar...
De espaldas al fuego,
    corriendo hacia atrás...

v.

Pero al fin de tanto
    sorber y soplar,
Cual asno que pudo,
    por casualidad,

En un basurero
	la flauta tocar,
Aquí nos ha dicho
	voacé la verdad:
Dice que doquiera
	que suela tocar
El Toro la puerta
	que se la abrirán:
Y yo le aseguro
	que de par en par,
Y como a un faldero
	le dirán "¡Quía, sal!"
Para que se vaya
	sus pulgas a echar
Al tórrido clima
	do está Satanás...
En fin, ya no quiero
	más tiempo gastar
De usted criticando
	las rimas de gas.
Mas siendo SOLDADO,
	cual díjolo ya,
Cuya SOLDADURA
	muy antigua está,
Voacé ¿cómo espera
	poder remendar
El roto registro
	de aquel Barrabás
Que usted denomina
	la misma "verdad!"...
En fin, no debemos
	en serio tornar
A quien sólo exhala
	vapores y gas...
Persista en su tema

tan digno de "un real,"
Que tal vez consiga,
　　con perseverar
En luengas estrofas
　　de humo y de gas,
Al buen San Gregorio
　　del "Toro" sacar:
Milagros patentes
　　bien puede forjar
Quien pudo ¡caretas!
　　la Patria salvar . . .
De espaldas al fuego,
　　corriendo hacia atrás . . .

Note

　1. [Editors' note: A verse that would clarify this metaphor appears to be missing, obfuscating Chacón's intended meaning.]

UN BAILE DE CARETAS

Era la ocasión de un concurridísimo baile de caretas, que cierta logia local verificaba en la casa de ópera de una mediana población del Estado de Colorado, en el año de 1898.

Muy divertido me sentía yo contemplando el singular espectáculo que presentaba una multitud de seres, ataviados en una extravagante diversidad polícroma de mil caprichos humanos: por aquí se veía un disfraz que representaba un salvaje de Borneo; por allá se veían dos que personificaban los "Gemelos de Siam"; más allá se veía otro que saltaba imitando una rana, cuyo verdor de manchas negras le daba conspícua prominencia, y por toda la platea se veían bailando caracteres alegó ricos de reyes, gitanos, turcos, indios, chinos y qué se yo, sin faltar el omnipresente "tramp," perseguido de listos polizontes (tales como rara vez existen), y un sinnúmero de otros más que no diré.

Estaba yo completamente obsecado por todo aquello, cuando de repente se acerca a mí una dama, al parecer joven, la cual, no obstante el disfraz que la cubría, se veía muy arrobadora, su talle tan esbelto y bien configurado, que me llenó al instante de embeleso. Me habló con voz ladina y placentera:

—Buenas noches, señor.

—Muy buenas se las deseo, le respondí con nervios agitados.

—Deseo hablar con usted unas palabras.

Yo, más que de carrera condescendí a que sus carminados labios se acercaran, si no a los míos, al menos a mi oído. Díjome quien era, y lo que deseaba, y todo vino a rematar en una grande risotada entrambos dos...

Reclinado a uno de los pilares del salón, observé a cierto conocido mío, llamado Pancho Morales: joven, cortés a lo palurdo; pulido y presuntuoso hasta ridículo extremo, y amante de las muchachas hasta la pared de enfrente, que éstas les hacía mil dengues, guiños y agasajos para granjear su cariño, pero como fuese por lo natural, torpe y desagraciado, todos sus esfuerzos y galanterías resultaban siempre en ridículo para él, y en disgusto para ellas. Pancho, como yo, andaba sin disfraz, habiendo ido más bien a presenciar el evento que a participar de él. Fuí a donde él estaba, mas como fuese corto de vista, no me vió sino hasta que me hube acercado mucho, y eso sólo cuando con voz fuerte le dije en forma de saludo:

—¡Hola, chico, qué tal! ¿Cómo la pasas?

—Qué, ¿la vista? Pues, la paso de un lado al otro del salón, mirando todo, me respondió con una explosión de risa, que en él era característica, siempre que creía haberse lucido en una agudeza.

—¡Hómbre de Dios, pues, nó te aplomes! Acabo de encontrarme con una señorita Carmen Hinojosa, extranjera en el lugar, y es ella uno de los tipos más amables y encantadores que ojos hayan visto. Es para bailar, una moderna Salomé, un verdadero Terpsícore. Vente con migo para presentarte a ella, y verás tú qué barbiana...

—¡Cáspita, bufón, no lo repitas, voy contigo aunque al punto me desnuque! exclamó Pancho ardiendo de entusiasmo. Presentarle yo a la señorita Hinojosa, y convidarla él a bailar la siguiente pieza, fueron una y la misma cosa.

Yo me quedé sentado haciendo el mayor esfuerzo por suprimir la risa que me ahogaba, al ver las ondulantes cabriolas, multiformes piruetas y risibles chicoleos con que el quijotesco Pancho trataba de agradar a su bella compañera. Bailó con ella cinco o seis piezas consecutivas. Por fin vino a donde yo estaba, y con el gusto cloqueándole al gargüero, y apretándome la mano brúscamente, así me dijo:

—No te puedes figurar cuánto he gozado... y además, capitán, ¿qué no te cuento? Le he ofrecido acompañarla a casa y ella ha recibido mi humilde cortesía con una amabilidad digna de un ángel. ¡Cuán feliz yo me siento en esta noche, después de tantas y amargas decepciones! Aunque todavía no puedo ver su cara, la regia simetría de su talle, y la rica melodía de su acento, me tienen ya volando en la ilusión...

Al terminar este interesante discurso, llega la media noche, la hora de partida, ¡hora feliz para el dichoso Pancho! Se marchan ambos muy ufanos con rumbo a la casa de la Sra. Petra Bustillos, en donde estaba hospedada la Sra. Hinojosa.

—¿Por que no se quita usted la máscara? pregunta Pancho.

—Tan pronto como lleguemos a la casa.

—No puede usted figurarse cuánto anhelo conocerla con intimidad, y cultivar relaciones mútuas a la vez que recíprocas con usted, tal vez hasta el amor; y más aún, hasta unir mi destino al suyo en los eternos vínculos del matrimonio, iba, diciendo Pancho, y continuaba:

—Perdóneme usted mi franqueza, pero en verdad le digo que al través del antifaz que oculta su cara, se trasluce un alma llena de virtudes, la diosa de mis más floridos sueños...

En esto llegan a la casa, y Pancho ansioso le pregunta:

—¿Dónde podré yo verla a usted mañana, en la mañana?

Quitándose la máscara, y con voz natural le responde:

—En el "Pool de la Esmeralda," como siempre; soy José Olivas, a tus órdenes . . .

Yo, con otros amigos, estaba, a la vuelta de una cercana esquina descostillándome de risa al ver los procedimientos; José echó a correr soltando al eco sabrosas carcajadas, mientras que el desvalido Pancho se quedó allí turbado, patitieso, aturdido y estupefacto, y por varios momentos no pudo realizar con plenitud lo que le había pasado. Por fin recobró sus facultades normales, hasta el punto de desembuchar varias indecibles imprecaciones: sapos, y culebras, con algunas víboras entremezcladas por añadidura. Acto contínuo, desapareció en la oscuridad.

Esa misma noche, Pancho empacó su baúl y maletas, y se fue de la población en el primer tren que pudo tomar. Yo mismo no le volví a ver por muchos años. ¡Fue tal el choque!

DON JULIO BERLANGA

Fue en agosto de 1918, cuando tuve el honor de conocer a don Julio Berlanga, de... en Las Vegas, N.M.

Era don Julio un hombre industrioso de 48 años, cerca de seis pies de alto, erecto de estatura, de complexión muscular, trigueño de tez, prominente de pómulos, espeso de bigotes y pelo negros, ojos vivaces, aunque algo hundidos en sus órbitas, ajeno a bromas y chanzas, aunque sabía apreciarlas en los demás, siempre cándido y serio en su conversación, aunque se tratase de frivolidades.

Al través de las buenas cualidades de don Julio, que era sobrio, laborioso y constante en sus ocupaciones, no dejaba de traslucirse una especie de inocente vanidad, que, en una persona de su serio índole, era muy divertida. Para dar una idea más clara de su carácter peculiar, es mi propósito relatar, en manera característica, la descripción que él mismo me dió del día más feliz de su vida.

Sentados estábamos los dos en la sala de espera de la estación del ferrocarril, conversando, cuando me dijo:

—Nunca se me olvidará a mí este lugar de Las Vegas, y ¿sábe usted porqué?

Yo le dí una mirada inquisitiva, y tras una breve pausa, prosiguió él: Porque aquí pasé, el año pasado, el día más feliz de mi vida. Verá usted que yo llegué aquí la tarde del día 3 de julio, de Guayuma [Wyoming], en donde había estado trabajando en las borregas durante un año. Vine con el fin de pasar unas dos semanas de recreo y descanso, atraído por la tan sonada reunión de vaqueros que se celebraba los días 3, 4 y 5 de ese mismo mes.

Tan pronto como llegué fuí y tomé la comida; después, fuí a la barbería y tomé un baño, me cambié de limpio, me hice el pelo y la barba, y en seguida fuí a un comercio a comprarme ropa. Compré un vestido que me costó cincuenta pesos, un sombrero que me costó diez, unos zapatos que me costaron doce, calcetines de seda, una camisa de seda morada, con su respectivo cuello y correspondiente corbata amarilla. ¡Gasté allí noventa pesos lo mismo que uno, amigo! Pero con trescientos más que traía con sigo, y trescientos más que había dejado en el banco de Rolin [Rawlins], ¿qué, me hacía el tiempo? Fuí a mi cuarto y me vestí de ropa nueva, de pies a cabeza, y como yo traía un reloj y una leontina que me habían costado sesenta pesos en Rolin, me vestí, amigo, ¡y no me las recargo! pero daba luz en aquel espejo...

Tanto en la barbería como en la calle, había oído hablar tocante a un baile que se iba a dar esa misma noche en un salón que llamaban "La Favorita." Después de vestirme, anduve paseándome en ambas plazas de Las Vegas, y aunque no conocía a nadie, por decir así, pasé muy buen tiempo, pues, fuí al parque de las carreras a ver los juegos de lareateo y la domación de caballos y reses por los vaqueros, y todo me gustó mucho.

Cuando venía del parque, se me puso en la cabeza ir esa noche a lucirme en el baile de La Favorita; porque hay ocasiones en que le dan a uno ganas de lucirse. Después de la cena fuí a las vistas, y sería las 9: de la noche cuando llegué al baile. Luego que entré en el salón, que estaba lleno de gente, todos me miraron de pies a cabeza, porque en verdad le digo, amigo, no había allí un solo hijo de vecino que se me acercara sin quedar "eclisado," por decir así, con el primor de mi vestuario y la elegancia de mi persona.

Estuve mirando a todas las damas que allí se hallaban, hasta que ví la mujer más hermosa que he visto jamás, conversando con otra en el costado del salón opuesto a donde estaba yo. Ví que me miraba y se secreteaba con su compañera; luego fuí y la convidé a bailar, y de una vez me tomó del brazo y nos fuimos paseando hasta el medio del salón. Todos nos miraban y nos admiraban, amigo, y yo luciéndome con aquella hermosa mujer. Por fin me detuve y dije:

—Amigos, ¡párense a bailar un vals todos los que gusten acompañar a este humilde servidor de ustedes, Julio Berlanga! ¡Párense todos los que gusten, ¡yo pago!

No faltaron dos o tres que gritaran—¡Que viva Julio Berlanga! Y aquello fue la mar, amigo, una de vivas por Julio Berlanga que aturdía, y yo luciéndome con aquella hermosa mujer . . .

Por fin llegó el colector y me dijo:—Se han parado veintiseis, ¿usted vá a pagar por todos? Yo le respondí que sí, dándole un par de pesos. Me devolvía setenta centavos, pero yo le dije:

—El cambio es suyo, joven. Por demás es decir, amigo, que aquel colector allí fue mío. Repetí la misma "aición" tres o cuatro veces, y aquel baile fue mi trono, amigo, todos me brindaban sus más amables atenciones y cortesías, y no más la mía venía. De las veinte o más piezas que bailé esa noche, en quince fue mi compañera aquella mujer hermosa que le dejo dicho. Por fin me permitió que la acompañara a su casa después del baile. Esta mujer era casada, pero hacía nueve que la había abandonado su marido y vivía con una hermana suya. Por fin la solicité a que se fuera conmigo para Guayuma, y convino. A los tres días me fui para San Luis a ver a mis gentes, y en tres días más volví y nos fuímos.

Pero esa mujer, amigo, por fin me pagó mal. Le puse casa en Rolin y la dejé bien abastecida de dinero y víveres inter volvía yo de las borregas: una ausencia de unas seis semanas. Como mi trabajo era ambulante, casi no esperaba recibir, carta de ella, pero a la semana de mi ausencia recibí una en la cual me decía que estaba bien, que me amaba lo mismo que siempre, v que esperaba que a mi regreso a Rolin me casara con ella. Yo le contesté que su gusto era el mío, pero a las seis semanas, que volví, hallé a otras gentes viviendo en la casa. Después supe que había vendido los muebles y todo y se había ido con un americano. ¡Me puse yo en sangre de perro con rabia! . . . y no la he vuelto a ver más. Pero nunca se me olvidará el día en que la conocí, ese día en que gocé a la medida de mi deseo, ni aquel baile, amigo, porque en ese baile yo fuí el rey, ¡el mero león!: no más la mía venía.

EUSTACIO Y CARLOTA

Novelita

I.

Fue en el año de 1897, que en una do las grandes casas de habitaciones tan comunes en la ciudad de Nueva York, y la cual, aunque grande, era tan sólo un átomo componente de aquella magnifica, pintoresca, y populosa metrópoli, vivía una pobre familia española que respondía al nombre de "Quintanilla." Esta familia so componía del padre, la madre, un hijo de ocho años llamado Eustacio, y una hija de dos años con el nombre de Carlota.

Como es de suponerse, esta familia vivía en medio de una laberíntica muchedumbre de gente vulgar, que es lo que caracteriza una fase de la vida, la vida de los "Slums," en esa prodigiosa urbe.

En una noche del mes de diciembre, durante un período de frío casi insoportable, hallábase la pobre madre a punto de dar a luz un niño. El aposento que ocupaba estaba tan escaso de víveres como de calefacción, y la pobre mujer lloraba su triste situación, acompañada solamente de sus dos tiernos hijos, Eustacio y Carlota.

El esposo y padre de aquellos infortunados pasaba la mayor parte de su tiempo en las tabernas de la famosa calle denominada "the Bowery," malgastando el fruto del poco trabajo que hacía, en carácter do mozo, en pasatiempos frívolos con los tertulianos comunes de aquella conglomerada región.

La angustia y sufrimientos que la pobre mujer pasara durante aquella noche de amargura, pueden más bien imaginarse que describirse.

Poco antes de la media noche la madre despertó a sus hijos, que se habían quedado dormidos al pie de la cama, diciéndoles que se acercaran a ella. Esto hecho, la triste mujer tomó dos medallitas de San Antonio de Padua, y las ató con mano trémula a los cuellos de los niños, diciéndoles, con las frases entrecortadas de la agonía:—Esta es la única herencia que alcanzo a dejaros, mis queridos hijos; que San Antonio os guarde y proteja en esta vida tan amarga que yo ahora estoy próxima a dejar. Nunca os quitéis estas medallitas, sino conservadlas siempre como un recuerdo de la triste madre que con ellas os dá su última bendición.

Dicho ésto, dejó caer la cabeza sobre la almohada, y expiró...

Los niños se quedaron de nuevo dormidos, casi sin realizar lo que había pasado, pero a las 6 de la mañana, Eustacio despertó sobresaltado, evidentemente por la ominosa impresión que en él hicieran las últimas palabras de su madre: comenzó a gritarle a ella, lleno de lóbrego presentimiento. Como ésta no contestara, Eustacio salió asustado de la pieza, y, con voz llorosa, comenzó a gritar a la puerta de una de las habitaciones inmediatas:—¡Vengan a ver qué tiene mi mamá!

Dos mujeres acudieron con el niño al aposento de los Quintanilla, en donde presenciaron una tristísima escena: la infortunada mujer había dado a luz una criaturita durante la noche, mas por falta de atención clínica, lo mismo que de adecuada alimentación, madre e hijo habían dejado de existir.

Uno de los cronistas del gran diario neoyorkino, "The Times," también fue atraído a la habitación por la conmoción de los habitantes, y después de anotar los datos de lo que acontecía, para elaboración de las novedades de aquel periódico, comunicó el caso a las autoridades municipales. Estas tomaron cargo de los restos de la finada y les dieron sepultura durante el día, en el cementerio de pobres, mientras que los niños fueron alojados en un orfanato de la ciudad.

Dos semanas después de estas ocurrencias, murió en un hospital un hombre que, habiendo participado en una riña de taberna, había recibido dos heridas de bala, las cuales resultaron fatales. Con esto terminaba por fin la inútil existencia de Alejo Quintanilla, padre de Eustacio y Carlota.

Cosa de tres semanas después de haber ingresado Eustacio y Carlota en el orfanato, el niño fue adoptado por una familia rica de Toronto, Canadá, que a la sazón se hallaba visitando en Nueva York. Esta familia, a su regreso a casa, se llevó consigo a Eustacio, causando así la separación de los dos hermanos.

Unas cuantas semanas después de la adopción de Eustacio, también Carlota fue adoptada: ésta por una familia de Denver, Colorado, que gozaba de gran prestigio y distinción en los círculos sociales y financieros de aquella ciudad, pues estos no eran otros que Mr. George Freeman, banquero y capitalista, y su esposa, la señora Consuelo Arlington Freeman, una de las primeras damas de la culta sociedad de aquella metrópoli capitalina. Los Freeman eran jóvenes aun; habían estado casados solamente cinco años. Dos años después de su unión matrimonial, la señora había alumbrado a una niña, a la que dieron el nombre de Amanda Consuelo. Esta niña, sin embargo, fue siempre muy delicada de salud, y por fin murió, antes de cumplir dos años. El matrimonio fue estéril después y por tal razón adoptaron a Carlota, a quien dieron en seguida el nombre de Amanda Consuelo.

Cosa de cuatro años después de la separación de Eustacio y Carlota, sucedió que allá en aquel gran naufragio de todas las naciones de la tierra, que es a lo que se concreta la ciudad de Chicago, al ir por una de las calles suburbanas, y de poco tráfico, de la misma, un jovencito de unos doce abriles, llamado Orlando Havens, observó un extraño objeto atravesado en los rieles de la vía de tramvías eléctricos, que parecía ser el cuerpo de un ser humano. Orlando fue apresuradamente a ver qué era lo que llamaba su atención, y para su mayor sorpresa y sobresalto, vió que era la forma de un muchacho, más o menos de su misma edad, que yacía en esa forma, en estado insensible, en un punto donde la vía doblaba una curva, y en donde en unos cuantos minutos más el jovencito hubiera sido destrozado por uno de los carros urbanos quo corrían por allí.

Orlando arrastró la forma del muchacho a un lado de la vía; en seguida llegó el tramvía, cuyo conductor, después de enterarse de la ocurrencia, asistió a Orlando en subir al jovencito al interior del carro, todavía privado del conocimiento.

En esta condición Orlando condujo al muchacho al consultorio de un médico, quien, sobre un ligero examen, halló que tenía una fea y honda herida en la parte posterior de la cabeza, de la cual manaba un copioso flujo de sangre. Después de curar la herida, quo hizo necesarias varias puntadas para juntar la rotura del pericráneo, el médico administró un alterativo, en virtud del cual el jovencito pronto recobró el conocimiento.

El muchacho, por largo rato no se pudo dar cuenta de lo que pasaba: en qué situación se hallaba, ni como había venido al lugar donde estaba. Por fin pudo decirle al médico y a Orlando que su nombre era Henry Collins; que vivía en la casa del licenciado Samuel Perkins, quien le daba asistencia y alojamiento en cambio por servicios en su casa y en sus despachos, en forma de quehaceres ordinarios. Dijo también, que el licenciado Perkins le pagaba una pequeña remuneración pecuniaria además de su alojamiento y asistencia, y continuó su información con el siguiente relato:

—Iba yo por la calle sonando algunas piezas de plata en el bolsillo. De repente sentí que alguien se acercaba a mí, por detrás, y no bien hube hecho impulso a voltear a ver, cuando sentí este golpe (indicando el lugar) en la cabeza: quo no supe más de mí.

Este relato aclaró el misterio: se vió luego que Henry había sido víctima de un salteador, que por robarle el dinero que llevaba en el bolsillo, le asaltó en la manera que dejamos dicha, y tal vez creyendo que le había matado, quiso ocultar el supuesto crimen atravesando el cuerpo en la vía de tramvías.

Henry por fin se sintió suficiente fuerte para irse a su casa, a donde, Orlando le acompañó, y ambos jóvenes fueron amigos muy íntimos todo el tiempo después, cultivando entrambos relaciones de verdadero cariño y hermanable afecto.

Un año después de esta ocurrencia, los padres de Orlando cambiaron su residencia de Chicago a Filadelfia, y los dos amigos no se volvieron a ver más, por muchos años.

II.

En el transcurso del tiempo, pasaron diecinueve años, desde que la niña Carlota, que ahora la llamaremos Amanda, fue adoptada por el matrimonio Freeman. Amanda, por lo tanto, ya frizaba en los veintiún años, y había recibido una educación y cultura extraordinarias, tanto en las letras y la música, como en lo más selecto de la etiqueta social.

Estos bellos atributos, agregados a su talento natural, daban a Amanda un ingenio notablemente feliz en la escritura, y sus contribuciones a la prensa, que consistían en interesantes e instructivos artículos sobre temas relativos a problemas sociales, cívicos y docentes, eran leídos con avidez por todos. De este modo, Amanda se había labrado distinguido renombre nacional, y una profusión de laureles de admiración.

Un día de tantos, los padres de Amanda resolvieron hacer un viaje de recreo al estado de California, acompañados, por cierto, de su hija, dando por resultado que, dos semanas después, la familia Freeman se hallara en San Francisco, gozando de la más completa dicha y felicidad. Muy ameno les había sido aquel viaje, y durante las dos semanas que pasaran en esta ciudad, Amanda había escrito y publicado varios artículos, típicos de su brillante estilo, altamente elogiando las múltiples bellezas del "Estado del Oro," que ella, en su admiración, denominaba "El Verjel del Mundo."

A este punto, hemos llegado ya al año de 1898, precisamente cuando terminaba la guerra hispano-americana, y el 12 de agosto, la familia Freeman se hallaba en ese puerto del Pacífico cuando el famoso regimiento de "Rough Riders" (Jinetes Intrépidos) del Coronel Theodore Roosevelt zarpaba en San Francisco a su regreso de Cuba.

Era capitán de una de las compañías de este regimiento, un elegante y primoroso joven de veintisiete años, a quien parecía que la naturaleza misma había dotado para la vida militar, con toda perfección. Tenía cerca de seis pies de alto; pesaba ciento setentitrés libras; era de índole activo; erecto de estatura, constitución muscular, formas simétricas; temperamento ecuánime y placentero. Este tipo de perfecta masculinidad, no era otro que Orlando Havens, de quien hablamos ya en otra parte de nuestra historia. Este, después de su alistamiento, fue designado Primer Teniente pero en virtud de su gran valor y admirable bizarría en las operaciones, había sido ascendido al rango de capitán, por la Superioridad.

Inmenso fue el entusiasmo patrio con que el Regimiento de "Rough Riders" fue recibido en aquella metrópoli costeña, toda la cual estaba inundada en un verdadero derroche de banderas y festones, que desplegaban con predominante esplendor los colores nacionales. Salvas de bienvenida tributaban sus vítores a los héroes regresantes, mientras las bandas de música preñaban el ambiente de patrias melodías.

Después de terminadas las ceremonias públicas del día, había de verificarse un lucidísimo banquete y un baile en el suntuoso auditorio X . . . , de acuerdo con el programa que habían dispuesto de antemano, el Concilio Municipal y la Cámara de Comercio. La familia Freeman, favor a una invitación particular del mayor de la ciudad, fue una de las más prominentes que presenciaran aquel esplendoroso evento. Y no será por demás advertir aquí, que Amanda se veía encantadora; ataviada de un traje de chifón azul celeste, güarnecido de finísimas blondas de seda; una soguilla de diamantes ceñida al marmóreo cuello, todo lo cual daba muy correspondiente realce a sus rasgados ojos, en los cuales brillaban el candor de la pureza y la perspicacia del talento, lo mismo que a las esbeltas ondulaciones de su venustio talle, el cual parecía haber nacido de los exquisitos pinceles de Rafael y Miguel Ángelo.

Muchas fueron las distinguidas personalidades que le fueron presentadas a Amanda durante la noche, y entre éstas, el Capitán Orlando Havens, que a su vez se veía como un verdadero Apolo, fruto de la bella escultura de algún moderno Praxíteles. Al ser presentado a ella, el Capitán Havens de una vez se sintió hondamente impresionado; bailó repetidas veces con ella, y cuando hubo terminado el banquete, se fue a su cuarto volando en las más floridas ilusiones, y no pudo dormir durante toda esa noche. Aquel indómito guerrero, que pudo arrostrar sin temor los horrores de la lucha, y salir avante, vencedor del enemigo en los campos de batalla, ahora se hallaba rendido incondicionalmente a los dardos de Cupido.

El día siguiente, la familia Freeman había de partir para San José, y Orlando fue uno de los primeros que fueran a la estación del ferrocarril a despedirse de ella. Antes de la salida del tren, Amanda le suplicó que fuera a visitarlos a Denver, asegurándole que sería cosa de su mayor placer el verle por allá. Por demás es decir que Orlando, de mil amores, accedió a tan halagadora súplica, prometiéndole cumplir con su amable solicitud tan pronto como obtuviera su licencia de la Superioridad, que sería dentro de tres semanas, más o menos. El tren partía, y con éste la familia Freeman.

III.

Diez días después de las últimas ocurrencias que dejamos narradas, ocurrió el terrible descarrilamiento de un tren de pasajeros, entre Los Ángeles y San Diego. Con este tren iba el coche particular de la familia Freeman, denominado "Anaconda." Este tren se componía de dieciocho vagones, incluyendo los de equipaje, correos, exprés y pasajeros, y el "Anaconda," que era el último del tren, y en el cual iba la familia Freeman. Al descarrilarse éste, la máquina y el ténder se precipitaron en una hondonada que estaba al lado de la nivelación de la vía, arrastrando a varios de los vagones por detrás; diez de éstos se precipitaron con gran estruendo en la hondonada y quedaron apilados en manera informe, más o menos destrozados; algunos de los demás se salieron de los rieles y quedaron atravesados en la nivelación, malamente averiados por el violento choque de consecuencia. Imposible sería describir con plenitud aquella aterrodora escena; los lamentos, de dolor, los gritos do la desesperación, los quejidos de agonía que se oían por todas partes, hendían el alma. Al caer la máquina de la nivelación, el maquinista brincó de la casilla del ingenio, en el esfuerzo de salir a salvo del peligro, pero la máquina le trampó las piernas, y en esa situación fue escaldado a muerte por el agua hirviente que se escapaba del caldero, mientras el infeliz pedía por Dios mismo que alguien le diera un tiro y le sacara de aquellos tormentos. Pero esta fue tan sólo una de las muchas espeluznantes escenas de horror que se desarrollaran en tan fatal suceso.

Para hacer más terrible aun aquel desastre, el descarrilamiento se incendió, y de este modo, ya por una causa, ya por otra, treintitrés personas por todas perecieron en ésta catástrofe, y cosa de cien más quedaron mas o menos seriamente lastimadas, de las cuales quince murieron después en un hospital de Los Ángeles. Solamente tréintidos de los doscientos pasajeros y miembros del servicio quedaron en condición de poder dar auxilio a los lastimados y salvar de las llamas a varios de los cadáveres de los muertos. Entre estos treintidos se contaban once mujeres, y entre todos ellos se distinguía un joven robusto, de unos veintesiete abriles, quien, no obstante una fea herida en la cabeza, que le dejaba el rostro ensangrentado, ponía en juego hercúleos esfuerzos, que descuellaban sobre los demás por su energía y denuedo.

Ahora, volviendo al coche particular de la familia Freeman, es decir, el "Anaconda," éste quedó sobre la nivelación, con la parte frontal incrustada en el coche que le precedía. La violencia del choque y el sobresalto, habían dejado a sus ocupantes privados del conocimiento en el interior. Estos eran, ademas de la familia Freeman, un señor llamado James Wilkins, la esposa de éste, y una hija, amigos de los Freeman y residentes de Los Angeles, que acompañaban a éstos en un viaje de paseo a Denver.

Cuando el "Anaconda" comenzaba a arder por uno de sus extremos, el joven que dejamos mencionado, entró en el coche por la entrada posterior y halló a los ocupantes esparcidos por todas partes, en estado insensible y próximos a morir quemados, o asfixiados por el humo de que estaba lleno el interior del coche. Este joven no era otro que Henry Collins, a quien Orlando, o sea el capitán Havens, había salvado la vida en Chicago, quince años antes. Luego se echó a hombros a la señora Freeman y la sacó del peligro; en seguida llamó a tres más de sus compañeros, con quienes logró rescatar a cuatro más de aquellas víctimas. Para este tiempo las llamas se habían desarrollado a grado tal que ya nadie se atrevía a entrar en el coche, y uno de los que habían entrado antes, afirmaba que no había quedado nadie adentro, mientras Henry sostenía que estaba seguro de haber visto a otra persona allí. Al impulso de esta convicción, entró precipitadamente en el coche, que ya esta envuelto en llamas, y dirigiéndose a donde creía haber visto la otra forma humana, logró dar con su objetivo. Aquel fue un esfuerzo de supremo heroísmo, pues en virtud del mismo, Henry, ya a punto de sucumbir a la asfixia, salió arrastrándose del coche, pero arrastrando consigo el cuerpo, casi exánime, de la preciosa Amanda. Una vez en la plataforma exterior, ambos fueron auxiliados y llevados a salvo.

El día siguiente toda la prensa del país daba a la estampa artículos más o menos detallados de la terrible tragedia; el diario, "Los Angeles Examiner," por ejemplo, daba una cuenta del caso que rezaba en parte como sigue:

Un tren de alivio fue llamado de Los Angeles ayer, a la escena fatal de un descarrilamiento del tren regular de pasajeros, No. 10, que partió de ésta para San Diego, a las 9:30 a.m. Este tren de alivio regresó a Los Angeles esta mañana, trayendo consigo los cadáveres de 24 personas que perecieron en el desastre, y más de cien víctimas que sufrieran serias, y aun graves, lastimaduras. Las víctimas han sido alojadas en los hospitales de esta ciudad, en donde recibirán propia asistencia clínica, y se hará todo lo posible por aliviar sus sufrimientos.

Uno de los rasgos que merece mención especial en conexión del trágico suceso, es, sin duda alguna, el valor y heroísmo de cosa de una veintena y media de personas que iban en el malogrado tren, y que pudieron rescatar los cadáveres de los muertos ya lastimados que llegaron en el dicho tren. Varias víctimas de tan lamentable catástrofe fueron devoradas por las llamas.

Entre este grupo de rescatadores, se distinguió, por su admirable energía e intrepidez, un agente viajero, de unos 27 años, representante de una fábrica de calzado de Boston, Mass., que responde al nombre de Henry Collins.

La condición de Mr. Freeman, su esposa y su hija, se considera crítica, pero de ningún modo grave, y los médicos creen que pronto recobrarán de sus lastimaduras y del efecto general de su dolorosa experiencia; pues, redúcese todo ésto a cortaduras superficiales y contusiones dolorosas, pero no de carácter alarmante.

El héroe de la catástrofe, Henry Collins, que a peligro de su propia vida salvó la de la señora y señorita Freeman, no obstante que sufriera una honda rotura del pericráneo y gran pérdida de sangre, favor a su robusta complexión, se halla en vías de recobrar próntamente su estado normal.

Tanto así por la relación del "Examiner." La familia Freeman y el joven Collins se hallaban convalecientes en el Hospital de San Lucas, en donde se les daba la más eficiente y esmerada asistencia que los conocimientos clínicos podían proporcionar.

Ahora volveremos nuestra atención al capitán Havens, que, en San Francisco, había leído con honda pena los referidos relatos de la prensa, y no pasaba un solo día sin que, por medio del teléfono distante, comunicase con el Hospital de San Lucas para informarse de la condición en que se hallara, tanto la familia Freeman, como Henry Collins, en quien Orlando ahora, con orgullo y admiración, recordaba, al íntimo amigo de una época pasada; ansiaba verle, con el mayor entusiasmo, para darle un fuerte abrazo y felicitarle, de todo corazón, por haber salvado la vida a la joven Amanda, ídolo de sus más floridos sueños.

IV.

Pasaron cuatro días, y los Freeman, lo mismo que Henry Collins, recuperaban muy satisfactoriamente. Amanda, lo mismo que sus padres, todos los días mandaban a Henry hermosos ramilletes de flores, y libros de amena lectura, para su solaz y recreo, no obstante que él les suplicara no se molestasen tanto por él.

Dos días más, y los médicos permitieron a los pacientes el salir fuera de sus cuartos, a recrearse en el invigorante sol y dulce ambiente de "El Verjel del Mundo." Lo primero que los Freeman hicieron, fue ir a donde estaba el libertador de sus vidas, a quien ansiaban conocer. Henry andaba paseándose en uno de los portales del hospital. Uno de los médicos de la institución, que había estado atendiendo personalmente a los interesados, se encargó de llevar a los Freeman a donde estaba Henry. Profusas y calurosas fueron las expresiones de gratitud con que Amanda y sus padres colmaban a Henry, mientras éste sólo respondía que, aparte de haber cumplido con un deber que las circunstancias le habían impuesto, no había hecho nada fuera de lo ordinario.

Pasaron dos días más, y las relaciones mútuas de Henry y los Freeman tornaban mayor incremento en la intimidad personal. Por fin los Freeman resolvieron partir de regreso a casa, pero no antes de hacer a Henry convenir en irse con ellos a pasar una temporada de visita en Denver, como su huésped. De conformidad con tal solicitud, los interesados partieron el día siguiente para su destino; pero algo más que el solo deseo de acompañar a los Freeman, impulsaba a Henry, pues la verdad del caso es que ya estaba enamorado de Amanda. En el tren que los llevaba, los interesados ocupaban un coche sala de los más elegantes, el coche particular de Mr. Freeman habiendo quedado reducido a ceniza y fragmentos como resultado del descarrilamiento.

Era esta una serena y hermosa mañana del mes de setiembre, y aquellos viajeros se sentían muy felices de que el siniestro acaecido no hubiera tenido para ellos fatales consecuencias, ya que, desafortunadamente, las había tenido para tantos otros, cuya triste suerte ellos deploraban.

Henry y Amanda ocupaban el mismo asiento, conversaban muy contentos, contínuamente, y en curso de su conversación por fin dijo ésta:

—¿Quién hubiera pensado que un paseo tan delicioso como el que estaba teniendo en California, viniera a tener un desenlace tan terrible y trágico!

—Pero no es remoto que todavía ni usted ni yo hayamos visto el desenlace, respondió Henry.

—Estoy segura, por cierto, que lo peor ha pasado ya—dijo Amanda, riéndose en manera significativa—pero la deuda que le debo a usted, jamás podré pagarla; a no ser que pueda hacerlo por medio de mi eterna gratitud, concluyó diciendo.

—Lo imposible no existe cuando hay la voluntad, repuso Henry.

Amanda le dió una mirada de sorpresa, manifestando no haber comprendido las palabras de Henry, mas por fin dijo:

—No veo porqué haga usted referencia a mi voluntad, como si pusiese en duda la sinceridad de mis palabras.

—No son pruebas de sinceridad las que anhelo, repuso Henry—su sinceridad está fuera de la cuestión; para no andar con rodeos, ¡quiéro que sepas, Amanda, que te admiro y te amo con todo el fuego de mi ardiente corazón; dime que serás mía, mi querida esposa, y convierte mi ventura en un mar de eterna dicha para el resto de mi vida!

Al oír Amanda tan seriamente amoroso discurso, quedó desconcertada por el momento, más recobrando su natural serenidad de ánimo, respondió:

—¿Pudiéra yo negar su felicidad a quien le debo la vida?

—No, Amanda, no quiero que accedas a mis deseos únicamente por esa razón; quiero que me digas—

—Que en verdad te quiero—interrumpió Amanda—y ya que me pides la verdad, confesaré la verdad: con nadie en este mundo podría yo ser más dichosa que contigo; de todo corazón, considérame tuya; tuya hasta la muerte...

Los dos amantes se abrazaron, y sellaron su compromiso matrimonial con un beso, y otro y otro, que parecían ser los dulces precursores de las románticas nupcias que pronto habían de convertir aquellas dos almas en una.

Acto contínuo, Henry puso en conocimiento de los padres de Amanda, lo que acontecía. Estos se manifestaron enteramente complacidos de tan interesante culminación, dando a los prospectivos cónyugues, con su consentimiento, su bendición.

Unos días después, el matrimonio Freeman formalmente anunciaba, los esponsales de su hija, y copiosísimas fueron las felicitaciones que recibieran, tanto personales como telegráficas y postales, de sus numerosas amistades.

El capitán Havens, recibió una de las esquelas de estos esponsales en San Francisco, y no obstante sus esfuerzos, se colmó de turbación y nerviosidad, con algo de vejación, sentimientos que calmaba tan sólo pensando en que la dicha que había. soñado para sí, estaba destinada a brillar esplendorosa en la vida de su querido amigo, Henry Collins. Por fin fue a los despachos de la Western Union, de donde mandó el siguiente telegrama:

Mr. y Mrs. George Freeman,
Denver, Colorado:

Permitidme expresaros mis más calurosas felicitaciones. Que la vida marital de su hija y Henry, sea un Edén abundante do todas las bendiciones de la vida, son los sinceros deseos de

Vuestro fiel amigo,
Orlando Havens.

Después de mandar sus felicitaciones, Orlando fue al hotel X..., en donde estaba hospedado otro capitán del mismo regimiento, llamado Melitón González, nativo de Nuevo México, a quien aquel estimaba mucho, tanto por sus buenas cualidades personales, como por el viril denuedo y valor con que se había distinguido en la famosa batalla de El Caney, en San Juan de Cuba. Era Melitón un perfecto contraste de Orlando: tenía el pelo rojo, lo mismo que las cejas y pestañas; la cara rubicunda como una remolacha, adornada por una abundante lluvia de pecas amarillas; era burdo de facciones, y no obstante la robusta simetría física de su persona, era verdaderamente feo, y tan extraño en sus ideas, como grotesco en expresarlas; más que todo, era, al paracer, enemigo implacable del bello sexo, como se verá más delante. Orlando, varias veces había confesado a Melitón el amor que le tenía a Amanda, pero éste más bien sentía simpatía que placer para con su amigo Orlando.

Serían las 9:00 de la noche cuando Orlando fue al cuarto de Melitón, a quien halló destendido en su cama, con los zapatos y el pantalón puestos, como era su costumbre hacerlo. Orlando luego dijo lo que acontecía, con respecto a Amanda.

—Ha sido para mí un rudo chasco, decía Orlando, el resultado de mi primer amor, y creo que con ésto he perdido la única mujer que yo pudiera amar en esta vida.

Melitón le escuchaba muy atento, y por fin comenzó a desenvolver su opinión en frases características:

—Mucho me sorprende—decíale—que un hombre de tu cuerda y madura sensatez, se encuentre amarrido y atolondrado porque cierta hembra que se llama Amanda, no se quiera casar contigo, cuando pudieras amarrarte con otra que se llamase Jacinta o Pancrasia, con los mismos resultados. Para mí, lo mismo es que sean Jerónimas que Amandas: las mujeres son . . . las mujeres, y nada más. Desde que la primera de ellas vino al mundo y se salió con la serpiente para embaucar al primer Orlando, las mujeres han sido fuente de todas las calamidades de la tierra. Aparte de ésto, ¿a qué vienen, pues, tus quebrantos y tus penas, cuando para cada Adonis hay una tonelada de Venus en el mundo? ¡Esto sí que está chistoso!: "¡Después que se fue el conejo, pedradas al matorral!" Si ella se casa con otro, haz tú otro tanto, y así serás . . . otro tonto. En cuanto a mí, si algún día me caso, será por la "platita" y no por el amor; sí, señor, dicen que "Por el dinero, baila el perro," y yo soy unos de los perros que quiere bailar la danza de los amores, siendo que los prospectos de la danza sean pecuniariamento remunerativos. De este modo me caso con la primer incauta jamona que me quiera, que hallará en este polio un maridito "tres piedras," y aunque la chica sea una tarasca espantosa, más horrible que un tiburón. De otro modo, ¡vayan todas ellas a "jondear" gatos de la cola a las regiones del Tártaro . . . !

Todo esto hubiera sido muy divertido, tal vez, para una persona que se hallara en otra disposición mental, distinta de la que ahora embargara a Orlando. Pero en aquellas circunstancias, la palabrería de Melitón poseía toda la sustancia de una sátira irritante.

—Y ¿a qué viéne toda esa ensarta de majaderías? pregunta Orlando, mal humorado.

—¡A mucho, hombre, a mucho! exclamó Melitón—te sientes atolondrado porque no te puedes casar con cierta liebre que se llama Amanda, que te pone el ejemplo casándose con otro. Esta pichona no es sino mujer como todas las mujeres; uno de aquellos seres tan comunes como los gatos caseros. Si ésta no te quiere, hay docenas de la misma especie, que están a dos manos, rezándole novenas a San Antonio, tratando de convertir al Santo en correchepillo, para que les consiga el amartelamiento de algún despavorido gaznápiro, de propensiones sentimentales como las tuyas. Y todo vá a parar en que, de aquí a mañana, te encuentras con una de tantas amorosas zánganas, que en eso do hermosura le dé cartas y espadas a la dichosa Amanda, y le saque adelante desde el pescuezo a la cola at cruzar la raya; y que te agarre, te enfrene, y te encille, y te cargue las mochilas, para que te dejes de tanto brinco estando el suelo parejo.

En el humor en que se hallaba Orlando, ésto bastó para exasperarle a grado de desesperación; se levantó de la silla en que estaba sentado y salió súbitamente de la pieza, sin dar las "buenas noches" a Melitón. Este se quedó destendido en su cama, como estaba antes, y con entera indiferencia y típico abandono se durmió cantando en sotto voce:

La nariz de Felonís
Es una nariz muy larga,
Pero qué me importa a mí,
Cuando ella es la que la carga.

Soy amigo de la luz,
La oscuridad desconsuela,
Pero estando yo con Luz
Aunque me apaguen la vela.

Al rico, don Juan Troselo,
Le pedí a su hija, Piedad:
Cogiéndome por el pelo.
Me hubiera arrojado al suelo,
Pero me tuvo piedad.

> El día que salí de Veracruz,
> Me vieron escapármelas al trote:
> Me seguía mi mujer con un garrote
> No más porque fuí yo a ver a Cruz.

Por su parte, Orlando llegó a su cuarto, se puso su ropa de dormir, y se sentó a un escritorio, en donde escribió los siguientes versos, que el día siguiente aparecieron en uno de los diarios de San Francisco:

ES MUY TRISTE

> Es muy triste, después de ya encendida
> La chispa del amor dentro del alma,
> Sentir ardiente su pasión crecida,
> Y que nos roba sin piedad la calma,
> En pos de una esperanza
> Cuyo límite alcanza
> Tan sólo a desplomarse donde nace
> La dura realidad que nos deshace...
>
> Es muy triste, después de haber soñado
> Una diosa que guiara mi destino,
> Y tal conio la había idealizado,
> La encontrara de pronto en mi camino,
> Para hallar invencible
> Un adverso imposible,
> Donde la dicha cuando ya florece,
> Se hunde para siempre y desparece...

El día siguiente, cuando el capitán González (Melitón) leyó estos versos, se llenó de disgusto y turbación, y exclamó:—¡Por el alto cielo y las canas de mi madre, Orlando se ha vuelto loco! Este sí que se ha trocado en Caballero de la Triste Figura.

Acto contínuo se puso a pasear de un lado al otro de la pieza, con las manos por detrás, muy pensativo. Por fin se sentó a un escritorio y se puso a escribir la siguiente interesante epístola:

Querido Orlando:

He visto por el periódico que ya te metiste a poeta sentimental, debido a que la Diana coloradense te volteó las espaldas por otro, y te dejó plantado con un palmo de narices. Estás luciéndote muy de lo lindo, lo mismo de melindroso que de objeto de irrisión. ¡Muy precioso está el fandango! Pero en fin, no hay que admirarnos: también don Quijote de la Mancha deliraba en Dulcinea del Toboso, y ¿por qué le has de ir tú en zaga a don Quijote, verdad!

¡Bueno, bueno! Pero ya que de versos se trata, con ésta te adjunto otro atropello a las Musas, para que lo publiques también sobre tu firma, ahora que estás de vena para tales desatinos. Hélo aquí:

Amanda:—
Quiero decirte
   Que yo no dejo de amarte;
   Que quisiera convertirte
   En diosa para, adorarte,
   Y con avidez asirte
   Y para siempre lazarte...
   Mas si al leer éste ensarte,
   Vas de mi amor a reírte,
   De plano quiero advertirte,
   Que muy lejos de olvidarte,
   Me voy al monte a gemirte,
   ¡A ver si un rayo me parte!
Tuyo, Melitón

La precedente comunicación tuvo el efecto que Melitón anhelaba: cuando Orlando la leyó soltó una risotada, con la cual se puso de buen humor. En seguida, salió en busca de Melitón, y al encontrarle, ambos se rieron con sabrosas ganas, se dieron un abrazo, y en seguida su conversación versó en asuntos muy distintos. Estos eran amigos sinceros, se amaban, y en todo caso, mútuamente se comprendían.

Aquí no será por demás advertir que el capitán González se casó seis meses después, en San Bernardino, con una de las damas más hermosas y distinguidas de esa ciudad, manifestando que no era, en su recóndito sentir, tan hóstil al bello sexo como presumía serlo; que fue uno de los mejores maridos que se han visto, siempre solícito de las cosas de la vida por el bienestar y la felicidad de su esposa. Su casamiento reveló su verdadero carácter: nobleza de corazón, cordura, y sensatez, y fidelidad al deber.

v.

Ahora volveremos nuestra atención a las ruidosas nupcias Collins-Freeman, que formaban una de las notas sociales de más interés en la capital de Colorado. El día en que éstas iban a verificarse, el mayor entusiasmo y animación reinaban en la mansión residencial de aquella distinguida familia, y como en este mundo todo cede dócilmente al poder de don Dinero, todo estaba listo y en orden para la esplendorosa culminación de aquel romance, a las 8:00 de la noche del día fijado. Las espaciosas salas de aquel hogar palaciego habían sido ricamente decoradas de rosas y azahares, dispuestos con delicado gusto y verdadero arte. Debajo de un bellísimo docel de aromáticas flores, en el centro de cuya bóveda colgaba una campana de rosas y azahares, estaba arreglado en altar do Himeneo. El novio, vestido de frac, era una de las personalidades más atrayentes del suntuoso evento: había ya recobrado de sus lastimaduras, salvo por la contusión de una pierna, que todavía, le causaba algún dolor, pero Henry, por medio de oportunos esfuerzos, disimulaba la cojera, porque ¿quién es el que no trata de conquistar hasta lo imposible, por parecer un modelo de perfección cuando anda de novio? Amanda, ataviada en las albas nitideces de su traje de bodas, con un par de delicados aretillos de diamantes en sus rosadas orejitas, y una soguilla de diamantes y rubíes ceñida a su cuello de marfil, parecía una visión fantástica del cielo de las hadas, en medio de transparentes celajes de inmaculado blancor: así como hiciera decir al tío Conde el Padre Luis Coloma, S.J., hablando de la casta Lulú en "El Primer Baile": "Hebe sirviendo la copa a los dioses, era menos hermosa... Ofelia apareciéndose a Hámlet, menos ideal ... Psíquis elevándose al Olimpo, menos vaporosa..."

Un coro de jóvenes amigos de los contrayentes, cantó el epitalamio, y de un modo general, jamás se han visto bodas más brillantes que las de Henry y Amanda en la ciudad de Denver.

Pasado ya el feliz evento, los dichosos cónyugues se retiraron a su tálamo nupcial, en el segundo piso de la casa. El día siguiente iban a partir en su viaje de bodas para Nuevo Orleáns, de donde intentaban darse a la mar con destino a la Isla de Cuba, con el fin de pasar su luna de miel en "La Perla de las Antillas."

Al estar cambiándose de ropa, Henry enseño a Amanda una medallita, diciendo:

—Esta es la única herencia que mi madre me dejara. Ella misma me la puso, ya en su lecho de muerte, cuando yo sólo tenía ocho años de edad, por lo tanto, la conservo como una joya de inestimable valor.

—¡Qué casualidad! exclamó Amanda, yo tengo una medallita lo mismo que esa, la cual mamá me dice que no me quite nunca. La traigo en este guardapelo ... Mírala.

Aquí consideramos propio advertir que Amanda no tenía ni el más remoto recuerdo de su verdadero origen, y estaba enteramente bajo la creencia de que era, en realidad, hija carnal de sus, padres adoptivos. Cuando le mostró la medallita a Henry, dijo éste:

—Es idéntica a la mía. Y te diré, Amanda, yo tenía una hermanita, de dos años de edad, cuando mi madre murió. También a ella le puso una medallita como esta. Mi hermanita fue adoptada de un orfanato de Nueva York, pero como las reglas y regulaciones de tales instituciones prohiben rigurosamente el que se divulguen los nombres de los interesados en casos de adopción, nunca pude yo conseguir informes que me encaminaran a descubrir su paradero.

—A poco crees que yo soy tu hermana, dijo entonces Amanda, soltando la risa.

—No quiero creer nada, repuso Henry, antes de ver a tus padres.

—¿Estás en serio, Henry? preguntó Amanda, y continuó, con palabras de risa. De veras que eres curioso.

—Ciertamente voy a ver a tus padres, repitió Henry.

—Déjate de eso, dijo Amanda, que te pondrás en ridículo.

A este punto Henry notó un lunar rojo, del tamaño de una moneda de plata de diez centavos, en la parte superior del brazo izquierdo de Amanda.

—Mira, Amanda, dijo Henry, estas no pueden ser meras coincidencias. Mi hermanita, cuyo nombre era Carlota tenía un lunar como este en el mismo lugar. Es preciso el ver a tus padres.

—Pues, voy contigo, dijo Amanda, todavía riéndose de lo que ella consideraba un imposible.

Salieron ambos de aquel recinto y fueron a la alcoba de los padres de Amanda. Tan pronto como entraron, Henry se dirigió a ellos diciendo:

—Quiero que me digan la verdad, ¿és Amanda hija carnal de ustedes?

La señora dió una mirada inquisitiva a su esposo, y por fin respondió:

—Yo soy la única madre que ella tiene. Sí, Amanda es nuestra hija.

Mr. Freeman no hallaba qué responder o decir, pero Henry, viendo que la respuesta de la señora Freeman era un tanto evasiva, dijo:

—Hay esto. Mi verdadero nombre no es Henry Collins, sino Eustacio Quintanilla. Cuando mis padres murieron quedamos huérfanos yo y una hermanita mía llamada Carlota, y fuimos alojados en un orfanato de Nueva York, de donde ambos fuimos adoptados después, y no he vuelto a saber más del paradero de mi hermana. Yo fuí adoptado por una familia de Toronto, Canadá; el hombre se llamaba Henry Collins, y a mí me dieron el nombre de Henry Collins, Hijo. A los doce años de edad, inducido por otros muchachos, y de ellos acompañado, me fuí de la casa de mi adopción, y por fin vine a parar en Chicago, donde había vivido antes de irme para Boston, o sea cinco años pasados.

Aquí no quedó más recurso a los padres de Amanda, que confesar lo que nunca habían querido dar ni siquiera a sospechar a su hija. Todos lloraron lágrimas de gusto y quebranto: gusto porque los dos hermanos se habían por fin encontrado; quebranto por el súbito chasco en que habían venido a quedar resueltas aquellas nupcias, que por la ley natural y la divina, eran nulas. Henry y Amanda, o sea Eustacio y Carlota, se dieron un abrazo y un beso, no ya arrebatados del amor ardiente del marido y la mujer, sino impulsados del cariñoso afecto de dos hermanos que habían estado separados desde su tierna niñez.

Aquella singularísima ocurrencia ha sido una de las más sensacionales que se han registrado jamás en los círculos de la culta sociedad de Estados Unidos.

Accediendo a las urgentes súplicas de Mr. y Mrs. Freeman, lo mismo que de su hermana, Henry por fin convino en quedarse a vivir con ellos permanentemente, y Mr. Freeman por fin le designó como gerente de sus grandes intereses de minería en Colorado y Nuevo México, ocupación en la cual logró Henry acumular una grande fortuna en pocos años.

VI.

Tres días después de este desenlace, el capitán Havens, que había conseguido por fin su licencia, permanente, vino a Denver a visitar a la familia Freeman, tal como lo había prometido hacer. El entusiasmo y placer de aquella reunión, excede toda descripción, pues allí se juntaban el libertador de las vidas de Amanda y sus padres: Henry, con el amigo íntimo y libertador de la vida de éste: Orlando. La dicha de aquella ocasión no tuvo límites.

———

En el año de 1908, fuí yo a la ciudad de Los Angeles. Un domingo por la tarde, al ir de paseo por una de las hermosas calles residenciales de la misma, ví un hombre que besaba a su esposa a la puerta de su casa, diciéndole:

—Mi vida, vuelvo dentro de una hora para ir a la matinée.

Cuando se retiraba, salieron de la casa dos preciosas criaturas, un niño de unos nueve años, y una niña de cosa de siete años, que corriendo fueron y le alcanzaron, gritando: —¡Un beso, papá, un beso! El papá afectuosamente los besó, y se fue.

Era aquella escena la manifestación de una dichosa familia, cuya vida doméstica era "un Edén abundante de todas las bendiciones de la vida": el esposo y padre era Orlando; la esposa era Amanda, y aquellas dos preciosas criaturas eran el bello fruto de su matrimonio, y sus nombres, respectivamente ... EUSTACIO y CARLOTA.

Finis

English Translation of Poesía y prosa

INDEX

Preface
Prologue
Ode to the Heroes
To the Homeland
To Santa Fe
Hobnobbers
Fragments
Jealousy and Love: A Song
To the Virgin at Her Altar
A Flowery Circumstance
Yesterday, Today
The Worker
Deceptions
To Mrs. Adelina Otero-Warren
Philosophizing
Autumn
Here's to the Month of May
The Ingrate
To New Mexico
Life (Sonnet)
To the Westward Explorer
Here's to Childhood
An Illusion
A Singular Moment
Christmas
Deception
A Tangled Affair

To the Lawmakers
A Nocturne to . . .
It's Love
A Sharp Edge
Paradox
In Memoriam
Dreams and Truth
Pleasure
Devotion
Indifferent
My Candidate and My Reasons
A Painful Affair
It Withdraws and Disappears
The Atheist and the Truth
Guardian Angel
Axioms
Anita
My Mother's Widowhood
To Ms. Adela Cruz
Creation
To My Daughter, Herminia
To My Son, Felipe
To My Daughter, Josefina
To My Daughter, Julieta
To My Daughter, Elvira
To My Elvira
To My Little Son, Buenaventura

To My Little Daughter, Melba
To My Goddaughter, Rosa Córdova
To My Godson, Jacobo Aragón, Son
To My Beloved Little Sister, Lucía
Psalm of Life (Longfellow)
To the Duchess of York (Dryden)
A Wise One (Origins unknown)
The House by the Side of the Road
   (Sam Wallis [sic] Foss)

Vision of Belshazzar (Byron)
On the Death of a Young Lady
   (Byron)
Mary Stuart and Her Mourner (E.
   Bulwer Lytton)
A Real Republican (Political Verses)
A Masquerade Ball
Don Julio Berlanga
Eustacio and Carlota: A Novelette

THE WORKS OF FELIPE M. CHACÓN, "EL CANTOR NEOMEXICANO"

Poetry and Prose

With a prologue by the Honorable Benjamin Read, author of "Illustrated History of New Mexico," "Sidelights on New Mexico History," etc., etc.

Published by F. M. Chacón,
Albuquerque, New Mexico
United States of America

© 1924 by F. M. Chacón

The ownership of this work is protected by law and the author reserves the exclusive right to grant, or withhold, permission for its reproduction.

The appropriate steps, as ordered by the law, have been taken to protect the rights to this work in the Republic of Mexico.

Preface

Upon presenting this book to those who might read it, I do so free from presumptions of vanity, which are so shocking in individuals.

I admit that the works that make up this collection suffer from imperfections, which emerge upon reading it with an eye toward fundamental restrictions. For this reason, I offer them only as a simple contribution to recreational reading for the popular masses of people, with apologies as warranted to theologians, philosophers, rhetoricians, and logicians.

With these brief clarifications, I hope that my book is received with the same spirit in which I offer it; and if it may provide solace and recreation, and make the hours dedicated to its reading pleasant, within its admitted limitations, then the modest effort of the author will be amply rewarded.

FELIPE MAXIMILIANO CHACÓN

Prologue

The author of this book has quite appropriately said the following, upon making available a certain newspaper to the public, and writing in it an article that came from the depths of his brilliant quill: "As the years pass, unfolding their path through the confines of time, they leave as footprints distinct epochs that characterize, in a particular manner, the ongoing succession of human progress."

Echoing the same sentiment, I do not doubt that, in the course of time's passage, the literary works of Felipe Maximiliano Chacón are destined to leave as their footprint a distinct epoch in the literary history of the United States of America.

I say a distinct epoch because a purely American genius has produced a work that gives glory to his homeland in the beautiful language of Cervantes.[1]

The poet Chacón owes no apology for having chosen the Castilian language to give form to the brilliant product of his talent. In his "Patriotic Hymns," Chacón has wished to affirm that the praises and words of adulation for American-born heroes—a group which includes him—are not limited to our own language, a language which we greatly love, but rather that the same praises are sung, with a surfeit of beauty, in other languages of the civilized world that the sons of America have successfully cultivated in the course of their numerous conquests.

Chacón was born in the town of Santa Fe, capital of the state of New Mexico, on the 6th of December of 1873, and as such, I have had the great pleasure of knowing him from his tender youth, and in the course of these long years have become accustomed to calling him simply "Felipe." His father was the late don Urbano Chacón, one of the first pioneers in the field of journalism in the southern part of the state of Colorado and in the northern part of the then-territory of New Mexico.

Don Urbano Chacón published *El Explorador*, in Trinidad, Colorado, in the last years of the 1860s and *El Espejo* in Taos, New Mexico, in the early 1870s. The latter newspaper don Urbano would later move to Bernalillo, New Mexico, later resulting in the great coincidence that Felipe would establish and edit another newspaper, *El Faro del Río Grande*, in the same locale exactly thirty years later. The father of the author of this book, don Urbano, also published *La Aurora* in Santa Fe during the early '80s and passed away at the end of 1886, when he was serving his second term as superintendent of schools in Santa Fe County, leaving Felipe orphaned of his father at the tender age of 13.

Felipe's mother is Mrs. Doña Lucía Ward, Viuda de Chacón, who currently resides in Albuquerque.

The author of this book received his primary education in the public schools of Santa Fe, and his more advanced instruction at the College of San Miguel, which the Christian Brothers of Saint John the Baptist of La Salle still direct in Santa Fe.

Felipe was always, of his own accord, very studious, and dedicated as much time as his occupations permitted to the study or reading of good books. A testament to how our poet has made the most of his time is the manner in which he has fruitfully learned and cultivated the Spanish language, without any formal instruction, in a country whose language is English and where there are few or no opportunities to learn Spanish formally.

He who writes this prologue has always regretted that Felipe has not been able to dedicate himself more exclusively to the creation of literature, having devoted the majority of his life to commerce. This has been, perhaps, more the result of the workings of Destiny, than a result of his natural inclination, for, as he himself says in one of his verses:

Destiny is a deaf man who does not hear
The voice of the suffering he inflicts
And there is no living beast
Who escapes from the fate devised for him.[2]

One of the things that all who know Felipe admire in him is the uniform ability with which he writes in Spanish and in English, and poetry as much as prose. Felipe has written many poems in English—serious ones, witty ones, and love poems—and to give an idea of his ingenious wit in particular, it does not seem amiss to me to reproduce, as an example of the same, the following three compositions, in respective order:

PARTING

Not dead but living whilst they be,
To me my loved ones die,
And one by one they pass from me
With but my last good-bye.
Yet feel disheartened? I refuse!
My haughty spirit soars on high,
And with each knock and slap and bruise
Unmoved I give my last good-bye.

IN MEXICO

We met: for me 'twas love at first sight.
She was divine;
I prayed her then my soul delight.
Asked her to make my future bright,
To be but mine,
Said she: "No entiendo!"

I love you more than tongue can tell,
I yield supine;
Without thee life, in sadness' spell,
Is but a winter's barren dell,
Won't you be mine?
Said she: "No sabe."

Unbounded wealth at your command,
Rich, superfine,
All at your feet, belle of this land,
You'll find anon as you demand,
If you'll be mine,
Cried she: "¡Ay Dios!"

Diamonds, gold, all to surprise,
A treasure's thine;
I'll give you, love, a paradise,
A home that queens may long for twice,
Won't you be mine?
Said she: "Oh! Yes me quiere."

These verses should be taken in the spirit in which the author intended them: as an instance of good humor and, in no sense, with the intent to offend. Among his love compositions, one finds the following sonnet:

WOULDST THOU?

Sad I long as in life I stroll
For the days of the past to return;
Not the time but its pleasures I mourn
In the folly so plain in the scroll

Of the woes I now sadly enroll;
Yet I see them but giving in turn
Recollections I willingly spurn
For another new hope in my soul.

Couldst thou only perceive in my heart
But to fathom my deepest regret,
Couldst thou only perceive ere we part

How it beats all alone for you yet,
Wouldst thou know why we drifted apart,
Then perchance you'd forgive and forget.

As a translator from English to Spanish and vice versa, we have but to read his translations of works by great English-speaking poets, which appear in this book, to fully appreciate the author's expertise, his intimate knowledge of both languages.

The compositions that make up this book have been written in isolated instances, and are best seen as accidental creations, rather than anything purposeful on the part of the author: they were not written with the intent to be published as a book, a fact that is evinced by the mere fact of the long period of their production, which covers a great many years; Felipe wrote the poem entitled "An Illusion," which appears in this book, when he was just 17 years old. He also wrote poems of a political nature when he was only 14, and these were widely celebrated in their time in New Mexico.

As far as his personal character goes, "The Neomexicano Poet" is philosophically inclined. This is clearly demonstrated in his own words: "I have suffered cruel and harsh blows of fate at several points in my life—he says—but I know of no grief that I could not overcome. I have known how to face down misfortune, bitter tribulations, sustained in the idea that things could have been worse still, and thus I have triumphed over adversity. It is useless to the point of foolishness for one to grieve over what has no remedy. In doing so, one only exacerbates the situation. One must defeat life's misfortunes in order to live for many years and be happy."

Another of Chacón's characteristics is his aversion to publicity, his loathing of seeming famous. His beautiful poem entitled "Ode to the Heroes," which he wrote under the influence of righteous patriotic sentiments, inspired by the victory of the Allies in the [First] World War, he did not publish prior to its appearance in this book. The author did not wish to give the appearance that he sought notoriety for trivial things; not because he considered his homeland's triumph in arms to be trivial, but rather out of his lack of appreciation for his own handsome efforts. Chacón is a genius, and like all geniuses, he does not know his own value.

A certain writer, who responds to the name Anita Acevedo, has said, regarding the theme of "Art and Poetry":

Art is a splendid sun that never sets, that dazzles the pupils of all eyes towards whose blazing and rough fire the colossal condors of legitimate aspirations extend their titanic and luminous flight; it is an immense ocean without shores, on whose limpid and sonorous surface white swans of longed-for purity glide, shedding blushing lyrical songs among the rumor of the waves and the kiss of the surf; in a luminous and vast rainbow hung on the blue diaphanous sky and towards whose vivid colors the powerful wings of butterflies of supreme desires beat; it is the radiant star that illuminates the broad course that leads to the sublime peak of glory and under whose vibrant golden kisses the adoring lilies of dreams open their grasp. And poetry, poetry is the most beautiful flower in the garden of lyric art; poetry is the flower of all times and all races, a flower that grows dazzlingly and nobly, as much under the burning rays of the tropic sun as under the glacial cold of the poles; it is the butterfly that has scattered upon the mantle of the ages the gold dust of its brilliant wings; it is the magic bird of white feathers, who in the sweet language of trills has revealed to all generations the secret passion of Romeo, Paolo's kiss, Abelard's promise, Othello's passion, blind with madness and armed with a dagger; the agony of Desdemona and Dante's triumphal voyage to Paradise, in Beatrice's amiable company.

Placing this assessment alongside Chacón's works, one may no less than see Poetry intimately connected to Art. The beautiful fantasy paintings that Felipe fashions stand out in his verses and serve as a lively inspiration for the arts of the paintbrush and chisel. Take, for example, these stanzas of "Creation," which provide characteristic scenes of epic beauty, luxuriant landscapes of picturesque naturalness, speaking of the effects of the sun's birth among branches, flowers, and waters:

   A dazzling ornament fell from
The quiet lake into its crystal waters below
Where the tree's branches, draped with delight,
Gave rest to the waves.

Extravagant blooms of flowers juxtaposed
Their whiteness with the green field,
Where jubilant wood nymphs
Sang pleasant praises from their lightning kiss.

And out of the countryside beautiful brocades
Made of palm trees and birches
Breathed in ecstatically, smiling:
Life growing in tinged tulle.

Who could read these stanzas without seeing in them the magnificent sustenance of Art's genius?

Felipe has dedicated seven years of his life to journalism: he was the associate editor of *La Voz del Pueblo* of Las Vegas, New Mexico, from the fall of 1911 to the spring of 1914; he founded and directed *El Faro del Río Grande* in Bernalillo, New Mexico, in 1914, and in the spring of 1915, he moved that weekly to Albuquerque. A short time later he sold his interest in this newspaper and returned again to Las Vegas, where he undertook *El Independiente* as editor and manager. He also had under his responsibility and direction *El Eco del Norte* from Mora, New Mexico, in 1918, but at the end of the same year, he retired from journalism and again dedicated himself to business interests. In November 1922, however, he finally returned to journalism, taking the helm of *La Bandera Americana*, a weekly that is published in Albuquerque, New Mexico, of which he is presently editor and manager.

In my humble opinion, the United States should be proud of having produced a fellow citizen who offers up glowing praise for his homeland through the talent of his literary production in the language of those kings, the Catholic kings, who so notably contributed to the discovery of America, the continent we inhabit.

Moreover, Spanish-speaking people—Americans as well as Europeans and *insulares*[3]—should openly embrace Chacón's works, as writing by one who, though from a foreign land, has honored the sweet language of Spain—that is, the language of their own countries—an accomplishment that of itself merits profound esteem.

Many of the poems that Chacón has written during his life will never see the light of day as published works: "They have been lost drowning in indolence," as he himself says, indicating that our poet has not much occupied himself with what we might have thought of as the merits of his work in the past; he has not appreciated them enough to keep the manuscripts, and in some manner or by some means to give them published form, apart from those which comprise this book, which, without attributing to myself the virtues of a prophet, is destined to carve out an everlasting memory for this favored son of the great state of New Mexico.

In conclusion, I wish to advise that this prologue has been translated to Spanish by the author of this book; I implicitly approve his version of my concepts and specific sentiments.

Benjamin M. Read
Santa Fe, New Mexico
18 February 1924

Notes

1. [Editors' note: It bears noting how Read is adamant in ascribing an innate Americanism to Chacón not because Read is unaware of questions of race and ethnicity, but because he is wagering on the full incorporation of nuevomexicanos into the US body politic. Conversely, and without contradiction, Read remarks on Chacón's ontological identification with the specific geographical space of New Mexico, insisting that the poet is a product of the land of his birth and, by consequence, of the complexities resulting from the history of how New Mexico came under the purview of the United States.]
2. [Editors' note: An excerpt from Chacón's poem "Dreams and Truth."]
3. [Editors' note: Spanish-speaking inhabitants of the Philippines and Marianas.]

PART I

Patriotic and Miscellaneous Poems

I dedicate these pages
to my mother, doña Lucía Ward Viuda de Chacón

—The Author

ODE TO THE HEROES

To the American Legion

octava real (section I)

1.

With my spirit brimming with pride,
Amid the joy of victory,
I praise your valor in song.

You have my undying admiration,
For I am witness to your eternal glory
Your deeds, left yonder on the fields of struggle
Are now a part of History.
Your loyalty, evident and consistent,
Burns bright over the Sunshine State.[1]

Our world twisted in anguish
At the action of a shameless tyrant
Who razed the tempestuous earth;
In vain that Prussian sought to satiate his fury
Ravaging the churches and homes of Belgium and France
And then, Germany horrified the world
With the cruel butchery that was the Lusitania.

The cosmos is filled with horror,
Seeing how the blood of innocents turns Neptune's waters red
And behind them, the Teuton's hard fists
Drum out these evil deeds.

Assassin, destroyer of homes,
Violator of beloved mothers, daughters, and wives,
Given to wild abandon that makes a mockery of that which is pure.

Growing and rising from the depths of the sea,
Wrenching cries drown the soul;
Civilization itself saw its foundations shake,
And heard the cries of a thousand *brenos*[2]
As they lament,
"Oh, pity now the conquered!"
They threatened as they roared in fury
As they sought to erase, crazed with mad temerity,
The very soul of Democracy!

Thus passed days and weeks,
And the months turned into years
And the despicable Teutons increased
Their inhuman submarine battles;
And bit by bit their insane forays
Violated America's rights
Such that Usona[3] issued its immortal proclamation:
"Shoulder your arms, for thy Homeland calls thee!"

II.

Then and there is when you answered
With American honor and resolve,
Then and there you stepped forward
To fight for the sovereign rights of men,
Offering to die to recover them;
As you left behind your wife and children,
And your beloved parents,
Leaving them
With your eyes turned toward your happy home hoping that
It would hold, in loving care, your beloved,
You said "good-bye" and with the resolute brow
Of the Spartan you raised up the flag,
The stars and stripes of the Nation you love.
"Here I am!" you replied, your farewell tinged with honor.

And so, you go now marching, glorious warrior,
To the blare of the bugle that arouses the spirit,
You head forth and take up the torch of Justice following this noble cause.
The whole world receives you with hurrahs,
There will be no hesitation, no quarter given, no break
Now that you have left behind industrious crafts
To take up the cause of the liberty of nations;
You now give all praises to Mars
As you turn your cannons against the enemy.

And so you go marching now, glorious warrior
Going far to cross untamed seas to reach
France, where that country awaits
With hope and joy amidst the many reasons to despair.

Dense clouds darken the sky again,
And as the hordes of enemies grow
And advance in power through the forests,
Now shouting a mantra, "On to Paris!"
A depleted nation, France, is weakened and bogged down,
Hearing but not trembling at the chant
That taps out retreat to the warriors.

But the scene changes unexpectedly
And the morning sun, like some divine torch,
Peeks out, pouring out rays of hope

Seeming like a victory call in splendid, far-off summer
On the first day of June and advancing from afar
Whose voices are heard rising up in military cadence?
What are these mystical stirrings?
The German hordes quake
As the sharp, resounding notes hie upward
For a moment, the beating fury stops
And from indigenous and remote lands

An unknown and brave army is singing
With the rumpus of their trucks.
"Not until we have finished them off,
We will not retreat until we are victorious!"

Flashes of light rise ever higher
Up from that fiery scene
Where you witnessed your exalted and strategic march
Blessed, as it were, on Mount Belleau,
And where you heard the cannons roar with patriotic zeal.
There, sons of America, you were crowned with glory
And there, too, in the land of Pluto, god of the underworld,
Now the place of a horrific battle
The steel of your sword strikes like a raging hurricane
In triumphal struggle, and there the shadow of the great Washington,
Unmoved and daunting, appears among his noble offspring
Striking fear in the German fighter, who retreats with his impious horde
Your bravery so great that even the Hun in his way
Paid you honor, naming you "Devil Dogs" in his language.

With heads raised, proud, you go forth, sons of New Mexico,
Fighting in Château-Thierry and in San Miguel
Joined as brothers you advance, winning laurels of victory.
And flashes of that burning world return
Upon seeing the brazenness of your guns
And upon hearing the solemn vow
Not to quit until the enemy is finished off
And the resolve not to sound a ceasefire until victory is at hand.

Each blow of your arms
Crushed the emerging Germans
Forcing the enemy to sound alarms after each sure defeat
And the throne of the Empire swayed
And hate heaped upon the world.
But then, the eleventh day of November arrived

And in one abject defeat the haughty Prussian nation tumbles
See how its crown rolls in the mud
And so, too, the kaiser, like Nero and Diocletian,
Is mocked and disrespected by Bellona;
The kaiser shamefully flees
And with him the flattened tones of a "De profundis"
Are dragged through the worm's muck
Sighing as he goes, the glory of the world is fleeting: "Sic transit gloria mundi."

The conquest is achieved,
Your holy mission is complete
Consider how your victory is crowned
And becomes a glorious epic!

Oh, how beautiful the colors wave
From the flag filled with stars,
As the world, rescued now,
Sings universal, ecstatic praises;
And in you, the sons of this earth,
And you, New Mexicans,
Sons of this land,
With the valor of true Americans
Were victorious in formidable combat;
That Olympus which showers you
With chorus of mounting hurrahs
Rains down upon you
A flood of glory!

Notes

1. New Mexico. [Editors' note: New Mexico was at one point referred to as "The Sunshine State," a nickname used by territorial governor L. Bradford Prince in the late nineteenth century.]

2. [Editors' note: Chacón is referring to the people of Brno in the Czech Republic and Moravia.]

3. A word composed of the initial letters of the United States of North America, and bearing the same meaning. —The Author. [Editors' note: It is interesting that Chacón here follows the Latin American convention of referring to the United States not as America, but rather as North America.]

TO THE HOMELAND

Fourth of July, 1776–1918

octava real

Allow me to strum, oh my Homeland!
The strings of my wanting lyre, to offer up to you
Harmony from its ardent tones,
Joyfully gripping your flag,
My chest radiates joy,
I seek to offer you, my native homeland, love
As the unequaled glories of your heroism
Overpower even the cynic.

I ponder your splendid annals
From valiant Napoleon's exploits
Which unsettled continents;
I see the souls of brave insurgents
Tinged with nobility;
Brave insurgents who built your greatness,
And erected a temple of freedom for mankind,
Where praises will e'er be sung in your name.

Tyranny roamed the land,
Upon hearing John Adams' eloquence
The precursor for that glorious day
In which Jefferson, full of prescience,
Drew out of his immortal wisdom
The great Declaration of Independence,
Blessed mother of those native lands
Where my muse, today, lifts her songs!

I wish that I had that splendid lyre
Which gave Homer eternal glory,
To sing to you that which inspires genius,
The brilliant nimbus of your history;
To paint you with the fire of he who admires
The laurels encircling your memory,
And in a beautiful and skillful Iliad,
Give to you in my ballad that which touches my soul.[1]

Yet, upon reflection, I bless that star
Which steers my destiny on this earth,
Which guides my steps along their footpath
Following the path of civic equality,
Beneath the august banner that stands out
As a divine symbol upon your altar,
Where Washington traced out, in letters of gold,
"Liberty," that unequaled treasure.

Receive, therefore, my Homeland,
The ardent notes of my patriotism,
On this anniversary of that day
On which the land's imperialism,
With its fatal yoke of tyranny
And its miserable shame of cynicism, was turned
And eternal American Independence
Rose like the morning sun!

Note

1. [Editors' note: This entire stanza appears in "To the Westward Explorer."]

TO SANTA FE

    octava real

Holy earth of ancient city,
History-filled garden where flowers gladly open to the bright sun
In patches of fragrance and color.
From earthen pots, grains and fruits grow with great love.
There under your blue fragrant sky,
The bed of my childhood is cradled.

Your lovely earth is holy for me,
Just as beautiful as the flower of your gardens,
Holy for the loving kiss upon my lips,
A child of maternal love nourished
In times when she suffered in her loving bed
To give me life from her noble breast.

Holy because you hold in your bosom
The dust of he who gave me life, and
Because you are the sweet reliquary of my dead brothers,
Inflamed, torn, as the voice of thunder snatches away the calm,
And your winters have frosted
The blessed tears my mother shed there.

And even though sad memories come back to me
When my thoughts return to the past
And form a scene that offers me
A thousand heartaches that pierce my heart,
Upon seeing the thorns that pain me,
I also see the fragrant rosebush filled with the joy
That my parents gave me as a child.

I never forget the fleeting tolling
Sent from your regal bell towers,
Nor the birds in vibrant song
That sweetly greet the first light of each new day
And the evening lullabies in the soft whisper of your orchards
That fill me with burning desire.

But if unavoidable fate sends my ship
Sailing from you with indifference,
And if the sad echoes of my nostalgia
Never again reach your soft embrace,
Look to the sky and you shall see the constant star of memory
Shining and you, alongside that blessing, will be there.

HOBNOBBERS

cuarteta

An old woman from Orizaba
So deaf she heard nothing,
When questioned
Would only reply "yes."

Once chagrined,
Her husband calmly told her,
"If they speak to you,
As has just happened . . .

Take my advice,
For I offer sound counsel,
Tell them once "yes"
And tell them "no" a thousand times.

FRAGMENTS

cuarteta

You should not criticize
What you see others do
For all that appears to be malicious
May not be so.

There are inoffensive things,
The offspring of good intentions,
That become harmful
Simply by negative judgment.

There is joy that is in truth sorrow
Just below the surface,
And some things that start out good
Seem from a distance quite evil.

To judge at first sight
Is to give false witness;
In all things in this life
The intent behind such things is what matters.

JEALOUSY AND LOVE

A Song

The butterflies that flit through your garden
    Watch over me
    Because they seek out flowers—
    They look for you;
    The robins who cheerfully come and go
    Watch over me
    Because they seek with me
    The lofty balconies of your home.

   Chorus
Because I, darling, go sighing,
    Anxiously seeking I go,
    As the butterflies and robins,
    Oh! seeking your eyes' simple love.
    Because your eyes speak,
    As two missives from the soul,
    I look to them in hope,
    Of that divine happiness I desire.

I wish I were a bee,
    And in the red and orange blossoms
    Of your nectar-filled little mouth,
    A sea of joy to sip!
    And if I were a swallow,
    I would ardently seek out
    The myrtle of your bosom
    A joyful place to nest.

   Chorus
Because I, darling, go sighing . . .

They tell me, darling, that heaven
  Is eternal paradise
  And the reward of the good.
  Do you think, darling, I might attain it?
  You know, because at your side
  There is an Eden of joy
  And in your love,
  All heaven above I come to possess!

  Chorus
For this, darling, I go sighing . . .

TO THE VIRGIN AT HER ALTAR

sextina/sexteto

Creature without equal! White lily!
Burning dawn that introduces the day,
Chasing away sorrowful hours,
Filling my soul with hope,
I lift up my voice to thee
And I celebrate your triumph with my song.

Though just a child upon the earth
Your dignity already soared above,
And by an archangel from heaven
You were proclaimed by the Divine Word
To be the mother of a Child sent to earth
To redeem mankind with the shedding of his blood.

Beautiful brooch of an august chrysanthemum
That displays its beauty as it unfolds its petals!
You, crowned by a magnificent diadem
Made from the stars and clothed by the sun,
I implore you to light my treacherous path
With your splendid celestial light.

I know that my human weakness is great
And that three dangerous enemies pursue me
With sweet and subtle adulation,
They set upon me with poisoned arrows
And I, in the rapture of their spells,
Fear that I will be dragged to the place of the eternal dead.

For this reason, sweet mother, bowed here,
Before your altar filled with flowers,
I ask in fervent supplication
that by the horrible sorrows you lived at the foot of the cross
I will not be blinded and fooled,
Nor my resolve weaken before the battle that
Lies ahead and to which you have enjoined us.

Most blessed[1] and pious mother!
I ask that when I reach the end of my life
That you not allow my odious soul to offend the sight
of your just Son;
But that a host of cherubs
Take my soul up into the white clouds.

Then I shall sing and praise your glory,
I shall in great joy raise up my eyes
To you who are full of grace and tenderness,
And I shall declare my good fortune
As you, graciously, gather up the
Tribute I offer in this humble song.

Note

1. [Editors' note: Chacón misconstrues the common and accepted invocations of the day, giving us "sacratísima" for "madre sacra" or "madre santísima."]

A FLOWERY CIRCUMSTANCE
redondilla

Soila was the treasured daughter
Of one Anselmo Corona,
And she was an attractive woman
Of around twenty years.

At last she was called upon
Taking stock of her loves,
By a young man, Jacinto Flores,
With whom she tied the knot.

And thus our lady's name
Grows in fineness,
As she now is called
"Soila Corona de Flores."

YESTERDAY, TODAY

copla de pie quebrado o estrofa manriqueña

Purple flower of the fields,
Chaste like the pure years
   of childhood,
I look upon your divine sunrise,
Wrapped in beauty,
   as if it were just yesterday.

Your vestal tomorrow has arrived
And your young womanhood
   draped you with ermine fur
And you praised the blithe butterfly
with gentle affection,
   all this, just yesterday.

You were but an innocent girl,
Running to and fro
   across the fields
Bounding across an ever-changing world,
That you could barely comprehend,
   All this just happened, yesterday.

But much too soon, early in your time,
Winter arrived with its frost
   withering some flowers,
That still cling to the dry, brown plant
That you have become,
   today.

THE WORKER

    sextilla de pie quebrado

Sunk among the rocks
    The drill explodes
Cleaving rocky faces,
    Opening mountains;
And the pick and shovel
    With great labor
Level the road
    Over mountain and desert,
And in their place
    Appear routes of iron
Cutting distances
    Into less than half;
Industry flourishes
    In a variety of ways
And with a thousand blessings,
    Thanks to the worker.

The wheels of manufacturing
    Of a rich tillage
Spin and fly
    Forging tools
Or primary materials
    Thus transforming
Into useful fabrics
    Cloth that the laborer wears,
Or the rich banker
    Parades at parties
All made possible by God and
    Thanks to the worker.

The skilled engineer
    Draws up his plans,
Those which an architect
    fashions;
The solid foundations
    Are dug and formed,
The grand walls
    Armed with steel,
And thousands of skyscrapers
    Haughtily reach up
To the firmament,
    Colleges and temples,
Their roofs and spires
    And royal cupolas,
And all is done
    Thanks to the worker.

If haughty tyrants
    From exotic lands
Threaten the Homeland
    In ominous tones;
If perchance the Government
    Recruits millions
To defend itself
    With firm resolve
Those who work
    Respond with zeal.
The worker foremost among all
    Is nothing less than a patriot.
And when the blaring triumph
    Sounds out with
Its ring of victory
    Following fierce combat,
The blood of the enemy,
    Streaming out,
Inscribes in glory,

"LONG LIVE THE WORKER!"

DECEPTIONS

madrigal

I knew you when you were still young and lovely,
It's been some time since first I saw you,
I asked you for your hand and you dismissed me
Turning me down flat.

And you took away the sweet nectar and the flower
Of that joyful feeling,
Leaving me with the bitter taste of your deed
In exchange for my love.

Life has passed and you now see
Bitter deception
Where the once sweet chalice of your dreams
Has changed to bitter gall.

And now that the noxious world so quickly
Has discolored your ermine skin,
No one offers you a hand as a friend,
No one, that is, except me!

TO MRS. ADELINA OTERO-WARREN

Woman Republican Candidate for Congress, 1922

serventesio

Your brow is encircled by laurels
And your name radiates honor;
Your star rises today over the threshold
Of a new day's triumphant dawn.

The world advances and so too human thought
And new things into this life are born;
Today reflects the morning light
Of a new dawn into which women are born.

Born into suffrage as man's equal,
But a more spiritually elevated soul;
Her name labors in moral purity
And the earth profits through her labors.

This meritorious evolution,
Marking the elevated path of Progress,
Will cover New Mexico in glory
By sending a woman to Congress:

Accomplished, capable, honorable,
Of graceful soul and sincere heart.
She is here, proclaimed by her people,
The emblematic lady, Adelina Otero!

Descendant of noble Spanish lineage,
And further, wholly American,
Yet, of what importance is this external garb
For she who deserves such echelons!

Human greatness is not bounded,
It is not limited by nation;
From on high its power emanates
And descends upon those whose beauty pleases it.

Yet this flattery is not meant for
The servile benefit of the ego.
Rather my lofty aim
Is to tinge Justice with idealism.

Hear, hear! A toast! A pledge of joy,
And gratitude from the progressive citizen,
Who sends you in this humble verse,
The salute of a sovereign people!

PHILOSOPHIZING

cuarteta

As Sophia studied
   Philosophy books,
Zenon, her husband,
   Sharpened his knife.

Drawing her attention,
   She asked what he was doing,
And Zenon replied:
   "Adding a bit more edge, Sophia."[1]

Note

1. [Editors' note: This poem is a play on words. Sophia is studying philosophy (*filosofía*), and when she asks Zenon what he is doing to the blade, he tells her he is making it a little sharper ("Poco más filo, Sofía"), which sounds like "filosofía."]

AUTUMN

redondilla

Leaves strewn by the wind:
Blemished, dry, broken,
Everywhere curl
As harsh fate seems to intend.

Days before they were a vivid green
Making forests leafy and verdant
Painting the horizon
With brilliant beauty.

The leaves gave cover to the songbirds
Hidden in the foliage,
There they paid tribute
With their morning songs of praise.

From them came forth
A pleasing perfumed scent
That the birds inhaled
Making their hearts beat fast with joy.

But those days have passed
And with them the happiness they brought
And they leave us in exchange
Only the memories of time past.

Now, upon an uncertain road
That travels through life,
The leaves move as I do, sighing,
Following the push of Destiny.

Thus, in this world where all must end,
The leaves are man's equal,
In the end we are mortals,
Leaves snatched away by the wind!

HERE'S TO THE MONTH OF MAY

   sextilla

Blessed month in which the flowers
With their many colors,
Unfurl and tinge everything,
Yours is the sweet balsam
That stirs my lyre
Its strains to sing to you.

Green adorns the mountain,
Gleaming in rich splendor
On the polychrome horizon,
And among living tapestries
Sing the larks,
Joyfully sings the nightingale.

Nourish with your enfolding perfume
And elixir that atmosphere
Which all creation breathes.
And in you, life itself is reborn,
Revived, gratified,
All is joy, where'er.

Ceres with fecund magic
Engulfs with a prodigious sea
Of unequaled riches,
Gardens and fields
That breathe in
Your springtime nectar
In ecstasy.

The liquid flowing
From the crystal spring
Sings praises at your feet,
And its murmur arrives to me
Like a heavenly lullaby
Over the transom of my window.

Blessed month in which the flowers
With their many colors,
Inspire rejoicing and pleasure,
You who bring new life
Grant that in my numbed soul,
God may be born again!

THE INGRATE

soneto

If in this life you have been disappointed,
You too must have experienced
That ingrate you thought friend,
He who, aimlessly meandering in years past,

Stepped on thousands of thistles along the way.
And you gave the scoundrel refuge, as a father would.
And did you also help him when he was a beggar?
Wait, then, for the coming years:

If someday destiny gets the best of you
And bad luck overwhelms you,
He who lacks a human heart

Will derive no pleasure from seeing you, his benefactor.
And if the world suffers unto you a stoning,
He, one more in the indifferent world, tosses his stone!

TO NEW MEXICO

Upon Being Admitted as a State of the Union

serventesio

At last, land of mine, I have lived to see
Your head rising to meet a summer sky
Crowned with glory and with a
Glorious and splendid star.

A rising star circled by morning lights
Now proclaims that you are a sovereign state,
May the homeland shine forever in the annals of history
And on the American flag!

An honor for your sons and daughters
That have suffered defeat with you
Only to have been rebuffed with
Injustice these many years.

Despite this, your children have
Offered you unquestionable loyalty,
Battling the indomitable Indian
And the secessionist American South.

Despite this they threw themselves against
Their ethnic brothers
And spilled their blood in Cuba
To show that they were true Americans.

Oh, how many times you were left
Hoping for a glimmer in the cloudy skies,
A light to raise your spirit
As you traversed the arduous path ahead.

Might we have caught sight of it? You saw it
Fading away into a thick fog,
Your hopes dashed
And you sighed deeply and bitterly.

But you battled against that hardened fate
Challenging the injustice of Congress
And the insults born of racial hate
So often invoked against you.

I suffered in your suffering,
I followed as you tracked the trail . . .
Until, at last, in a far-away clearing,
That precious star shone forth.

Rising out of eastern forests,
Destiny now happily takes hold
And gives you its celestial fires
Flooding your road with glory . . .

Now I desire, dear homeland,
That your government, worthy of that glory,
Stretch its wings across the heavens
And bury in the gulf of eternity[1]

The unjust laws that tarnish your name.
I want to see your archives gleam
With resplendent accomplishments bearing your name
Into the centuries to come.

And I hope that history will compose
With the pure light of its sable brush,
Works and deeds that elevate the gaze,
Making you an eminent example for the Union.

Meanwhile, your children rise up today
With the hurrahs of a fervent chorus
Whose jubilant echoes sound out:
Long live the state of New Mexico!

Note

1. [Editors' note: Chacón chooses an awkward verb form in "sepulte" and ends up with the clunky "Y sepulte en el golfo de lo eterno," literally, "And bury in the gulf of eternity."]

LIFE

Sonnet
soneto

It roamed about in a frenzy,
Changing course in its incessant flight,
Like a bold dove who dreamed only of
A nectar-filled garden.

It sallied forth full of pride and without concern,
Then night overtook it and, unable to rest,
It entered my home, where, still filled with ambition and zeal,
It mistook the candle's flame for the petals of a spring blossom.

Its wings fluttered, its flight turned.
In anticipation of its promised love,
It nosedived into the candle flame.

Now tattered and scattered in burned pieces,
I later found the dove, and I exclaimed,
This life is but a fraud of deception and sorrow!

TO THE WESTWARD EXPLORER

octava real

Brave explorer, how we admire thee!
You arrived in enduring glory
On the shining pages of the West's history,
Yellowed by time,
Its history inscribed on eternal papyrus,
Begun in Lexington and Concord
And carried on by great patriots.

You had home, its blessings,
Tender offspring, dear wife,
All those worldly gifts
That nestle within the quiet life.
But you had more—your convictions,
And the unflagging resolve
To undertake unknown adventures
And turn them into constructive realities.

Thus upon thinking, I can well imagine
Your titanic heart, weighed down
By a penetrating sigh and quiet
Reply to the tender good-bye
Of the home you left to follow your creed,
An inspired belief born
In the gleam of some florid dream
That shared with you its promise of many colors.

And like the Magi making for Judea,
Guided on their path by a star,
You followed the enticement of an idea;
And like Columbus following the wise way
Provided by the Sun's luminous torch,
You happily arrived to your destination,
And with indomitable feats
Your army took for its own self the West's riches.

You ascended a rocky and steep path
You followed intrepidly, with resolve,
And you suffered the rigors of the desolate mountain,
Sick and numb,
Exposed to that savagery embodied
In the heartless, stupefying blow,
Which gave Custer his eternal memory
In terrific slaughter.

A thousand ways you defied death,
Crossing mountains and thickets
And the arid grasslands where you began everything
You—a figure of movement
Against a fixed landscape.
You united the deep oceans
And sowed over half a continent
The magic flowering of progress.

This continuous, painful march
You led resolutely and valiantly,
Finding pain in place of love,
Worry instead of domestic repose.
Yet out of this sea of troubles
And your energetic, laborious effort
You marked out a precious footprint for all to see,
Elevating your immortal star.

Webster's legacy has been undone—
The West met him with misfortune,
Endless snows over never-ending ground . . .
Now your rough shacks are cities,
And the grasslands a fecund paradise,
And you have already bequeathed to posterity
A treasure of magnificent worth
Cutting through to the Pacific coast.

I wish that I had that splendid lyre
Which gave Homer eternal glory,
To sing to you that which inspires genius,
The brilliant nimbus of your history;
To paint you with the fire of he who admires
The laurels encircling your memory,
And in a beautiful and skillful Iliad
Give to you in my ballad that which touches my soul . . .

Intimidating, severe, unschooled, undaunted,
A spirit distinguished on earth,
A titan unvanquished by danger,
A battle-hardened victor;
Today your name is assured,
Your place in the annals of life
Shaped in valor and suffering
And raised in enduring monument.

Today this modern architecture
Flaunts itself in its haughty cupolas
Its magical figures chiseled
In delightful friezes and frescoes;
And thus as with the eternal cynosure
Your being is listed among brilliant heavenly figures.
Shine today, from continent to continent,
You, the great explorer of the Occident!

HERE'S TO CHILDHOOD
quintilla

    Childhood, you are that sacred time of life
Filled with innocent hopes and dreams,
When the heart surges with joy
Because it beats without afflictions.

    White doves fly across
Your clear, open mind;
Notes springing from an innocent soul
That sound and vibrate through the air
As if they rained down from heaven.

    Your pains are fleeting,
Rather you are given to pleasing times,
A tear that springs forth
Is followed by laughter
And the two are rather alike.

    Sorrow does not overtake you,
And your whims are simple,
Mere hopeful fancy.
They emerge like tears from the eyes,
Not from the heart!

    Joyful and tender feelings
Stir in the soul of the child
That happens upon a butterfly
Feeding on the roses
And spinning the stitched brocade of its weave.

Fly! You fly after the butterfly
Full of immense delight,
Following its path from flower to flower,
Its one true goal,
Its only love in all the world.

Sweet hours of morning,
Hours without worry, without sleeplessness,
In which mortals have only
To enjoy the abundance
Of drums, little cars, and treats.

Because you are so precious,
Nothing is worth more of my affection;
What would I give, lovely childhood,
At this turbulent time of life
To relive childhood once more?

All was flowers,
Oh! thornless flowers,
Born at first light,
Still their perfume and colors
Died even as they began to bud . . .

Even knowing all this,
Childhood, you are the sacred time of life
Filled with innocent hopes and dreams,
That time when the heart beat and surged in joy
Without dread of afflictions.

AN ILLUSION

serventesio

Why does your smile enchant me so,
Pouring from the gleam of your spell,
As soft as a breeze's kiss
Born of flowers' perfume?

Is the ground upon which you were born,
Perchance, a transcendent glory,
Or is it that your encompassing gaze
And voice are celestial melodies?

Are you, perhaps, that Venus of the divine heights
Who pagans worshipped in another age,
And who by unequaled beauty,
Imbues all with love on extending your hand?

I see beauty in your eyes,
A lightning bolt of irresistible light,
Whose wonder changes my fortunes
To a chaos of burning passion.

I see the image of your chestnut curls:
A tender wave of mild calm,
An evening of magic spells
That shakes my soul with ecstasy.

You have superhuman magnetism,
And even as I study you, I remain awake and restless,
You are a woman and thus a mystery
That I, a man, cannot unravel.

Yet if you are that goddess the Romans adored
When you were no more than a passing myth,
I would gladly become a pagan
And raise you to the eternal!

May the Heavens forgive this crazy affair
Which your beauty sparks in me,
The Heavens made your burning wonder
And the Heavens' handiwork drives me mad.

Oh! but my heart throbs in vain
When I see your wondrous image
With its firm beating bosom
And the innocence radiating from your face . . .

Perhaps it is better to consign you to the future
As a fleeting dream of the past,
Born at night under a mantle of darkness,
Born only to be dreamed.

Farewell! thus I bid you,
I nip this flower in the bud,
I will erase your image by my absence
So that time may expunge . . . an illusion!

A SINGULAR MOMENT
quintilla

An old gentleman was advising
   a habitual drunk,
   and he spoke against that vice
   like a father would:

"Human beings become brutes
   with that infernal juice
   that dulls reason,
   makes the mind go mad
   and turns man into a beast."

But the drunkard, a slave to Bacchus,
   staggers and responds:
   "Mister Paco, you just don't get it
   the way an itsy bitsy drink,
   stirs up Climaco.

My debaucheries are all but divine,
   I have been at them since I was a boy
   and the taverns' sweet juice
   causes me no greater ill
   than to turn my legs to jelly."

CHRISTMAS

quinteto

The night rested
the sky shone clearly
at glorious midnight,
mankind was blessed
with Christ at his Nativity.

Beneath the diaphanous, handsome sky,
an angel shines glorious light,
and speaking to the shepherds, says
I bring you glorious news:
Jesus is born today in Judea!

A heavenly chorus sings out
its sweet, divine antiphon,
GLORIA IN EXCELSIS!
a resounding echo
reverberates its golden notes
over all the earthly sphere . . .

Full of joy, faith, and hope,
the shepherds travel to Bethlehem,
and there, kneeling in praise,
they muse over their fortune
adoring their Messiah.

Caesar Augustus went unknown
and the chaste shepherd was acclaimed:
he who makes himself great shall be humbled
and he who humbles himself shall be exalted
by the Redeemer's proclamation!

The angelic notes of
that message of love and peace
flew o'er war-torn nations whose battles
hemorrhage torrents of red blood
and rain down ruin with audacious fury.

　　May the song of the angels be, this glorious day,
a shining beam of inspiration;
transform the horrible, impious battle
into sweet songs of joy,
deserving heavenly benediction!

　　In holy jubilation, let us nurture
temperance among men;
let us forget our petty rancor
so that with the angels
we may lavish upon the helpless
goodness and love.

DECEPTION

    ovillejo mayor

On the night of a summer moon
    in the month of June
I saw the full moon
Drop into a dense fog
    where its beauty
was extinguished . . .

And so, too, the moon of my affection
    I had lost
some days before,
Vanished into the clouds of deception
    whose grief
I so very much deserved.

I saw the illusion
    of my thousand fiery passions
sink away amid rebuffs.
And as with the moon,
    a delicate, jittery, flirtatious woman
also fell away!

A TANGLED AFFAIR

cuarteta

At a doctor's appointment,
A doctor told a young bachelor
With a shattered memory
The following:

"Take this prescription.
It's an effective remedy
That costs mere pennies
And will leave you in peace" . . .

Three short days later,
The young man, afflicted, returned
And told the doctor: "This has gone quite poorly,
In fact, it's the opposite of a remedy.
Why don't you first cure
The illness?
Then, I can remember to
Take the medicine on time
Because today
I forgot to take it" . . .

TO THE LAWMAKERS

At the First Legislative Session for the State of New Mexico

    You are set in place
You, the chosen members of the sovereign
Legislative body of the State.
You are crowned with laurels
For the people have entrusted you
With the honor of their faith and their confidence,
For they are convinced by your integrity,
Which has given them cause to praise you
Placing you atop the pinnacle where the great Solon[1] was made immortal.
With spontaneous esteem, I raise you up
So that you can labor to eternal fame.

    Do you wish to enjoy that renown
And hope that it remains clean and pure
Across the centuries?
Do you want to be worthy of the respect
And admiration of the future nation?
This all depends on you.
You are aware of what this obligation demands
And know that in this life he who fulfills the promise
Rises up and the pride of his descendants will never die.

    Today, the eyes of the world
—just and watchful may they be—
are fixed and observe with profound interest
the first acts you undertake in your posts.
Therefore, heed my words,
Hispanic Americans,
The children of noble and valiant parents,
Brave and free,
People who have never bowed

And for many centuries have held no one as superior.
They are the free sons of those sea captains
From the land of El Cid and Guzmán
Who sailed the untamed seas,
People who on this American continent
Have gifted you with blessed homes
Won in blood and sacrifice
Under the pure blue New Mexican sky.

   Be on guard against the evil designs
Of petty tyrants of yore
Who with false gentility
Sought with vulgar deception
To make you pawns in their designs.

   Remember your beginnings with pride,
Acknowledging those limits,
And raise them like a banner to the infinite
As pure as a budding flower,
But stronger than a granite stone.
You must be the measure of the model,
Not to be led by others,
And raise your names to the heavens
And be anointed with the holy oils of honor.
And your glory in this present moment
Will shine like a faithful new dawn
That will gleam through time,
A light that was born in the East
But has yet to see its setting in the West!

Note

   1. [Editors' note: An Athenian statesman.]

A NOCTURNE TO . . .

*A Political Satire, an Adaptation of
"Nocturne to Rosario" by Manuel Acuña*

alejandrino

I.

Fine then! I must tell you
    that if I weep,
And with my sighs
    wound the frigid north wind,
Consider that cruel Fate
    pulls me from my seat
Taking my treasure from me
    and I vanish into nothingness
A fleeting chimera.

II.

I wish all to know
    that I have been dazed
For many days
    by lack of sleep;
The Devil has made away
    with my hopes.
My foolish exploits
    inscribed on my headstone
Sealed Oñate's[1] fate
    forevermore.

III.

At night, when I rest
    my temples upon the pillow,
Willing Morpheus
    to calm my suffering,
Horrible nightmares
    interrupt my labors,
Menacing ghosts
    laugh at me
And I wake again
    Crazed and stunned.

IV.

I understand that the place
    I leave vacant
Will never again be filled
    by my corpulent body . . .
Yet I love it
    and regarding it from a distance
I bless its countless scorns
    with a sobbing soul
And instead of loving it less,
    I love it that much more.

V.

At times, I think of making
    a final good-bye,
Erasing this place
    from my memory . . .
But if all is in vain
    and the soul never forgets
The trodden people
    I leave on my departure,
What on earth should I do
    with this pain!

VI.

And once my stay
    is concluded,
And I have gone to my joy
    like a god upon his altar,
Sucking from the Government
    my jolly fat salary,
Skillfully taking from the people
    of all the places
I could possibly legislate . . .

VII.

How beautiful it would have been
    to live beneath that roof
With Pancho and don Jacinto
    who now whimper over my fortune!
Both of them privileged,
    and I deeply satisfied,
The trio of us a single soul
    (a third in each chest),
And I, like a tsar,
    receive their flattery!

VIII.

Imagine how beautiful
    the hours of this life are!
How sweet and beautiful the journey
    through a land like this!
But seeing my promised land
    buried in the graveyard,
Oh how I wish
    that devastating spark
Would burst into a quivering fog
    for me, alas, not for me!

IX.

Only God knows
    that was the sole dream
That could sustain me,
    like Sancho Panza . . .
God only knows
    that my true zeal
Lay only in FILLING MY POCKETS
    in the fecund land
That wrapped me in diapers
    when I was born.

X.

That was my hope . . .
    but now its brilliance
Is opposed by "Teddy" Roosevelt
    from far-off Washington.
I bid good-bye, one last time,
    to flattery and jealousy,
My chiefly reign,
    my flaws, my glories,
My executive grasp
    on my power—Farewell!

Note

    1. Fictional names have been substituted for real names, out of respect for those individuals, with the exception of Roosevelt, who is only mentioned in passing. —The Author.

it's love

   octava real

   A fever, a fit of laughter and tears;
The cause of an insomnia that pulls you towards madness;
A sweet pleasure and a pain that wounds
When suddenly it sets the heart to spinning.
It is like an itch that slithers
Going from the eyes to the soul and making the spirit dizzy
An itch that cannot be soothed, the first of many missteps;
A bed of thorns that feels like a bed of flowers.

A SHARP EDGE

cuarteta

With a pitcher in each hand,
And Josefita in the middle,
She set out to break up the tedium
By joking with her brother.

"Hey, Juanito,
Why don't you repeat
What I'm going to tell you,
But say it as you hear it:

'I come from Guadalajara
Bringing pitchers, pitchers to sell.
Wedged between two pitchers, I.
What expensive pitchers I sell!'"

And as brother Juanito
Was more of a Juan than a Juanito,
And more than a Juan a rascal,
Replied thus to her:

"I come from Guadalajara,
Bringing pitchers, pitchers to sell.
And between these two pitchers
What a tired face I see!"[1]

Note

1. [Editors' note: "A Sharp Edge" is another example of Chacón's wit: here he creates wordplay with the words *jara*, *ajada*, and *cara* ("face") and *cara* ("expensive"). So, the lines "¡Qué jaras tan caras vendo!" (What expensive pitchers I sell) and "¡Qué cara ajada estoy viendo!" (What a tired face I see) are juxtaposed for humorous effect.]

PARADOX

quinteto

Frequently, regrettably, all too often,
Once you've tasted life
And the hard truth of your life's journey,
You will unhappily find how upsetting
The false gratitude of men is.

Don't think of the loyal and grateful dog,
You will believe you have found unfailing gratitude
In whatever man you have put your trust in,
But your mistake will be made clear,
The dog, you'll learn, is more humane than any man.

IN MEMORIAM

octava real

There is nothing strange in seeing you there,
Stretched out, changed into inanimate material;
The course of your life ended,
Your mission carried out;
At night your lantern would pour out
The mutable light that was its duty and destiny,
Today, seeing its globe extinguished
I see that morning has arrived.

And yet my chest feels heavy,
My soul battered with pain;
Who would not ache when a beloved one
Leaves forever on their journey?!
I know, too, that
Upon leaving this miserable dwelling
From tender lips your soul enjoined a "good-bye" to my name
As your final breath spilled out.

I was absent; nor did you even cross my mind
In that trance of ineffable shame
When death came too early
Entering the last scene of your life.
Neither when your ashes were tendered
To the earth in a final tribute,
But I will lift up to the heavens now a prayer for the dead
That will serve you before Christ on Calvary . . .

    Adorned with noble sentiment
Your soul crossed this ephemeral existence,
And extraordinary intelligence
Shone out through your ill-starred life;
Your heart
Held a simple loyalty of conscience,
Your sincere heart a welcoming asylum
From the pain borne by your human companions.

    In light of such beautiful virtues,
Which adorn a part of your history,
I reflect that over time's passage
Each cursory shining star
That makes up the myriad Pleiades
Has had with it a brief shadow:
They have switched between the cloak of daylight
And the full moon against deepest darkness.

    I saw the jewel buried in the mud and muck
That sullied its diamond-like fineness,
Even as my soul regretted its mistakes;
I saw the lymph, its crystalline boil,
Run its chaos across your temples,
And I understood that Whoever
Trucks in destinies sacrificed your life in exchange for vice,
As an example to the world.

    This has been your sublime mission!
Great are they who live for the good of mankind!
May your name be written
—Without letters, without show, without renown—
In a book of maxims, leading others
To elevate your name and dismiss your shortcomings.
You are the lamp that illuminates the cliffside
Where the seafaring skiff is apt to wreck.

    Sleep soundly!
The heavens will calm with compassion
The bitter tears
Concha and René[1] have poured out;
The eternal return of the sun will console them
Dissolving their tears into the humid ground.
A sigh will rise up out of this ground,
A white canopy covering the dreadful tomb
Where your body rests in peace.

Note

1. Wife and daughter, respectively.

DREAMS AND TRUTH

silva in part I, redondilla in part II

I.

    Destiny, that king of kings
Spoke to man on the morning of the first day
And said, "Get up and walk."
Following that most powerful prod
Man arose and began to walk,
He traversed time and epoch
With only the light that fell upon his narrow trail
Leading him to the future he faces.
He thinks of a great truth spoken by Iriarte,[1]
Which reveals all truth
Since death, in the end, "uses the same yardstick to measure
the straw-thatched hut and the royal palace of the king."[2]

    And so it seems that by caprice Destiny
Lifts up from the sea of men in this life
A powerful Caesar, a haughty titan
To rival the genius of Hannibal in war
And the art of Cicero in the Senate.
Exceeding Alexander in conquest
And defeating Pompey's forces at Munda;
That bold and bellicose warrior who opposes
The feared desert storm and formidable typhoon at sea,
In fearsome battle has breached
The haughty home of the enemy
To conquer all the known world.
And even after countless victories,
Crowned by eternal laurels,
At the end of his triumphs
He will be found traversed by pain, dejected . . .

It is the ides of March; it is now the time
And the place, the Senate:
The protagonists of this tragedy prepare,
Hiding steady daggers under their togas
Ready to burn the victim of this play.
Caesar enters the proscenium unaware
And finds his friends:
He expects a smile from each
As with the blessed smile of a brother,
But the icy wind of winter arrives
To snuff out the flowers as they bud
And to darken their emerald green leaves
Leaving behind only thorns
As the rest evaporates into nothingness . . .

　　Caesar resists the first wounding blow
His fastness holds,
But then he feels the stab from his beloved Brutus
Which goes much deeper into his soul than into his flesh,
And he exclaims with deep emotion,
With his soul brimming with feeling,
"Et tu, dear Brutus, you sentence me to death?"
His voice fills with the pain of his lament,
He falls to the floor without a whimper, lifeless:
Victories and grand deeds and all that remains tumble
At the foot of Pompey's statue!

　　And thus, this king issues his decrees,
Indifferent to everything.
And yet who would call them indiscreet?
Destiny is a deaf man who does not hear
The voice of the suffering he inflicts
And there is no living beast
Who escapes from the fate devised for him.

II.

    As Mother Nature
Is a rich source of virtue
She has sprouted from her slopes
A torrent of beauty.

    It is she who has given the day its brilliance,
Borrowing the Sun King's light,
The rainbow its beautiful colors
And the birds their song;

    To the plain, she gave sands,
And to the grasslands, vast expanse
And to the mountains, greenery
With its pleasing smells;

    Thunderheads to the firmament,
And brilliance to the moon,
And she is the Universe's crib
From its very birth.

    On dissipating the first serene flashes
Of one daybreak,
Nature strolled contentedly
Among perfumes and flowers;

    The first glimmers disappear
Into the sweet-sounding stream,
And the light's brilliant gold gleams
Off her blonde tresses;

    And her changing forms,
Her white skin displayed,
Were contemplated
In the crystal waters.

Michelangelo and Raphael painted
That day in beautiful colors,
The glory that still shines forth today
Where their names inscribed it . . .

Lost in rapture
And burning with passion,
Destiny admired that moment
When glory was born.

III.

And the two, linked by the Heavens,
From that day they first saw each other,
Accompany mankind.
As much for the shepherd in his cottage
As for the magnate lost among his riches,
Through time's transitory path
She shares her beauty with all
And he traces out their lives.

Notes

1. [Editors' note: Tomás de Iriarte y Oropesa.]
2. [Editors' note: Chacón inserts a found line from Iriarte that has a consonant rhyme between "iguales" and "reales." The rhyme and symmetry of the saying, which was quite important to Chacón, is lost in translation to English.]

PLEASURE

    serventesio

    A young dandy who passed through the park,
His step light and springy,
Upon encountering a young woman,
Immediately offered this cheeky greeting:

    "Oh how I admire, Miss, your eyes,
Which the God of beauty gave you,
Their gaze soothes what pokes me
For it comes from those BLACK EYES I love."

    Far from gracing him with a smile,
The young woman turned to the chap
And, making a spirited fist,
Gave him two BLACK EYES!

DEVOTION

Sonnet

soneto

There is in this world a small and beautiful garden,
One that I cultivate with love and care,
Neither the world nor its pomp nor its money
Equals this, my own precious treasure.

But it is at the same time also a painful chalice
That I venerate fearfully in my soul,
And my noble heart blesses it
With tears fed by my sobbing.

Heavens, what treasure has this refuge
Of beloved dust taken from me,
This place festooned with flowers!

Her precious body sleeps here
Under the vault that I have watered
With tears I have poured from my soul.

INDIFFERENT

serventesio

Conceited people do not move me,
Those who are intoxicated by their own importance,
Who like vain, puffed-up peacocks
Would pour their contempt on me.

Because I don't offer myself up for that,
Let them fatten themselves on their empty pride,
May disdain, hidden under the threefold cloak
Of indifference, repay them.

Poor little ridiculous pygmies!
More deserving of pity than censure,
Who think themselves distinguished coryphaei,[1]
Full of themselves if only by their lowly servility.

Yet I revel in the little frog puffing himself up,
Stretching to be the size of an ox,
Who through his efforts ends up bursting,
His dreams dying with him.

Keep on, then, carry on with determination,
Murmur from the heights of your pleasure,
But know that your ill will and scorn
Mean less than nothing to me.

Note

1. [Editors' note: Chacón here uses a classical term for "spokesmen."]

MY CANDIDATE AND MY REASONS

To the Honorable Octaviano A. Larrazolo

Read by the author before the "Larrazolo Society"
in Las Vegas, New Mexico, in October of 1908.

    Hail, illustrious champion, be welcomed!
If thou hearest the voice that calls thee,
Proclaiming that you are the chosen one,
Know that it is not the mere echo of a Party
That praises thee
As you again are chosen
For the congressional delegation.
If the Democrats wished
To brandish your name on their banner,
Then it is the people's love for you that shouts:
"Long live Larrazolo and Progress!"
And with enthusiastic pride the people clamor,
The unanimous voice of the historical and erudite
New Mexico!

    Two years have passed since you were nominated,
Against the will of the predominant faction,
And in the fight that followed
You gained on that very faction.
But thanks to organized pillage
By the villainous, driven by their ego,
The servant of the most vile
Now takes your spot with chilly cynicism;
The people's vote disparaged,
The apostle of bribery triumphs,
And propagated by the most abhorrent sucking up,
The public's will is undone.

But today you return to battle
Armed as though Minerva were your teacher,
Born from Jupiter's temples
With her victor's lance and shield;
Today you firmly hold in your fist the scepter
Belonging to Pallas, the founder of Athens,
And you gain her favor like Achilles;
Today you return as a reflection of the dawn
That rises out of hope to the blue sky,
The idol of all nuevomexicanos
Who, adverse to revenge,
Love justice above all!

How much more pleasing and admirable
Would the issue seem in retrospect
In the minds of all conscientious Americans (excepting Andrews)?
How much more exalted
In the hearts of a grateful people
If its desires had been met
And triumph conceded to Larrazolo,
And if his opponent had renounced,
Acceding to the voice of his conscience,
The false victory awarded him
From the theft of votes in Colfax and Valencia Counties?

When those frauds came to light,
Like some dirty act of History,
If he [Andrews] would have then, with virile nobleness,
Repudiated his false modesty,
And—giving his soul voice and greatness—
Exclaimed:
"I am not he who sanctions these offenses,
They are the products of craven spirits,
Forbidden by Honor and Morality!
I am not he who wishes to see

The people's desires mocked
To realize his own ends!
I confirm that I was elected delegate
By a dishonorable system.
I would exchange this exalted reward,
The fruit of a shameful origin.
I took the place of he who was the people's choice,
The voice of the people is law, and I respect it.
And if they have decided against me,
I sincerely approve of their decree!"
Oh! Think how much admiration would come to surround him
With a nimbus of glory,
Oh yes—the shining brilliance of "Bull" Andrews
Would ever adorn our memory!

But a magnanimous action such as that
Would have to come from a generous spirit,
Noble and virile in its integrity;
Holding within itself the beautiful attributes
That you, Andrews, can't even grasp at,
And from this clear light to those glimmers
Can you now see, perchance, where you find yourself?

What is lost when one is robbed of one's victory?
What is an ill-won victory worth?
Has the world forgotten the honorable Genovese
Who gave Spain the lands it fancied,
Who defied the seas' furies
And counted as accomplished
The glory oustanding among all glories
Because Vespucci wished to snatch away
The immortal diadem which now shines forth
On Columbus's temple, he who perches upon an altar?
Today, that sun sends forth its triumphs,
Sending out its rays to eternity,

Its impartial and justice-seeking rays
Place the other in the shadow of History,
Elevating Columbus's genius
To the august pinnacle of glory.

    So it is with you, Larrazolo, your blood
Already burning as it circles through your veins.
In that Iberian blood tinged with the
Nuevomexicano's, break the chains
Of feared oppression
That tyrants enjoined upon the freeman,
To vindicate the offense committed against you
When your victory was thwarted.
And at the end of your career already undertaken,
That Coroebus[1] of Olympian honors
Your proud forehead crowned with laurels,
With Themis handing down just ruling,
The expressed will of the people having been fulfilled,
You *will* enter Congress, your insignia extolled,
Radiating honors.

    The June sun just breaking
Its rays across the limpid horizon
Has created in you a Pericles,[2] he of Athens,
One who confronts enemies without fear;
It has given us your rational eloquence,
The beautiful gift to which the "native" inclines,
To destroy the contemptible belief
That the Latin American is inferior to the Anglo-Saxon
On the basis of his intellect.
Just as the condor daringly soars
Over the Andes' proud heights,
You uplift the "native" to the summit's clouds,
With the great resounding knells of your mind.
And today as the ardent campaign advances,

The people are your faithful herald,
And the voice of those people praises you,
Offering you its ardent salute:

    Hail, illustrious champion, be welcomed!
If thou hearest the voice that calls thee,
Proclaiming that you are the chosen one,
Know that it is not the mere echo of a Party
That praises thee
As you again are chosen
For the congressional delegation.
If the Democrats wished
To brandish your name on their banner,
Then it is the people's love for you that shouts:
"Long live Larrazolo and Progress!"
And with enthusiastic pride the people clamor,
The unanimous voice of the historical and erudite
New Mexico!

Notes

    1. [Editors' note: Coroebus of Elis, who won the first stadium race in the first Olympic Games.]
    2. [Editors' note: A famed Athenian statesman.]

A PAINFUL AFFAIR

   redondilla

Little Dolores, the beloved daughter
   of Mister José Armando Fuertes,
   was married, but you'll never guess to whom,
   yes, someone that is a very respectable person.

It was to Gonzalo Ijar, the attorney,
   a son of that same place,
   who has joined in wedded vows to her,
   and so her name is now
   "Dolores Fuertes de Ijar."

IT WITHDRAWS AND DISAPPEARS

Life is an iris of changing colors,
The varying wonders of a minuscule prism,
A short-lived dream of tears and laughter,
And thus it slips away . . . it withdraws and disappears.

That unique mirage which captivates the eye
Of he who, following, walks anxiously,
Like a mist that traverses the firmament,
And in a mere instant . . . it withdraws and disappears.

It is a passing dream, golden and bedecked with flowers,
That man has never achieved,
A confusing sight fraught with battles
That bit by bit becomes nothingness . . . it withdraws and disappears.

But I speak now of men who let life pass them by,
Consumed with idleness,
Their vain existence, a wobbly tale
That is quickly forgotten . . . it withdraws and disappears.

Because only the man who fights each hour
And with this makes improvements for posterity
Sees his name written forever in the books of History.
His memory shall never withdraw nor disappear!

THE ATHEIST AND THE TRUTH

serventesio

"It's a lie. There is no beyond," the atheist says,
Puffing himself up with a serious-sounding tone,
He babbles on with that fallacy
In the hope of converting the entire world.

Thus overflowing with blinding fancy,
With bold arrogance and evil presumption,
He denies the reality of the One who made him
And kills all hope of the world to come.

Feeding himself with this unhealthy effort,
The pastime of his crazy thinking,
He does not understand that he disdains the Heavens
And slashes away at divine and eternal wisdom.

He reduces the ways of the just-minded to nothing,
And destroys all recompense for people's good will,
Everyone, the just and the unjust, he pushes toward the void,
Leaving them without either a just reward or a just punishment.
But he argues:

"Where did God come from? Who made God?
Might there be another more powerful being
Who made the Being, and leads us to believe
That this world is truly one of sorrows?

They call this God just and good,
And yet he created a world of naïve folk
Who he then destines to suffer all manner of indignities
Sent from the God of the believers.

Would a God of mercy condemn us
To suffer the woes of this world?
And then, in his righteousness, condemn us
To face torments in the depths of Erebus'[1] eternal darkness?

This is absurd! Nature in its fullness
Is the only power that gives us life;
It is the mother of the abundance
That makes up the Universe.

And when this source is exhausted and
All the vigor at its core has lost its energy,
Say good-bye to dreams of another form of life
As all will end with this existence!"

I say only a mirage can live this way:
The unsustainable, substanceless doctrine
That this miserable matter purports to offer
As the only source of all Divine Creation.

To the contrary, nature supports the former
Unfolding a grand and wise design
That holds within it billions of stars above,
And the fields of crops that daylight feeds.

And so, too, nature's power
Gives man his intelligence,
His subtle creations, his ideals,
And builds into his heart the voice of conscience.

Here, then, reason must recoil
And bring forth a strong rebuke,
With the soul's conscience contesting
And with justifiable reason inspiring us.

If all were to end in death,
If there is no life beyond the grave,
Of what consequence is good or evil
If in this, our fate, Justice is overthrown?

What would be the fate of the wretched, imperfect human being?
A being who does not even understand his very nature
Nor is able to apprehend this grand Mystery
If his thinking redounds in cynicism.

Great is the man who is able to comprehend
The vast smallness which is his lot,
And upon consideration praises the Heavens
And in return the Heavens are elevated.

He who thinks well of himself as a piece of this finite world
Stakes out his reasons well
Since, in any case, it remains impossible
To understand the infinite by human measure.

Now we have before us the truth that clears the way ahead
And frees us to clearly see:
God is a light of such brilliance that it blinds
   The poor judgment of the human mind.

Note

   1. [Editors' note: God of darkness.]

GUARDIAN ANGEL

serventesio

On a serene and placid evening,
Along a particular street
A young woman strolled,
Coming from her convent school.

Her attractive and modest charms,
With her angelic scarlet lips
And the deepest black splendor of her hair,
Set fire to one's heart . . .

How many men are there in this depraved world,
Prisoners of their rapacity, who would ravage a virgin's virtue
To satisfy some insane desire,
And who will be eternally damned?

But another person accompanied
This young, attractive, agreeable young woman;
None less than her sainted mother,
Her guardian angel!

AXIOMS

cuarteta

Never seek to praise yourself for wisdom,
Always be mindful
That while there is much you do know,
There is much more that you don't.

Don't puff yourself up with things that
Casually come your way,
Things gain in meaning and
Are much more valuable
When they spring from dedication and work.

He who overestimates himself
And presumes to be a legal mind
Deceives himself in his own sight
When he's just an insignificant clerk.

No honor accrues to the one
Who puffs up and parrots the saying
"You can put lipstick on a pig, but it is still a pig."[1]

Note

1. [Editors' note: Chacón ends his admonishment against false pride by inserting the common rhetorical expression "aunque la mona se vista de seda . . . mona se queda," literally, "if a monkey puts on a dress, it remains a monkey." The corresponding saying in English involves putting lipstick on a pig.]

ANITA

octava

I saw a virgin, immaculate, beautiful,
Captured in a magnificent painting:
The work of some fine brush,
Like that of Raphael.
And in her exquisite countenance,
Eyes radiant with beauty,
I saw a reflection of mystical purity.
I saw your portrait, Anita!

MY MOTHER'S WIDOWHOOD

cuarteto

In days past, I saw only pristine blue sky
Unspotted by blue clouds,
My splendid sun did then burn,
A beautiful torch shining against sapphire tulle.

The soft air embraced me, imbued
With unequaled good fortune,
With the beloved whom I adored
As the flower worships the flowing spring.

But the soft air becomes a blasting gust
That swirls around me,
And the roaring hurricane
Leaves only a tomb, a wilted flower.

A shadow moves across the skies
With its black cloak,
Bringing ominous clouds instead of light
To my sad suffering.

Pierced by a thousand sorrows,
Alone, all alone, I cried
And as the night hung its dark curtain about me,
I was overcome by sobs and sighs.

Its lullabies of pain thus fed,
The north wind departs
Its dismal intensity diminished,
And I am given to the shadows, sighing.

TO MS. ADELA CRUZ

On the Day of Her High School Graduation

serventesio

There you are, crowned with Minerva's laurels,
Seated at her temple on high,
Admired by your parents and friends
For earning great success.

There you stand, an unblemished lily
That opens its bud with the dawn,
Your tender life filled with hope
As you stand before the journey of your bright future.

Now sixteen springs have passed
Since you first came to live in the bosom of your home,
So great is the honor you have won,
Equal to the pride you have kindled in your parents.

At once you are a perfect emblem,
The symbol of that parental love
That guided your footsteps and forged and shaped
The diadem that now crowns your head.

You have been diligent in your studies,
Which are the laurels that today crown your schooling,
Showing how your life is now a prelude
To a beautiful voyage over the seas of the world.

As you celebrate seeing your efforts realized,
Adela, do not forget that it was your parents
Who, day after day, watched your steps,
Leading to these beautiful results.

Today, their hopes rest in you,
Covering their hearts with love,
Be worthy of their tender praises
And in this life you will receive yet more reward.

Continue as you now go: a garden flower that endures
The elements unharmed.
Conquer admiration with your beauty:
A sweet nectar of peerless purity.

And you are a flower, a delicate flower
That sways in sweetness and honor.
And you should keep immaculate
That virtue that flowers in its whiteness.

I congratulate you and your parents,
Begging that you have in fate's book
A sea of good fortune on your path,
Written in shining fixity.

CREATION

lira irregular

I.

    The Lord fixed his divine, earthen gaze
On the forlorn atom,
A craggy, formless mass,
A fruitless effort, immersed in thunder
Born out of nothingness.
All was darkness in that embrace,
Save the gleam of burning spark
That Jupiter sent along with the thunderclap
Of his booming voice,
And the explosion of a roaring volcano.

    And yet upon seeing in his mind
Beauty's endless brilliance,
The God of seven colors combined
Brought forth a creature
That transformed that shadowy abyss
Into a realm of splendid light.

    Then the second day dawned
Bathed in clear, soft light,
And the edge of the earth emerged
Outlined against the diaphanous depths.

    And all was well: God, satisfied,
Continued on the path of Progress,
And there in the vastness he left stretched out
A mantle enveloping the Universe.

That mantle of most delicate blue,
Arching its vault on high,
Studded with innumerable suns
And with cloudscapes of peerless white.

And with the breeze's soft kiss,
As seductive as a virgin's
Tender flattery,
He gave us the divine second dawn . . .

II.

The Lord then said,
    "Onward! To the summit!"
With this joy, out
    of the seas a rumor was born,
That the earth would be traded
    for an inherited empire
Where Neptune would govern
    as the Universe's monarch.
But these vast domains
    the Lord wished to divide
So that the earth
    would also be productive.
Collecting the waters
    in a separate space,
The wide grasslands were born,
    richly ornamented in emerald green.
Flowers of great beauty
    and delightful gardens were formed
And the expansive valleys
    shone their colors;
At Ceres' hand
    cornfields were born

Trapped
   by drops of dew.
Hillsides carpeted,
   the formidable primitive mountains
Gave rise
   to their regal high crests,
And all around
   they displayed the rich
Unrivaled, radiant velvet carpet
   of botanical beauty.

The sonorous murmur
   of a crystalline spring
That gladly fed
   the flowers along its slope;
Lakes appeared
   and rippling seas
Where the firmament's
   sparkling lights are reflected;
The immensity of the ocean
   was majestic,
A fantastic ideal
   of mystic potency.
The gentle whisper
   of cypress foliage,
Its Aeolic lullabies
   playing a divine lute
Between one horizon and another,
   spanned by a matchless green,
All, silent, told
   of the omnipotence of the Heavens . . .

III.

    On the fourth day, the most dazzling star
Appeared, embedded in the ether,
And upon seeing the beam of its burning light
Its own Maker was amazed:

    He creates a splendid design
And calling up his immense power
He orders that, obeying his behest,
The handsome Monarch of Summer, the sun, be born.

    And out of the countryside beautiful brocades
Made of palm trees and birches
Inhaled ecstatically, smiling:
Life growing in tinged tulle.

    And the roses with their scarlet petals
And the irises with their purple flush
Bathed in the morning light
Surrounded by diamond-like crystals.

    A dazzling ornament fell from
The quiet lake into its crystal waters below
Where the tree's branches, draped with delight,
Gave rest to the waves.

    Extravagant blooms of flowers juxtaposed
Their whiteness with the green field,
Where jubilant wood nymphs
Sang pleasant praises from their lightning kiss.

    From the immense sea with its curling waves,
Its brilliant, nascent glow fell
Upon a cradle of lacy wheat fields,
Creating a scene of immeasurable beauty.

Later, it sank into the crescent moon,
Hiding its last glints,
And a magnificent vision appeared,
Adorning the heavenly vault from afar.

With its speedy light, my fantasy crossed
The centuries of the past
To see the splendors of that day
Which I pondered in awe:

"Could this be a shower of diamonds
Falling from places ignored,
Or perchance the brilliant, tender tears
Wept of happiness by innocent fairies?"

"Could this be the horoscope that tells
Of human destiny,
Which predicts the individual luck of the pilgrim
Through mysterious signs?"

"Reflections of hope, perhaps,
Which give sudden start to genius,
Or the Muses' brilliant sparks
Which illuminate the divine field?"

I know not what they might be; I, a poor human
Who cannot even comprehend himself.
How could I possibly grasp such a vast mystery,
Lacking sufficient tools?

It seems more funny than serious to me,
The mortal man with his many limitations,
Who seeks to parse out that Mystery
And who is thus consumed and lost in the infinite.

Great is the man who in trying
Achieves the great smallness which is his lot,
And, in so doing, praises the Heavens
And therefore is raised up to Heaven.

  The moon is born where'er the beautiful light
Of Phoebus, moving in the distance, is reflected,
And inspires the Creator's great axiom
With a countenance of faithful beauty.

IV.

The moon and the stars
   who were born shining
And who strikingly adorn
   their field of sapphire
Turn pale at last
   as the darkness abates.
At the sun's radiance
   they suddenly sink,
Spreading their light
   over the Antipodes.

The sun again brandished
   its proud rays
And presented its rich splendor
   to the world.
Vast numbers of
   aquatic creatures
Filled the wide ocean
   with their species,
Born amidst the waters
   surrounding the world.

Polyhymnia of Delphi,
    Apollo's inspired one,
Gave to us the sweet trills
    so easily sung,
God of harmony,
    that desirable art,
A divine dispensation
    admired by all,
Created the songs
    the nightingale spills forth.

The peacock with its
    dazzling feathered garb,
The swan in the lake with
    its enchanting whiteness,
The panther and the errant gazelle
    playing together,
The timid doves
    perched on a bold summit
Greet the condor
    with mutual affection.

The tigers and lions
    lived side by side,
Caressing the lamb with their tongues
    in brotherly care;
This was a paradise
    of unlimited love,
Wonderfully suffused
    with brotherly life,
A celestial offspring
    brought to earth . . .

V.

 Here thou hast transformed the earth
Changed it into an Elysian field;
Virgin that she was, immaculate,
Her breast full of innocent life,
Bathed by the limpid cascade
Of a fountain where a Nereid,
Delighting in its music,
Exchanges maidenly flattery with her . . .

VI.

 Taking mud from the blessed breast
Of that young maid, God made man,
And with his prodigious, pleasant breath,
He gave immortal soul to that pure mud,
"Adam," he told it, "shall be your name."

 He made him in his image; to that which he created
He gave complete domain and prosperity;
Thus from the Lord and through his pleasure
His works culminated in mankind,
And man is made in God's likeness.

 On the seventh day the Lord rested
Full of tender contentment;
Later his eyes looked to Olympus
And he blessed that Eden where all delighted
For the good of mankind.

VII.

    And all the Universe was satisfied,
Intoning jubilant alleluias,
Blessed by Heaven's hand,
Endlessly changing its gala garb,
Drunk with joy, it sang on . . .

VIII.

    But God was not satisfied,
Not even by giving Adam plants,
An Eden bursting with beauty
Which he could contentedly rule.

    Because man, that sublime creature,
The breath and image of God,
Merited even greater favor,
Yet more excellent fortune!

    The Heavens bathed the womb
Of that florid valley
With splendid light,
Creating an ineffable, indescribable dawn.

    A soft, balm-filled breeze,
Perfumed by bright flower
With its amorous hint,
Electrifies the air Adam breathed.

    A sonorous fountain he adds,
Its burbles a soft lullaby,
And giving in to this beautiful dawn,
Adam sinks into a deep sleep.

God draws near, and finding him asleep,
Decides to make out of him another being,
To give a wife to the husband,
To give a queen to the king.

But meanwhile Adam dreamed
That a cherub descended from the sky,
Signaling with his right hand
Two stars hanging in a blue sky.

The cherub, aloft, tells him,
In a shining whiteness of ethereal vapor,
"This sky with two stars united
Reveals Adam's destiny" . . .

The joy Adam felt,
Contemplating such a pleasant vision,
Was like that of an infant smiling while dreaming,
Like the flower smiles before the Heavens.

But suddenly an ominous cloud arrives,
Propelled by a strong north wind,
And in its tempestuous hurry,
That shining sky darkens.

Immediately an archangel appears,
Adorned in diaphanous tulle,
And it seemed that in his hand
Shone the light of a burning sword.

A devastating thunderclap,
The fatal rumble of a volcano,
And Adam foresaw in his dream
That the earth would shake.

Not knowing what he was seeing,
In that strident lightning's voice,
He awoke and at his side
Was she more beautiful than the celestial sun.

   Mother foremost of creation,
Eve, given by the Heavens,
Whose eyes took their brilliance
From two stars in an inspired dream.

   She has the form of Venus Citerea,
The soul of an innocent child,
And her almond-shaped eyes
Gaze gladly over all Eden.

   Her copious brown hair
Frames her marble skin,
Her lips a rich carmine, accompanied by
Her rosy cheeks.

   Man overflowed with gratitude,
With contentment, with joy, with love . . .
Ah! The clouds had not yet arrived . . .
And the pair remained in bliss . . .

IX.

   And all the Universe was satisfied,
Intoning jubilant alleluias,
Blessed by Heaven's hand,
Endlessly changing its gala garb,
Drunk with joy, the cosmos sang on . . .

PART II

Songs of Home and Translations

TO MY DAUGHTER, HERMINIA

alejandrino/quintilla

Little sea pearl
   enigma of my life,
Corporeal gift
   of the triumph of my love,
You are held in my being
   as the most prized jewel,
A living symbol of purity
   born of childhood's
Fleeting, chaste innocence.

A soft expression
   springs from your eyes,
Resplendent with beauty
   and brilliant as the sun.
They fill my life with such joy
   that casts away my grief
And turns my path
   that has been full of setbacks
Into a celestial delight
   of fatherly love.

Herminia, little button-nosed girl,
   the fuel of a thousand loves,
Aurora circling my blazing heart,
   I wish my words of praise
Could match the way
   the flowers of the fields equal your beauty.
Alas, I fall short,
   since you are greater yet,
A master work
   of heavenly creation.

In a few days it will be
    three years that you have been with us,
A gift inspiring
    new hope in my soul.
You have filled my heart
    with happiness and joy
And with your presence you
    have turned our home into an Edenic paradise.

Since your coming,
    we, your mother and father, live
Days filled with good fortune and weeks
    that go by in peace.
At the clearing of the sky at morning
    we saw your bright fire
Shine so powerfully that
    I am left lacking the words to sing your praise.

May heaven entrust her to us
    with a pure and radiant soul,
She brings us perfect,
    unending joy,
May her virtues shine
    constant like a star,
May her good fortunes
    flow in torrents
And may God keep this pearl angel
    from all harm!

TO MY SON, FELIPE

octavilla

In the shade of a fern
That majestically rises
Alongside where doth flow
A fast-flowing river,
I sit upon the grass
With my rod and hook,
Anxiously awaiting
A treasure from my fishing.

The afternoon was serene,
And my pleasure grew
With the pleasant caress
Of the occasional breeze.
I was distracted
When suddenly
A spiritual vision
Appeared on the near slope.

A group of white nymphs
Floating on ethereal clouds
Gradually came closer to me
Without hesitating;
I guessed that they might be
Proud little water nymphs
Who came to gaze
At the crystalline waters.

Later the scene changed:
I spied a grove of trees;
In a field decorated
With a garden of flowers
A bee wandered
From white lilies
To violets, sipping
Their honey nectar.

   Walking among the flowers
Here and there I followed,
Hoping thus to find
The bee's workshop.
But again there appeared
The nymphs I saw before
Floating on ethereal clouds,
And they came flying toward me.

   A honeycomb of rich syrup
They placed in my hands
And, singing, told me:
"Flowers provide you with this honey."
For a moment, I was stunned,
Witnessing such a curious scene,
I was lost in the mystery
And then immediately, I awoke.

   Awake, I saw nothing,
And my efforts were in vain,
For I wished an explanation for that dream
But I never received it.
But now, as I recall
What happened that day,
I surmise that this
Is what I saw in that dream:

The garden was our home,
And all the flowers
The symbol of two loves
That the heavens united in our home.
The bee was my destiny
That I followed in my longing,
When the heavens sent our
Son, the product of our love.

Yes, the honeycomb was, without a doubt,
Our adored son:
Honey which has sweetened life,
Wax which spills light,
Light that dissipates the shadows
That cross our path.
He is the fruit of our love,
Who will bring hope in our world of conflict.

TO MY DAUGHTER, JOSEFINA
quinteto

It was a spring morning,
And April's light dawned,
And I hoped that a flower would bloom
In a pot in my delightful garden,
As so much life was reborn.

I saw among its leaves
A jasmine bud hanging down
And I inhaled in ecstasy
The pleasant aroma that emanated from it,
Dreaming dreams of hope.

Distracted by this
I saw that the space darkened,
And I remained immersed in the shadows,
I felt my chest split with sadness
And everything left me . . . left me . . .

But all this happened in an instant,
A brief puff from a gale,
And the sun again came out, shining brilliantly,
Reverent of new life,
Typical spring life.

My eyes turned again to the flowering plant,
Drawn there as if by love,
And—how can I explain how I felt?—
Seeing the moment when my little bud
Became a fragrant flower!

A flower that gave me happy fulfillment,
Utter joy to my being,
It was Melba, my pure daughter,
My Josefina, a sun of beauty,
Precious jasmine, light of my home!

Two years had passed since that morning,
A steady stream of thousands of delights;
She brought pleasure to my life,
Sweet humor, pomegranate red lips,
Blonde hair, the ideal of beauty . . .

My longings were at last satisfied
By the same Heaven who gave her to me
That after much living
She returned to Heaven's breast as she came,
As pure as she was born!

TO MY DAUGHTER, JULIETA

A Soliloquy

terceto with closing cuarteto

I see you are smiling in your sleep:
You sleep the sleep of innocent calm
In your little cradle of soft feathers.

You dream, perhaps, of whitest doves,
Who sing their coo-coo-coos at your side,
In an Eden full of perfumes,

Perfumes that dahlias and roses
Offer as incense to your smile
In the innocent sleep in which you rest.

Three months since you came into this world,
A heavenly emissary of our joy,
A beautiful cherub of deep love.

And if a royal king were to offer me
Riches and his throne in exchange for you,
I would hurl my curse at such an insult!

Your ancestors and I,
When we see each other in your wise eyes,
Offer you an immense sea of love,

In exchange, we receive, enraptured,
Your smile, in triple recompense,
More precious than the world and all its kingdoms!

Today, two souls joined together form one,
And together watch over your happiness
From the side of your beloved crib.

We call on God for your destiny
That beautiful gifts shower upon your soul from on high,
And that where'er your path may lead
He pours down his blessings upon you.

TO MY DAUGHTER, ELVIRA

Sonnets

sonetos

I.

   Diaphanous, a cloud-striped sky spirals
Up to a high dome
Where some rough-hewn wisps of cloud become
Pure, holy and white forms leaving only waves above.

   Beauty spills onto that sky rotunda
That breaks at odd and rough spaces
At the place where the green hue of pine trees gleams,
Awash with the sun's fertile light.

   Just so, my dear, with peaceful tenderness
You radiate your own flowery essence
Over the rough path of my life.

   I am a dome onto which your radiant beauty projects
A loveliness that embraces my brokenness with its light
And soothes my worries with joy.

II.

   A kiss upon a breath, quick and sweet,
And white vapor turns to a pure drop
Of crystalline liquid,
Magnified by a prism.

Where an iridescent splendor is born
And the heights and scenic valley breathe in its radiating balsam,
And the valley radiates
A flowering sea of blessings.

If my soul has sought greatness,
Or if I find a gentle flower in this arduous life—
The fruit of some virtue that aids my soul—

It is but the heavenly manna rained down by your virtues,
The comforting balm I take from the lily
That is your angelic soul, my dear Elvira.

TO MY ELVIRA

quinteto

I have a pair of stars
Which shine brighter with each passing day
In the loving sky of my soul;
They lay out a path for my footprints
Through a valley filled with pleasures and calm.

They are a pair of stunning suns;
On my path of rough peaks,
They are the light on my dark journey,
And through them a sea of colors
Marks the dawn of my every day.

If my home has a bit of heaven,
Glowing with domestic charms,
To which I secretly dedicate my desires;
If there is a plant sown in my arid being
Which gives my life its everlasting bloom;

If my fields are bedecked with flowers
And if Phoebus spreads his
Rich brilliance upon them;
If my heart overflows with love,
I owe it all to those two little stars.

They are the lively, spirited
Sparks that cleverly laugh
When they conspire to tease me;
That heaven where doth audaciously twinkle
My Elvira's light-filled eyes!

TO MY LITTLE SON, BUENAVENTURA

redondilla

   You have flown to heaven, dear angel,
Taking with you the pure, sun-crested dawn,
The earth has been made dark and more somber
With your absence.

   Your parents and grandparents
Are pierced by sorrow,
Your absence reminds them
How many of their ardent desires are now snuffed out forever.

   We will not for an instant
Forget your heavenly grace,
Your noble glances
Nor the sound of your voice.

   You had been our delight,
The light of our days,
A sun we now see extinguished
By waves of tears of anguish.

   But my soul is comforted
When I consider
That while we gave the world a son
We sent an angel into Heaven.

TO MY LITTLE DAUGHTER, MELBA

redondilla

It was a fall night when I saw
With great pain and concern
That a freezing wind
Withered a tender shoot.

A sprout that had been born
In the garden of my love,
As pure as the flower
That it would have become.

It lived a few days
In this valley of tears,
When, full of joy, its white wings
Carried it aloft to heaven.

Today her ashes rest
At the edge of a sad forest,
But the soul of my little Melba
Is now a glorious star.

This little one did not find her place
In this world's coming and going,
Because an angel has no place
In this earthly life.

TO MY GODDAUGHTER, ROSA CÓRDOVA

I.

cuarteto

Imagine and try to understand
Why the noble hearts of your parents
Race and beat, urged on by tender emotions
Stirring within the deep sea of their love.

Imagine and try to understand
Why each new smiling dawn,
The kiss of the sweeping breeze,
And the entire course of a single day's glimmer has them under its spell.

It is for you, lovely Rosa, that their lives
Are a dream of yet-to-be-fulfilled hopes,
That their hearts joined together,
Creating a soul—yours—in which their love rests.

II.

serventesio

Do you see how the field and garden
Filled with jasmine offer you love?
And how in the stands of pine trees
The songbirds offer you their sweet melodies?

Your beauty is greater than that of the flowers,
Purer still is your honesty;
I heard your voice so mystical and holy
That it denies the songbird its song!

Go forth following the path you are on,
Perfumed rose, lovely vision,
And you will be the joy of your beloved
When love strikes the opening bud of your heart.
It flowers now . . .

　　This is why
The noble hearts of your parents
Race and beat, urged on by tender emotions
Stirring within the deep sea of their love.

TO MY GODSON, JACOBO ARAGÓN, SON

serventesio

So great is this joy, dearest godson,
That I feel it beating in my chest,
Seeing the possibility in your childhood
Of a future full of good fortune.

It is pleasing to see in your early calling
The flowering within you
Of healthy and beneficial teaching
That today shines forth as an example in your behavior.

That behavior is the fruit that, with much effort,
Your parents have cultivated in your being,
The rich flowers of sincere love that crown
You, the reflection of their efforts.

Thus, godson, I wish to suggest to you today,
As you climb your pristine steps,
Recall that you must first fulfill your obligations
To them in future years.

Know that they who gave you your being,
Full of faith, love, and trust,
Have hidden within you their own hopes,
From the cradle where they rocked your little soul.

The desire that they have most deeply guarded
Is to see their Jacobo grown,
Admired among men,
Distinguished for wonderful talents.

Their joy is made up of your joy,
See the love with which they follow your every step;
Never forget that upon you depends
The blooming of all they so desire.

Pledge that your sublime affection for them
Will always be your loyal, shared principle.
Ensure that over the course of your life
You offer them full gratitude and sustenance.

With this, your duty will be complete
And for this, they will live blessed:
Your beloved being will be the fulfillment
Of that with which they adorned their most beautiful dreams . . .

Dawn broke and at that moment
The meadow filled with life and flowers.
The serene morning sun announced
The day's early awakening.

I confidently foresee
Your future path free from thorns,
And thus I toast you with my wish,
You, who are your godfather's pride!

TO MY BELOVED LITTLE SISTER, LUCÍA

A poem that I greatly appreciate because my cherished uncle, the deceased don Pedro C. Chacón, wrote it as a gift to my mother, whom he affectionately called "my little sister." My uncle Pedro was an inspired poet: he wrote a number of poems of great merit and fine taste, most of which died with him, as the manuscripts were not preserved. This is the only poem of his that I have been able to find, as it was saved by my mother. —The Author

    Lift, sister, your divine forehead,
Listen carefully to my plaintive song,
I speak to you with ardent love
About things that have been cloaked in silence;

    I gather here the purest sentiments,
Thoughts that had been long afield,
They are echoes sounding out from the core of my being,
Listen to them graciously, my sister:

    Fate descended, bedecked with fury,
In that time of pleasing joy
That was snatched from me—Oh tragic misfortune!—
Gone was my good fortune, my peace, my contentment.

    Fate descended ferocious, inexorable,
And killed the soul of one I hold dear,
My mother, whom I love more than riches,
She to whom I owe my being.

    And that was not to be the end of it all, for as I awaited
My life's fortune to shift,
Death descended, intrepid, homicidal,
And . . . killed my beloved father!

With that sad and fatal event
A mortal dart shot through my heart . . .
Oh what an unhappy weight and what torment
When I saw my glory end!

   Upon seeing myself alone, poor, abandoned,
All was sadness around me;
My fate was an austere gloom
Bellowing out into the torment.

   And in the midst of this dense fog,
My soul withering without refuge . . .
An angel with tranquil gaze descended
And calmed the unending mist.

   You were that angel, my beloved sister,
You the rainbow that, in the valley of pain,
Emerged, a sign of comfort,
Restoring my skies to turquoise.

   You, on seeing my life in such pitiable state,
Moved by pity and tenderness,
You told me in sweet words:
"Poor thing, you must come lie by my side."

   I heard your sweet, bewitching voice,
And I ran, longingly, to your refuge,
In you I found—happily, fortunately—
A mother full of love and faith.

   Yes, you have been my mother, dear sister;
You have comforted my sorrowful life,
The tears from my wasted eyes
You have dried with heavenly goodness.

You are the author of my new life story:
You have given back to me the peace that was lost,
I see now my life gloriously stretched before me
Seeing myself, happy, by your side.

And the foul funereal memories
Of lost glories, of days past,
Are changed into happiness
In your presence, angel woman . . .

Heroic, kind, incomparable soul,
Who are you that you discerned
My anguish and, filled with mercy,
Heard the voice of my heart?

Upon seeing the greatness of your soul
My being is filled with emotion,
And I rise up to the heavens
To proclaim you my redeeming angel.

And although I cannot in my eager desire
Provide recompense for your goodness, as you deserve,
My burning heart has beat a thousand times
Filled with your love and in gratitude.

Only God can reward your deeds
So heroic, so noble, so faithful;
Your virtue will surely be crowned with laurels
In the sweet hereafter.

—Pedro C. Chacón

PSALM OF LIFE[1]

Tell me not, in mournful numbers,
    Life is but an empty dream!
For the soul is dead that slumbers,
    And things are not what they seem.

Life is real! Life is earnest!
    And the grave is not its goal;
Dust thou art, to dust returnest,
    Was not spoken of the soul.

Not enjoyment, and not sorrow,
    Is our destined end or way;
But to act, that each to-morrow
    Find us farther than to-day.

Art is long, and Time is fleeting,
    And our hearts, though stout and brave,
Still, like muffled drums, are beating
    Funeral marches to the grave.

In the world's broad field of battle,
    In the bivouac of Life,
Be not like dumb, driven cattle!
    Be a hero in the strife!

Trust no Future, howe'er pleasant!
    Let the dead Past bury its dead!
Act,—act in the living Present!
    Heart within, and God o'erhead!

Lives of great men all remind us
    We can make our lives sublime,
And, departing, leave behind us
    Footprints on the sands of time;

Footprints, that perhaps another,
    Sailing o'er life's solemn main,
A forlorn and shipwrecked brother,
    Seeing, shall take heart again.

Let us, then, be up and doing,
    With a heart for any fate;
Still achieving, still pursuing,
    Learn to labor and to wait.

—Henry Wadsworth Longfellow

Note

1. [Editors' note: Henry Wadsworth Longfellow, "Psalm of Life," in *Poems* (T. Y. Crowell, 1901), 3.]

TO THE DUCHESS OF YORK[1]

So when the new-born Phoenix first is seen,
Her feather'd subjects all adore their queen,
And while she makes her progress through the East,
From every grove her numerous train's increast:
Each Poet of the air her glory sings,
And round him the pleas'd audience clap their wings.

—*John Dryden*

Note

1. [Editors' note: John Dryden, "To the Duchess of York," in *The Miscellaneous Works of John Dryden, Esq.: Containing All His Original Poems, Tales, and Translations*, ed. S. Derrick (J. and R. Tonson, 1760), 50.]

A WISE ONE[1]

Freely Translated

Perched so discreetly in the oak tree where he nests,
A Mexican spotted owl views everything below,
Still and quiet he hears every sound,
The owl remains transfixed,
Grateful that the folly, the misguided ways, of others,
Did not befall him,
All who blunder, who then murmur and backstab
Should learn the ways of the screech owl.

Note

1. [Editors' note: This text is a translation into English of Chacón's translation into Spanish. Chacón did not provide an author for the poem, and a definitive source could not be located. However, given the similarities in theme and content, it is possible that he interpreted a poem similar to this popular rhyme:

A WISE OLD OWL

A wise old owl lived in an oak
The more he saw the less he spoke
The less he spoke the more he heard.
Why can't we all be like that wise old bird?]
   —Origins unknown

THE HOUSE BY THE SIDE OF THE ROAD[1]

There are hermit souls that live withdrawn
In the peace of their self-content;
There are souls, like stars, that dwell apart,
In a fellowless firmament;
There are pioneer souls that blaze their paths
Where highways never ran;—
But let me live by the side of the road
And be a friend to man.

Let me live in a house by the side of the road,
Where the race of men go by—
The men who are good and the men who are bad,
As good and as bad as I.
I would not sit in the scorner's seat,
Or hurl the cynic's ban;—
Let me live in a house by the side of the road
And be a friend to man.

I see from my house by the side of the road,
By the side of the highway of life,
The men who press with the ardor of hope,
The men who are faint with the strife.
But I turn not away from their smiles nor their tears—
Both parts of an infinite plan;—
Let me live in my house by the side of the road
And be a friend to man.

I know there are brook-gladdened meadows ahead
And mountains of wearisome height;
That the road passes on through the long afternoon
And stretches away to the night.
But still I rejoice when the travelers rejoice,
And weep with the strangers that moan,
Nor live in my house by the side of the road
Like a man who dwells alone.

Let me live in my house by the side of the road
Where the race of men go by—
They are good, they are bad, they are weak, they are strong,
Wise, foolish—so am I.
Then why should I sit in the scorner's seat
Or hurl the cynic's ban?—
Let me live in my house by the side of the road
And be a friend to man.

—Sam Walter Foss

Note

1. [Editors' note: Sam Walter Foss, "The House by the Side of the Road," in *Dreams in Homespun* (Lothrop, Lee & Shepard, 1897), 11–12.]

VISION OF BELSHAZZAR[1]

The King was on his throne,
The Satraps throng'd the hall;
A thousand bright lamps shone
O'er that high festival.
A thousand cups of gold,
In Judah deem'd divine—
Jehovah's vessels hold
The godless Heathen's wine.

In that same hour and hall
The fingers of a hand
Came forth against the wall,
And wrote as if on sand:
The fingers of a man;—
A solitary hand
Along the letters ran,
And traced them like a wand.

The monarch saw, and shook,
And bade no more rejoice;
All bloodless wax'd his look,
And tremulous his voice:—
"Let the men of lore appear,
The wisest of the earth,
And expound the words of fear,
Which mar our royal mirth."

Chaldea's seers are good,
But here they have no skill;
And the unknown letters stood
Untold and awful still.
And Babel's men of age
Are wise and deep in lore;
But now they were not sage,
They saw—but knew no more.

A captive in the land,[2]
A stranger and a youth,
He heard the king's command,
He saw that writing's truth;
The lamps around were bright,
The prophecy in view;
He read it on that night,—
The morrow proved it true!

"Belshazzar's grave is made,
His kingdom pass'd away,
He, in the balance weigh'd,
Is light and worthless clay;
The shroud, his robe of state;
His canopy, the stone:
The Mede is at his gate!
The Persian on his throne!"

—Lord Byron

Notes

1. Last king of Babylon, whose reign was heralded at a sumptuous feast with the words "Mane, Thecel," Phare, 538 before Jesus Christ. —The Author. [Editors' note: George Gordon, Lord Byron, "Vision of Belshazzar," in *The Poetical Works of Lord Byron, with Life* (W. P. Nimmo, 1881), 246.]

2. The Prophet Daniel.

ON THE DEATH OF A YOUNG LADY[1]

Hush'd are the winds, and still the evening gloom,
Not e'en a zephyr wanders through the grove,
Whilst I return to view my Margaret's[2] tomb,
And scatter flowers on the dust I love.

Within this narrow cell reclines her clay,
That clay, where once such animation beamed;
The King of Terrors seized her as his prey;
Not worth nor beauty have her life redeem'd.

Oh! could that King of Terrors pity feel,
Or Heaven reverse the dread decree of fate!
Not here the mourner would his grief reveal,
Not here the muse her virtues would relate.

But wherefore weep? Her matchless spirit soars
Beyond where splendid shines the orb of day;
And weeping angels lead her to those bowers
Where endless pleasures virtuous deeds repay.

And shall presumptuous mortals Heaven arraign,
And, madly, godlike Providence accuse?
Ah! no, far fly from me attempts so vain;—
I'll ne'er submission to my God refuse.

Yet is remembrance of those virtues dear,
Yet fresh the memory of that beauteous face;
Still they call forth my warm affection's tear,
Still in my heart retain their wonted place.

—Lord Byron

Notes

1. [Editors' note: George Gordon, Lord Byron, "On the Death of a Young Lady," in *The Poetical Works of Lord Byron, with Life* (W. P. Nimmo, 1881), 10.]

2. Margaret Parker, daughter of Admiral Parker, with whom Byron was enamored in 1802, when the author (Byron) was only 14 years old.

MARY STUART AND HER MOURNER[1]

Mary Stuart, queen of Scotland, was decapitated at the age of 44, on the orders of her cousin Elizabeth, who was then queen of England (1523–1603). Her servants, whimpering, begged Elizabeth to allow them to take care of her remains and give them burial, but she denied this request. The body was covered with a piece of green felt fabric hastily yanked from a billiard table, and left completely alone, save for a lapdog that could not be induced to abandon the remains of its mistress. This faithful little animal was found dead two days later, at the side of the corpse, and the incident made such a deep impression, including on Elizabeth's hardened ministry, that it was mentioned in the official registry. —The Author

The axe its bloody work had done;
    The corpse neglected lay;
This peopled world could spare not one
    To watch beside the clay.

The fairest work from Nature's hand
    That e'er on mortals shone,
A sunbeam stray'd from fairy land
    To fade upon a throne;—

The Venus of the Tomb[2] whose form
    Was destiny and death;
The Siren's voice that stirr'd a storm
    In each melodious breath;—

Such was, what now by fate is hurl'd
    To rot, unwept, away.
A star has vanish'd from the world;
    And none to miss the ray!

Stern Knox, that loneliness forlorn
    A harsher truth might teach
To royal pomps, than priestly scorn
    To royal sins can preach!

No victims now that lip can make!
    That hand how powerless now!
O God! and what a King—but take
    A bauble from the brow?

The world is full of life and love;
    The world methinks might spare
From millions, one to watch above
    The dust of monarchs there.

And not one human eye!—yet lo
    What stirs the funeral pall?
What sound—it is not human woe—
    Wails moaning thro' the hall?

Close by the form mankind desert
    One thing a vigil keeps;
More near and near to that still heart
    It wistful, wondering creeps.

It gazes on those glazed eyes,
    It hearkens for a breath—
It does not know that kindness dies,
    And love departs from death.

It fawns as fondly as before
    Upon that icy hand;
And hears from lips, that speak no more,
    The voice that can command.

To that poor fool, alone on earth,
    No matter what had been
The pomp, the fall, the guilt, the worth,
    The Dead was still a Queen.

With eyes that horror could not scare,
    It watch'd the senseless clay;—
Crouch'd on the breast of Death, and there
    Moan'd its fond life away.

And when the bolts discordant clash'd,
    And human steps drew nigh,
The human pity shrunk abash'd
    Before that faithful eye;

It seem'd to gaze with such rebuke
    On those who could forsake;
Then turn'd to watch once more the look,
    And strive the sleep to wake.

They raised the pall—they touch'd the dead,
    A cry, and both were still'd,—
Alike the soul that Hate had sped,
    The life that Love had kill'd.

Semiramis of England, hail!
    Thy crime secures thy sway;
But when thine eyes shall scan the tale
    Those hireling scribes convey;

When thou shalt read, with late remorse,
    How one poor slave was found
Beside thy butcher'd rival's corse,
    The headless and discrown'd;

Shall not thy soul foretell thine own
    Unloved, expiring hour,
When those who kneel around the throne
    Shall fly the falling tower;

When thy great heart shall silent break,
    When thy sad eyes shall strain
Thro' vacant space, one thing to seek,
    One thing that loved—in vain?

Tho' round thy parting pangs of pride
    Shall priest and noble crowd;
More worth the grief, that mourn'd beside
    Thy victim's gory shroud!

—E. Bulwer Lytton

Notes

1. [Editors' note: E. Bulwer Lytton, "Mary Stuart and Her Mourner," in *The Poetical and Dramatic Works of Sir Edward Bulwer Lytton* (Chapman and Hall, 1852), 319–22.]
2. Libitina: goddess who presides at funerals.

PART III

Political Arrows and Prose

A REAL REPUBLICAN

Well, fine! Such is the case
That in a past time,
When a fierce,
Unequaled war raged,
A republican,
Offering solidarity to the
Fatherland,
A republican
Who says that he is worth a "real,"
When it's more like a quarter
Or penny, no more,
Says that he went to war . . .
Was it to fight?
With his back to the fight,
Running away,
His eyes open,
His mouth more so,
Trembling with the shock
Of seeing the explosion
Of the pounding,
Lethal shrapnel;
And within this exceedingly
Ridiculous figure
Dense clouds
Of steam and gas,
Were swallowed up
Through his pores,
Such that leaving the war,
Returning home,
He was an immense sack
Filled with gases.
Today the veteran

In his advanced age,
Hallucinates that he is a poet
Because in a hallucination
Anyone could save
The Homeland . . .
With his back to the fight,
Running away . . .

II.

Our military suffers
From this delirium,
So painful to witness
In recent days,
Mendacious news
Arrived
That William, the Bull,
Managed to increase
—How awful!—
His forthcoming pension,
For the bizarre reason
That he knew how to show
His back to the fight,
Running away . . .

III.

Upon reading the news
Our military
Danced and spun in the air,
Singing and shouting
With such joy,
First a jig

And then a cancan,
A bit of this and that
And perhaps a stumble or two,
Falling to the ground
Breaking a rib
With a crash
Satan would be proud of!
And from the Bull a vast wealth
That those who misfire in war
Tend to swallow,
With long stanzas of steam and gas,
That the Bull, in jest,
Began to praise!
And puff after puff
Of gas and more gas
Without thinking
At all about charity
Thanks to the Press
And to humanity,
He filled a gazette
With his yammer
Which seems to be
The Story
That Never Ends!
So, the stanzas
Now number
Twenty-two more
Of absurd repetition
That smells like a corral;
And in these he affirms
—What temerity!—
This same Bull
Says that it is "the Truth"
The very "Honor"
And "Honesty!" . . .

But this doesn't matter,
Mr. Military Official,
The people already know
That the Bull
Is incapable of the green
Tomatoes he is peeling,[1]
And you—oh!—
Can't eclipse the sun
With these verses of
Steam and gas,
It matters not that
He was brave in making war . . .
With his back to the fight,
Running away . . .

IV.

He says he is the Bull
"Without any exaggeration,"
The valiant Cid,
If one could imagine!
We all know
The Cid is dead,
And because he is dead,
I admit in all truth,
There is some similarity
Between the Cid
And the Bull,
That I do not deny,
Mr. Military Officer.
But here
We will come to a point,
A delicate point, in fact,
—Be careful in joining in!—

Because the women
You have described as
"Crybabies who only
Know how to cry,"
Well, one might as well
Put into verse,
That in the end,
The women will lynch you
Or at least remove all your clothes
With a curt "whack!"
Cover you with tar
And feathers;
And then take
This figure,
In its triumphal march
Through the streets:
A funereal dishonor
For a soldier
Who bravely saved
The Homeland...
With his back to the fight,
Running away...

v.

But at the end of much
Sucking and blowing,
Whatever ass
He came across,
Playing the flute
In a trash can,
He has given us
The voice of truth;
He says that wherever

The Bull knocks
A door
Will be opened to him;
And I assure him
That at every open door,
He will be given a
"Shoo, get out!"
Like a little lapdog
So that he can go
Shed his fleas
In that torrid clime
Where Satan resides . . .
Anyway, I do not wish
To spend more of
Your time critiquing
Gas's rhymes.
But being a SOLDIER,
As he has frequently reiterated,
Whose MILITARY SERVICE
Is very ancient indeed,
My liege, how should one hope to fix
The broken record
Of that Barabbas
Whom you call
The very "truth!" . . .
Anyway, we should
Not take seriously
He who only exhales
Steam and gas . . .
He persists in his subject matter,
So worthy of one "real,"
And perhaps will achieve,
With his long verses of
Steam and gas,
The removal of the "Bull"

From Saint William:
Such miracles
Could be forged
By one who
—Pouting!—
Saved the Homeland . . .
With his back to the fight,
Running away . . .

Note

1. [Editors' note: A verse that would clarify this metaphor appears to be missing, obfuscating Chacón's intended meaning.]

A MASQUERADE BALL

The occasion was the well-attended masquerade ball that a certain local lodge held at the opera house of a small Colorado town in the year 1898.

I felt quite amused gazing on the singular spectacle of any number of attendees decked out in extravagant, multicolored styles dictated by a thousand human whims. Nearby was someone disguised as a native of Borneo; a ways over, two people dressed as the "Siamese Twins"; further on, another who jumped like a frog, his shiny green and black spots making him all the more conspicuous; and throughout the ballroom all danced: the allegorical characters of kings, gypsies, Turks, Indians, Chinese, and who knows what else, including the ever-present "tramp," chased by smart cops (who rarely ever exist), and a multitude of others whom I will not mention.

I was completely absorbed watching all this, when suddenly a young lady came up to me. She appeared young in spite of the mask on her face, quite enchanting, tall, svelte, and well-shaped, so much so that I was immediately struck by her charms. She spoke in a pleasant and sweet voice:

"Good evening, sir."

"I wish you the same," I answered, agitated and nervous.

"I'd like to speak to you a moment."

In haste, I complied hoping that her red lips would draw close, if not to my lips, then at least to my ear. She told me who she was, and what she wanted, and we both had a good laugh.

I noticed a certain friend I knew named Pancho Morales was leaning against one of the pillars in the ballroom. He was young. He was neat but vain in the extreme. He loved all the girls as they came through the door. He flirted with them in a thousand ways, using winks and caresses, trying to win their affection; but as might be expected given that he was awkward and lacked grace, all his efforts, his gallant gestures made him look foolish and made the girls disdain him.

Pancho, like myself, had no mask. He had gone more to witness the event than to be a part of it. I went up to him, but since he was nearsighted, he did not see me until I was upon him, and then only when I greeted him in a loud voice:

"Hello there, buddy! How are you getting by?"

"Say what? The view? Well, I scan it from one end of the hall to the other and catch every little thing," he answered with a burst of laughter as he usually did, believing he had said something witty.

"God, man, don't be so dull! I've just met a young lady named Carmen Hinojosa, a stranger here, and one of the most lovable and charming women that anyone has ever seen. When it comes to dancing, she's a modern Salome, a true Terpsichore. Come with me, I'll introduce her to you, and you'll see how easy she is . . . "

"Whoa, say no more, fool! I'll go with you, even at the risk of breaking my neck," exclaimed Pancho, unable to contain his glee.

Introducing him to Miss Hinojosa and him asking her to dance the next number became one and the same thing.

I stayed seated, making the greatest effort to hold back the laughter that was choking me up as I watched the undulating capers, many-stepped pirouettes, and childish gestures with which the quixotic Pancho tried to please his beautiful companion.

He danced with her five or six consecutive numbers. Finally he came back to where I was, and cackling with joy, he grabbed my hand and said:

"You can't imagine how much I have enjoyed myself . . . and besides, Captain, what can I tell you? I've offered to walk her home, and she has accepted my humble courtesy with the kindness of an angel. I feel so happy tonight, after so many bitter deceptions! Although I have yet to see her face, the magnificent symmetry of her figure and the sweet melody of her voice have me floating through the air . . . "

The clock struck midnight as he finished this interesting speech—it was the end of the ball, and a happy moment for lucky Pancho! They both proudly departed in the direction of the home of Mrs. Petra Bustillos, where Miss Hinojosa was staying.

"Why don't you remove your mask?" Pancho asked.

"As soon as we reach the house."

"You can't imagine my great desire to get to know you and to build a mutual and reciprocal courtship with you, perhaps even leading to love; and furthermore, even to uniting my destiny to yours in the eternal bond of matrimony," Pancho said and then went on:

"Pardon my frankness, but to tell you the truth I believe I can see coming through the veil covering your face, a soul full of virtues, the goddess of my most cherished dreams . . . "

They had by this time reached the house, and Pancho anxiously asked:

"Where can I see you tomorrow morning?"

Removing the mask and in a normal voice, his companion answered:

"At the 'Emerald Pool Hall,' as always; I am José Olivas, at your service . . . "

I was with some other friends at the corner of a nearby street, bursting with laughter at seeing what was taking place. José began to run away, leaving in his wake boisterous laughter while a helpless Pancho remained still, confused, stiff, stunned, and stupefied, and for a time was unable to really understand what had happened. Finally, he recovered his senses, and he began to spew forth some unrepeatable damnations: toads and snakes, with some serpents mixed in for effect. This went on even as he disappeared into the darkness.

That same night, Pancho packed his suitcase and his bags, and he left town on the first train out. I myself did not see him for many years. So great was the shock!

DON JULIO BERLANGA

It was in August 1918 when I had the honor of meeting don Julio Berlanga from ..., in Las Vegas, New Mexico.

Don Julio was a hardworking man, forty-eight years of age, around six feet tall, of straight stature and muscular build, dark skin and prominent cheekbones, a thick mustache, dark hair and vivid eyes—though somewhat sunken in their sockets. He was not given to joking or jests, although he could appreciate them in others; he was always frank and serious in his conversation, even when dealing with frivolous matters.

Given all of don Julio's good qualities—he was sober, hardworking, and constantly busy at his work—one could still see in him a kind of innocent vanity, which was quite amusing in a person of such serious aspect. To give a clearer idea of his peculiar manner, I aim to present, in a characteristic way, the description which he himself gave me of the happiest day in his life.

We were both sitting in the waiting room at the railroad station, engaged in conversation, when he told me:

"I'll never forget this place, Las Vegas, and you know why?"

I gave him a puzzled look, and after a pause, he continued: "Because last year I spent the happiest day of my life here. You see, I got here in the afternoon on the third of July from Wyoming, where I had been working on a sheep ranch for a full year. I came here to enjoy a couple of weeks of rest and recreation, attracted by the famous Rough Riders reunion which was celebrated on the third, fourth, and fifth of that same month.

"As soon as I arrived, I went and had dinner; later, I went to the barbershop and took a bath, changed clothes, got a haircut and a shave, and then I went to a mercantile store to buy some clothes. I bought a suit that cost fifty dollars, a hat that cost ten, some shoes that cost twelve, silk socks, a purple silk shirt with a collar, and a matching yellow tie. I spent ninety dollars like I was spending a dime, my friend! But with the three hundred I had with me, and another three hundred more I had left in a bank in Rawlins, what did it matter? I went to my room and put on new clothes from head to toe, and as I had a watch and a gold chain which had cost me seventy dollars in Rawlins, boy was I dressed up, and I'm not kidding, my friend, but I even glowed in that mirror!

"At the barbershop and on the street, I had heard people mention a dance which was to be held that same night at a dance hall called La Favorita. After getting dressed, I went walking through both of Las Vegas's plazas, and even though I didn't know a soul, I can report that I had a great time. I went to the rodeo park to watch the roping contests and see the cowboys ride wild horses and bulls, and I enjoyed everything.

"As I was coming back from the park, I got the notion to go and show off that night at the dance at La Favorita, because there are times in life when one just wants to show off. After supper I went to the movie house, and it must have been about nine o'clock when I got to the dance. As I entered the dance hall, which was packed, everyone looked me over from head to toe, because—I tell you, my friend—there was not one child of God there who could match me and who I didn't outshine, to put it that way, with my flashy clothes and the elegance of my person.

"I kept looking at all the women there, until I came upon the most beautiful woman I've ever seen. She was talking with another gal on the opposite side of the room from where I stood. I saw her looking at me and whisper something to her companion, and that's when I went and asked her to dance with me. She immediately took my arm, and we walked to the middle of the dance floor. Everyone was watching us, admiring us, my friend. Oh, how I was showing off with that beautiful woman! Finally, I stopped and said aloud: 'Friends, everyone get up and dance a waltz, those of you who wish to join this humble servant, Julio Berlanga! Anyone who wishes to do so, get up. I'll pay!'

"Immediately two or three shouted, 'Long live Julio Berlanga!' and that turned into a deafening sea of 'vivas' for Julio Berlanga, and there I was showing off with that beautiful woman.

"Finally, the ticket collector came and said to me: 'Twenty-six people stood up to dance. Are you paying for them all?' And I answered, 'yes,' giving him a couple of dollars. He wanted to give me back seventy cents, but I told him: 'Keep the change, young man.' Needless to say, my friend, that I bowled that collector over. I did the same thing three or four times, and that dance hall became my throne, my friend: everyone offered me the kindest attentions and courtesies, and I ruled the night. Of twenty or more songs that I danced that night, that beautiful woman was my partner for fifteen of them. Finally, she agreed to let me accompany her to her house after the dance. She was married, but it had been nine months since her husband had abandoned her, and she lived with her sister. Finally, I convinced her to go to Wyoming with me, and she consented. Three days later I went to San Luis to see my relatives, and three days after that I came back and we left.

"But in the end, that woman betrayed me, my friend. I set up a house for her in Rawlins and left it well stocked with groceries and plenty of money until I could come back from herding sheep: an absence of some six weeks. As my job moved from place to place, I really didn't expect to get any mail from her, but a week after leaving, I received a letter from her telling me she was all right and that she loved me as much as ever, and expected me to marry her when I got back to Rawlins. I wrote back that her wish was my command, but when I got back six weeks later, I found other people living in the house. Later, I found out that she had sold the furniture and everything, and she had taken off with an American. I was as rabid as a dog! . . . And I have never again seen her. But I'll never forget the day I met her, that day when I enjoyed myself to my heart's content. I can't forget that dance, my friend, because I was the king of that dance, a lion, and I ruled supreme."

EUSTACIO AND CARLOTA

A Novelette

1.

It was the year 1879, and in one of the large tenant houses so common in the city of New York, that though big was but an atom making up that magnificent, colorful, and populous metropolis, there lived a poor Spanish family named Quintanilla. That family consisted of the father, the mother, an eight-year-old boy named Eustacio, and a two-year-old daughter named Carlota.

As one might imagine, that family lived in the middle of a labyrinth, a multitude of common folk, typical of a way of life, the life of the "slums," in that amazing city.

One night in the month of December, during an almost unbearable cold snap, the mother was about to give birth to a child. The room she occupied lacked provisions such as heat, and the poor woman lamented her sad state, accompanied only by her two young children, Eustacio and Carlota.

The husband, and father of those poor children, spent the greater part of his day in the taverns of that famous street called the Bowery, squandering the fruit of the little work that he did as a waiter, in frivolous pastimes with the daily clientele that choked the district.

The anguish and suffering that poor woman would endure that bitter night are easier to call to mind than to describe in words.

Shortly before midnight, the mother woke her children, who had fallen asleep at the foot of the bed, and called them close to her. At this, the sad woman took two small medals with the image of Saint Anthony of Padua and with shaking hands tied them around the necks of her children, telling them, in words interrupted by pangs of pain: "This is the only inheritance which I can leave you, my dear children; may Saint Anthony keep you and protect you in this bitter life which I'm about to leave. Never take these little medals off, but always guard them as a reminder of the mournful mother who with them gives you her last blessing."

Then she lowered her head on the pillow and died.

The children went back to sleep, almost without realizing what had happened; but at six in the morning, Eustacio woke up frightened, evidently because of the frightful lasting impression his mother's final words had made upon him. Filled with sorrowful foreboding he started calling her. Since she did not answer, Eustacio ran out of the room, terrified, and in a tearful voice started crying next door, "Come see what's wrong with my mother!"

Two women followed the child to the Quintanilla apartment and witnessed a very sad scene: the unfortunate woman had given birth to a child that night, but due to the lack of medical help, as well as of adequate nourishment, both the mother and the child had perished.

A reporter from the big newspaper, the *New York Times*, was drawn to the house by the commotion of the tenants, and after taking notes on what had happened, and owing to the newspaper's investigation the case was reported to the municipal authorities. These took charge of the funeral arrangements and buried the dead woman in a paupers' cemetery that same day, while the children were taken to a local orphanage.

Two weeks later, in a local hospital, a man died who, having been in a barroom brawl, had received two gunshot wounds that proved fatal. That was the end of the futile existence of Alejo Quintanilla, father of Eustacio and Carlota.

About three weeks after Eustacio and Carlota entered the orphanage, the boy was adopted by a rich family from Toronto, Canada, that was visiting New York at the time. Returning home, this family took Eustacio with them, thus separating the two children.

A few weeks after Eustacio's adoption, Carlota was also adopted, by a family from Denver, Colorado, that had prestige and distinction among the social and financial circles of that city, for the couple was none other than Mr. George Freeman, a banker and venture capitalist, and his wife, Mrs. Consuelo Arlington Freeman, one of the eminent ladies of the cultured society in that metropolitan capital city. The Freemans were still a young couple that had been married only five years. Two years after their marriage, Mrs. Freeman had a daughter, who was given the name of Amanda Consuelo. This child, however, was always very sickly and eventually died before reaching the age of two. The marriage was fruitless afterwards, so Carlota was immediately given the name Amanda Consuelo.

Some four years after the separation of Eustacio and Carlota, in that great swirl made up of all nationalities (something that the city of Chicago had been reduced to) and while going through one of that city's little-traveled suburban streets, a twelve-year-old boy named Orlando Havens happened upon a strange-looking object resembling a human body on the tracks of the electric trolley. Orlando ran hurriedly to check what had caught his attention, and to his great surprise and amazement, he saw that it was the figure of a boy, more or less his own age, lying in this manner, in an unconscious state, at a spot where the lane curved and where a few minutes later, the boy could end up being crushed by one of the streetcars that ran through there.

Orlando dragged the boy to the side of the road, and a moment later the trolley arrived, and its conductor, after learning what had happened, helped Orlando lift the still-unconscious youth inside the car.

Orlando took the boy in that condition to a doctor's office, where, after a quick examination, it was found that he had a deep and ugly cut on the back of his head, from which much blood flowed. After treating the wound, which required several stitches, the doctor administered a drug which helped the boy soon regain consciousness.

For a long while the boy could not tell what had happened, did not know where he was, or how he got there. At last he was able to tell Orlando and the doctor that his name was Henry Collins, and that he lived at the home of the attorney Samuel Perkins, where he earned his room and board by doing ordinary chores. He also said that Mr. Perkins gave him a small salary besides his room and board, and he continued on with his informative account:

"I was going down the street, jingling some silver coins in my pocket. Suddenly I felt that someone was following me, and I didn't even get a chance to turn around and look, when I felt this blow (touching the spot) to my head; and I lost consciousness."

This account cleared up the mystery. Henry had been the victim of a mugger who assaulted him in the manner described, and in order to steal the money in his pocket and, perhaps thinking that he had killed him, the assailant wished to cover up his deed by placing Henry's body across the trolley tracks.

Henry finally felt strong enough to go home with Orlando, and the two boys became very close friends, cultivating a relationship of true concern and brotherly love.

One year after this event, Orlando's parents moved from Chicago to Philadelphia, and the two friends did not see each other again for many years.

II.

In the course of time, nineteen years went by after the young Carlota, whom we should now call Amanda, was adopted by the Freeman couple. Amanda, therefore, was nearing the age of twenty-one and had received an excellent education and preparation both in letters and in music, as is common in the highest social circles.

These lovely attributes, coupled with her natural talent, armed Amanda with a considerable creative flair for writing, and her contributions to the newspapers, interesting and instructive articles on themes related to social, political, and educational problems, were read eagerly by everyone. In this manner, Amanda had earned a national reputation, had gained fame and abundant expressions of admiration.

One day Amanda's parents decided to take a pleasure trip to the state of California, in the company of their daughter, of course; and so two weeks later, the Freeman family was in San Francisco, enjoying unbridled happiness and joy. The trip was very pleasant, and during the two weeks they spent in that city, Amanda wrote and published various articles, and in her typically brilliant style greatly praised the many wonders of the "Golden State," which in her admiration she called "The Garden of the World."

At this point, we are in the year 1898, precisely when the Spanish-American War is drawing to a close. On the twelfth of August, the Freeman family found itself in that Pacific port as the famous regiment of Colonel Theodore Roosevelt's "Rough Riders" landed in San Francisco upon its return from Cuba.

The captain of a company in this regiment was an elegant and handsome young man, twenty-seven years old, who it seemed nature itself had gifted for military life with every perfection. He was almost six feet tall, weighed 170 pounds, was of active disposition; he had good posture, a muscular build, and a well-proportioned figure and was of even and pleasant temperament. This model of perfect masculinity was none other than Orlando Havens, whom we have talked about elsewhere in our story. After his enlistment he was designated first lieutenant, but in virtue of his great courage and admirable fortitude in army operations, he had been promoted to the rank of captain by his superiors.

Great was the patriotic enthusiasm with which the regiment of Rough Riders was received in that city on the coast, that port city completely inundated by an outpouring of flags and wreaths, all decked out with the splendor of the nation's colors. The returning heroes were greeted with shouts of welcome, while orchestras filled the air with patriotic tunes.

At the end of the day's ceremonies there was to be a most splendid banquet held at the luxurious auditorium X—, as part of the program presented by the Municipal Council and the Chamber of Commerce. Thanks to a special invitation from the mayor of the city, the Freemans were counted among those most fortunate to attend that splendid event. And needless to say, Amanda was enchanting. She was dressed in a sky-blue chiffon dress trimmed with fine silk lace, and she wore a diamond necklace around her marble-white neck—all setting off the splendor of her large eyes that shone with the purity of her soul and the sharpness of her intellect. Then, too, the genteel undulations of her graceful figure that could have been sculpted by Raphael's or Michelangelo's exquisite chisels could be noted.

Many were the distinguished personalities presented to Amanda that night, among them Captain Orlando Havens, who in his own way truly resembled an Apollo, appearing like a work of fine sculpture made by the hand of some modern Praxiteles. Upon meeting her, Captain Havens at once felt deeply moved. He danced with her several times, and when the banquet ended, he went hurriedly to his room filled with wonder, and he could not sleep at all that night. This indefatigable warrior, who could face the horrors of war without fear, defeat the enemy, and emerge triumphant, now found himself weakened by Cupid's darts.

The following day, the Freeman family had to leave for San Jose, and Orlando was one of the first to show up at the train station to bid Amanda farewell. Before she left, Amanda asked him to visit them in Denver, assuring him that it would be a delight to see him there. Needless to say, Orlando, bowled over with infatuation, accepted the flattering invitation and promised to comply with her kind request as soon as he obtained leave from his superiors, which would be within three weeks or so. The train departed, and so too the Freeman family.

III.

Ten days after this, there was a terrible derailment of a passenger train between Los Angeles and San Diego. On the train was the Freemans' private car, called the "Anaconda." This train consisted of eighteen cars, including those for baggage, mail, express shipments and passengers, plus the "Anaconda," which was the last car and the one in which the Freeman family rode. When the train derailed, the engine and the tender fell headlong down a ravine to the side of the track, dragging several cars behind. Ten of these suffered heavy damage as they fell and landed akimbo, one on top of another, each more or less a total loss; other cars jumped the rails and were left blocking the track, badly damaged by the violent shock of the moment. It's impossible to fully describe that dreadful scene: the moans of pain, the screams of despair, the cries of agony that were heard everywhere would break a heart. When the engine fell, the engineer leaped from the cab, trying to escape the danger, but the engine crushed his legs, and in that condition he was boiled alive by the hot water escaping from the boiler. The wretched fellow begged God for someone to pass by and shoot him and remove him from those torments. That was only one of the many hair-raising scenes of horror that unfolded in that fatal event.

To make matters worse, the wreck caught fire, and so, for one reason or another, thirty-three persons perished in this catastrophe, and about one hundred were seriously injured. Of these, fifteen died later at a Los Angeles hospital. Only thirty-two of the two hundred passengers and employees were able to help the injured and rescue several people from the flames. Among these thirty-two were eleven women; and among them all was a robust young man, about twenty-six years of age, who distinguished himself and, despite an ugly wound on his head which left his face bloodied, acted with Herculean action, surpassing the rest in energy and courage.

Meanwhile, the "Anaconda," the private car of the Freeman family, remained on the tracks. Its front end had been rammed into the car in front of it. The surprise and the force of the shock had left its occupants unconscious inside. There were, besides the Freemans, a man named James Wilkins, his wife, and a daughter—all friends of the Freemans and residents of Los Angeles who accompanied them for the ride to Denver.

When the "Anaconda" caught fire at one end, the young man mentioned earlier entered the car through the rear door and found the occupants scattered throughout in an unconscious state and about to be burned to death or asphyxiated by the smoke which filled the inside of the car. (This young man was none other than Henry Collins, whose life Orlando, or Captain Havens, had saved in

Chicago fifteen years before.) He then lifted Mrs. Freeman to his shoulders and took her out of danger; then he called three of his companions and with their help he was able to rescue four more of those victims. By this time the flames had spread to such an extent that nobody dared to enter the car, and one of those who had gone in before affirmed that there was nobody left inside, but Henry insisted that he was sure of having seen another person there. Convinced of this, he rushed inside the car, which was already in flames, and heading to the spot where he believed he had seen another human body, succeeded in finding his objective. It was a feat of supreme heroism, since Henry, who was just about to succumb to asphyxiation, came forth dragging himself outside the car, but bringing with him the near-lifeless body of the precious Amanda. Once on the platform outside, they were both helped and taken to safety.

The following day, all of the nation's newspapers carried articles, more or less detailed, on the terrible tragedy. The daily *Los Angeles Examiner*, for example, gave an account of the occurrence which read in part:

> An emergency train was called from Los Angeles yesterday to the fatal scene of a derailment of the regular passenger train No. 10, which departed east of San Diego at 9:30 a.m. This rescue train returned to Los Angeles this morning carrying the bodies of 24 persons who died in the disaster, and more than 100 victims suffering serious and even grave wounds. The victims have been taken to various hospitals in this city, where they will receive proper medical assistance and everything possible will be done to reduce their suffering,
>
> One matter deserving special mention in connection with the tragic event is undoubtedly the courage and heroism of some twenty-five passengers on the ill-fated train, who helped rescue the bodies of the dead and the wounded from the said train. Several victims of this horrific catastrophe were devoured by the flames.
>
> Among this rescue team, there distinguished himself, through his admirable strength and courage, a traveling salesman some 27 years of age named Henry Collins, a representative for a shoe manufacturer from Boston, Massachusetts.
>
> The condition of Mr. Freeman, his wife, and his daughter is considered serious, but in no way critical, and doctors believe that they will soon recover

from their painful experience, as all had but surface cuts and painful bruises, nothing of an alarming nature.

The hero in this catastrophe is Henry Collins, who risked his own life to save those of Mrs. Freeman and her daughter, although he suffered a deep cut on the forehead and a great loss of blood; thanks to his robust constitution he is on his way to recover soon to his normal state.

This much is known from the account in the *Examiner*. The Freeman family and the young Collins were recovering at the Saint Lucas Hospital where they received the finest care that medical science can furnish.

Let us now return to Captain Havens, who had read the sad newspaper accounts in San Francisco with deep sorrow, and did not let a single day go by without calling the Saint Lucas Hospital long distance to inform himself of the condition of the Freemans as well as of Henry Collins, whom Orlando now remembered, with pride and admiration, as a close friend from a former day. He was anxious to see him, to give him a firm embrace and wish him well, with all his heart, for saving the life of the young Amanda, the idol of his most vivid dreams.

IV.

Four days passed, and the Freemans and Henry Collins were recovering quite satisfactorily. Looking out for his well-being and enjoyment, Amanda and her parents would send Henry beautiful flowers as well as books for his reading pleasure, even though he asked them not to trouble themselves so much for him.

Two days later, the doctors permitted the patients to go out of their rooms and delight themselves in the invigorating sun and the gentle environment of "The Garden of the World." The first thing the Freemans did was to go visit their deliverer, whom they wished to meet. Henry was walking across the front entrance of the hospital. One of the doctors there, who had been in charge of attending to the victims, arranged to take the Freemans to Henry. Amanda and her parents conferred lavish and warm expressions of gratitude upon Henry though he answered only that, apart from having complied with an obligation brought on by circumstances, he had done nothing out of the ordinary.

Two more days went by, and the relationship between Henry and the Freemans grew into a personal friendship. At last, the Freemans decided to return home, but not before they had convinced Henry to go with them and spend some time visiting Denver as their guest. With all in agreement, the group left for their destination the following day, but something more than the simple desire to accompany the Freemans moved Henry because the truth of the matter was that he was already in love with Amanda. On the train they took, the party occupied one of the most elegant large coaches, since Mr. Freeman's private car had been reduced to pieces and ashes in the derailment.

It was a peaceful, beautiful September morning, and those passengers felt very lucky that the past wreck had not had fatal consequences for them, as it unfortunately did for so many others, whose sad fate they lamented.

Henry and Amanda sat together and talked contentedly the whole time. In the course of their conversation, Amada at last said: "Who would've thought that such a delightful trip to California would have such a terrible and tragic ending?"

"But it's quite likely that neither you nor I have seen the end of it," Henry answered.

"I'm sure, quite certain, that the worst is already over," Amanda said, as she knowingly smiled. She ended by saying, "But I can never repay my debt to you, unless I can do so by means of my eternal gratitude."

"Where there's a will, there's a way," Henry answered. Amanda returned a look of surprise, feigning she had not understood Henry's words and finally said: "I don't see why you should doubt my desire or question the sincerity of my words."

"I need no proof of your sincerity," Henry answered. "Your sincerity is beyond question. Coming straight to the point, I want you to know, Amanda, that I admire and love you with all my heart. Tell me that you'll be mine, my beloved wife, and turn my fate into a sea of eternal bliss for the rest of my life!"

Upon hearing such serious talk of love, Amanda was momentarily at a loss for words, but recovering her natural clarity of mind, she answered: "Could I deny any happiness to the man who saved my life?"

"Amanda, I don't want you to give in to my wishes just for that reason. I want you to tell me . . . "

"That I truly love you?" Amanda interrupted. "And since you ask me for the truth, I'll confess the truth. There is no one in the world I could be happier with than with you. With all my heart know that I am yours always and until I die..."

The two lovers embraced, and they sealed their promise to marry with a kiss, then another and another kiss, the sweet precursors of the romantic nuptials that would soon meld two souls into one.

Next, Henry informed Amanda's parents of their plans. They were very pleased with how things had turned out and gave the prospective couple their blessing and their consent to marry.

A few days later, the Freemans formally announced their daughter's betrothal, and received many congratulations from their many friends, many in person and others by telephone and mail.

Captain Havens received a wedding announcement in San Francisco, and though he tried otherwise, he became confused and nervous. He felt vexed and anxious, feelings he could pacify only by thinking that the future he had dreamed of for himself was destined to be for his dear friend Henry Collins. Finally he went to the Western Union office and sent the following telegram:

Mr. and Mrs. George Freeman
Denver, Colorado

Allow me to express my warmest congratulations. That marriage may be a paradise full of all life's blessings for your daughter and Henry is the sincerest wish of

Your good friend,
Orlando Havens

After sending his congratulations, Orlando went to Hotel X—, where another captain from his same regiment was staying, named Melitón González, a native of New Mexico, whom Orlando held in high esteem for his good personal qualities and for the virile boldness and courage with which he had distinguished himself in the famous battle of El Caney at San Juan, Cuba. Melitón was a perfect contrast to Orlando: he had red hair and red eyebrows and eyelashes; his face, like a red beet, was adorned by a full shower of yellow freckles, coarse features; and despite his robust physical symmetry, he was truly ugly, and he was as strange in his ideas as he was grotesque in expressing them;

most of all, he was, to all appearances, an implacable enemy of the fair sex, as will be seen later on. Orlando had confessed his love for Amanda to Melitón on several occasions, but he felt sympathy rather than joy for his friend Orlando.

It was about 9:00 p.m. when Orlando went to Melitón's room and found him stretched out on his bed, with pants and shoes on, as was his habit. Orlando then told him what had happened with Amanda.

"The result of my first love has been a cruel joke played on me," Orlando said. "And now, I believe that I've lost the only woman I could ever love."

Melitón listened closely, and finally started expressing his opinion in his characteristic way:

"I'm quite surprised," he told Orlando, "that a man of your temperament and mature judgment should find himself dejected and stunned because a certain female named Amanda doesn't want to marry him, when you could just as easily hitch yourself to another named Jacinta or Pancrasia and end up at the same place. For me, it's all the same, be they Gerónimas or Amandas: women are women, and nothing more. Since the first of them came into the world and allied herself with the serpent to deceive the first [man], Orlando, women have been the root of all evil in the world. Besides, why all your heartbreak and woe, when for each Adonis there's a load of Venuses in the world? What a joke! Beating the thicket for a rabbit that's already gone! If she marries another, do likewise, and you'll be . . . another fool. As for me, if I should marry someday, it will be for money and not for love. Yessir, it's said that 'Money makes the dog dance.' I'm one of those dogs that's ready to dance the dance of love, as long as the prospects of the dance is rewarded in cash. And so I'll marry the first unsuspecting hog that comes along and finds me to be a 'swell' husband, even if she's a fright to look at, uglier than a shark. Otherwise they can all go swing cats by the tail in Tartary . . . !"

All this might have been very funny to someone in a frame of mind other than the one that now consumed Orlando. But in this case, Melitón's preaching was nothing but irritating satire.

"And what does all this string of nonsense amount to?" Orlando asked, in a bad mood.

"A lot, man, a lot!" Melitón exclaimed. "You're harebrained because you can't marry a certain rabbit named Amanda, who carries on and marries another. This bird is just a woman like any other: as common as a house cat. If this girl doesn't love you, there are dozens of others praying novenas to Saint Anthony, trying to bribe the saint to be the go-between to secure the infatuation of some frightened simpleton with sentimental tendencies like yours. And it'll end up with you between now and tomorrow finding one of those lovey-dovey girls surpassing Amanda in beauty from head to toe, who'll grab you, bridle you and pack you with saddlebags and break your habit of bucking on level ground."

Given the mood he was in, this was enough to drive Orlando to the point of despair. He stood up from his chair and suddenly left the room, without bidding Melitón good-night. Melitón remained stretched out on his bed as before, and with complete indifference and typical detachment he fell asleep singing in sotto voce:

> Felonís' nose is truly big,
> But what's that to me,
> If she's the one who carries it?

> I'm a friend of light,
> And darkness is afflicting,
> But when I'm with Luz,
> My candle is aflickering.

> I asked rich Mr. Troselo
> For his daughter, Piedad:
> He grabbed me by the hair
> And would've thrown me on the ground,
> Had it not been for pity.

> I was in a hurry the day
> I left Veracruz:
> My wife came after me with a stick
> Just because I went to see Crucita.

Orlando went back to his room, put on his pajamas, and sat down at his desk, where he wrote the following verses, which appeared the next day in one of the San Francisco newspapers:

IT'S QUITE SAD

It's quite sad, after the spark of love catches fire,
To strongly feel its burning passion,
Which shows no mercy in robbing us of our tranquility,
In pursuit of a hope
That's capable only of collapsing
Where the solid reality which destroys us begins.

It's quite sad, after having imagined
A goddess who would guide my fate,
And, such as I had idealized her,
I'd meet her soon along the way,
Only to find invincible an adverse impossibility,
Where happiness, upon blooming,
Is crushed forever and fades away.

The next day, when Captain Melitón González read these verses, he felt very uneasy and disgusted, and exclaimed: "By the high heavens and my mother's white hair, Orlando's gone mad! He's mistaken himself for the Knight of the Rueful Figure!"

Then he started walking from one side of the room to the other, hands behind his back, and deep in thought. Finally he sat at his desk and started writing the following curious letter:

Dear Orlando,

I see from the newspaper that you've reduced yourself to a sentimental poet because that Diana from Colorado has turned her back on you, gone for another and left you flat-out busted. You're looking sad, a prude and an object of ridicule. What a lovely party! But let's not fool ourselves: don Quixote of La Mancha also raved about Dulcinea of El Toboso, but why must you madly follow don Quixote?

All right, since we're trading verses, with these I attach another insult to the Muses, and you can sign them too, since you're given to such mistakes. And so:

Amanda:
I wish to tell you
>   that I never stop loving you;
>   that I'd like to make you a goddess
>   and adore you
>   and seize you avidly
>   and bind you forever...
>   but if you should laugh
>   at my love
>   when you read this line,
>   let me make it clear to you,
>   that far from forgetting you,
>   I'll go to the mountains
>   and moan my loss,
>   hoping that a flash
>   of lightning might strike me!

Yours, Melitón

The preceding communication had the effect that Melitón was looking for and upon reading it, Orlando burst into laughter and thus set himself in a good mood. Then he went looking for Melitón, and upon finding him, both laughed heartily, embraced, and then their conversation turned to other matters. They were good friends, loved each other and, in any case, had a mutual understanding.

It is not in vain to observe that Captain González got married six months later in San Bernardino to one of the most beautiful and distinguished ladies of that city—showing that deep down he was not as hostile to the fair sex as he pretended to be; he was one of the best husbands ever known, and always sought happiness and good things in life for his wife. His marriage revealed his true nature: his nobility, his big heart, clear judgment, and unwavering loyalty.

V.

Now let us return to the Collins-Freeman nuptials since they became one of the most important social items in the capital of Colorado. The day of the ceremony there was great enthusiasm and energy at the mansion of that distinguished family, and as Mr. Money takes center stage in everything in this world, everything was ready and in order for the glorious culmination of that romance by 8:00 p.m. The vast halls of that splendid residence had been richly decorated with roses and orange flowers, arranged with delicate taste and true art. Beneath a gorgeous canopy of aromatic flowers, in the middle of whose arch hung a rose and orange bell, stood Hymen's altar. The groom, in a tailcoat, was one of the most attractive personalities at that rich gathering: he had already recovered from his wounds, except for a bruise on the leg, which still caused him some pain; but Henry, by means of reasonable effort, disguised his limp—for who does not try to conquer even the impossible to appear like a model of perfection on his wedding day? Amanda, adorned in the pure white of her wedding gown, along with a pair of exquisite diamond earrings on her rose-tinged delicate ears, and a diamond and ruby necklace around her ivory neck, seemed like a vision from a fairy tale in the midst of what seemed transparent clouds of immaculate purity and with the words Father Luis Coloma, S.J., had given the count in *The First Dance* to describe the Lulú family clan: "Hebe, upon serving the cup to the gods was not as fair . . . Ophelia, upon appearing before Hamlet, not so ideal . . . Psyche, upon reaching Olympus, not as sublime."

A chorus of young friends who were present sang the epithalamium, and generally speaking, a more beautiful wedding than that of Henry and Amanda has never been seen in the city of Denver.

Immediately following the joyful event, the happy married couple returned to their bridal suite on the second floor of the house. The next day they would leave for New Orleans on their wedding trip, and from there they would sail to the island of Cuba and spend their honeymoon on the "Pearl of the Antilles."

While changing clothes, Henry showed Amanda a small medal, saying, "This is the only inheritance that my mother left me. She herself put it on me, when she was on her deathbed, when I was only eight years old. For that reason, I guard it like a priceless gem."

"How strange!" exclaimed Amanda. "I've got a small medal just like it, which my mother asked me never to remove. I have it here in this locket . . . Look."

At this point we consider it necessary to point out that Amanda had not even the most remote remembrance of her true origin, and she was entirely under the belief that she was the real daughter of her adopted parents. When she showed Henry the small medal, he said: "It's just like mine. And you know what, Amanda, I had a sister who was two years old when my mother died. She put a small medal like this on her too. My sister was adopted through an orphanage in New York, but as the rules and regulations of such institutions utterly forbid that the names of adopting couples be released, I could never obtain information to lead me to her whereabouts."

"Don't tell me I'm your sister," Amanda said then, bursting into laughter.

"I can't say anything until I see your parents," Henry answered.

"Are you serious, Henry?" Amanda asked, and kept on laughing as she said, "You're really strange."

"I must see your parents," Henry repeated.

"Stop that," Amanda said, "if you don't want to make a fool of yourself."

At this point Henry noticed a red birthmark, the size of a silver dime, on the upper part of Amanda's left arm.

"Look, Amanda," Henry said. "This can't be a mere coincidence. My sister, whose name was Carlota, had a birthmark like this in the same place. I must see your parents."

"Well, I'll go with you," Amanda said, still laughing at what she considered an impossibility.

Together they went to the Freemans' bedroom. As soon as they entered, Henry approached them and said: "I want you to tell me the truth. Is Amanda your real daughter?"

Mrs. Freeman gave her husband a puzzled look and finally answered: "I'm the only mother she has. Yes, Amanda is our daughter."

Mr. Freeman did not know what to say, but Henry, seeing that the wife's answer was a bit evasive, said: "This is the case. My true name is not Henry Collins, but Eustacio Quintanilla. When my parents died, my sister, Carlota, and I became orphans and were taken to an orphanage in New York, from where we were both adopted later, and I've been unable to learn anything about my sister's whereabouts. I was adopted by a family from Toronto, Canada; the man was named Henry Collins, and I was given the name Henry Collins Jr. When I was twelve, persuaded by other boys and with them, I ran away from my adopted home and finally ended up in Chicago, where I lived before I moved to Boston about five years ago."

Amanda's parents had no other choice now but to admit what they had never wanted their daughter to even suspect. They all cried with joy and compassion: joy because brother and sister had finally met; compassion for the sudden disappointment in which the wedding had resulted, voided by both natural and divine law. Henry and Amanda, or be it Eustacio and Carlota, embraced and kissed one another, no longer seized with the ardent love of man and wife, but moved by the natural affection of brother and sister who have been separated since tender youth.

That strange incident has been one of the most sensational ever registered by the upper circles of society in the United States.

Acceding to the repeated requests of Mr. and Mrs. Freeman, as well as of his sister, Henry finally agreed to stay and live with them permanently, and Mr. Freeman finally named him manager of his large mining concerns in Colorado and New Mexico, a job in which Henry was able to accumulate a great fortune in a few years.

VI.

Three days after this unraveling, Captain Havens, who had finally obtained his permanent discharge, came to visit the Freeman family in Denver, as he had promised to do. The enthusiasm and joy of that reunion exceeds all description, for there was Henry, who had delivered Amanda and her parents, and Orlando, his close friend and deliverer. The happiness of that occasion was boundless.

―――――

In the year 1908, I visited the city of Los Angeles. One Sunday evening, as I walked through one of the beautiful residential areas there, I saw a man kissing his wife at the doorstep, saying to her: "My love, I'll be back within an hour, so we can go to the matinee."

As he was leaving, two precious children came out from the house, a boy about nine years old and a girl about six, who went running and caught up with him, shouting, "A kiss, Daddy, a kiss!" The father kissed them tenderly and left.

That scene was the manifestation of a happy family, whose home life was "a paradise full of all life's blessings": the husband and father was Orlando, the wife was Amanda, and those two precious children were the glorious fruit of their marriage, and their names, respectively, were EUSTACIO and CARLOTA.

The End

APPENDIX

"La navidad," *La Bandera Americana*, Albuquerque, New Mexico, December 24, 1923 (facsimile).

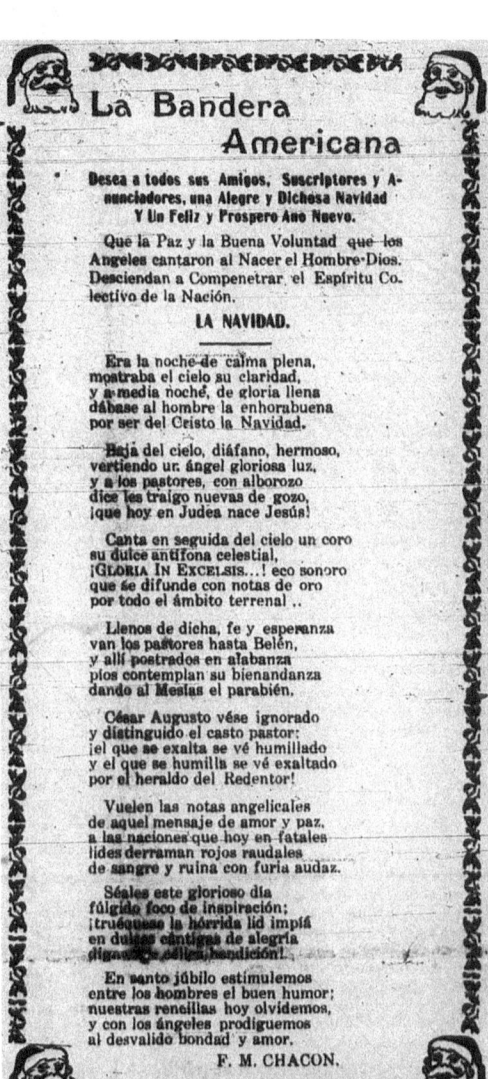

"La Señora Adelina Otero-Warren," *La Bandera Americana*, Albuquerque, New Mexico, November 3, 1923. This facsimile did not reproduce the correct title of the poem, which is "A la Señora Adelina Otero-Warren."

La Señora Adelina Otero-Warren
Candidata Republicana para el Congreso

Ceñida está tu frente de laureles
y tu nombre de honores irradia;
hoy se asoma tu estrella en los dinteles
de la aurora triunfal de un nuevo día.

El mundo avanza con la idea humana
y nacen nuevas cosas en la vida;
hoy refleja la luz de la mañana
en otra esfera la mujer nacida.

Nacida en el sufragio, igual al hombre,
pero en lo espiritual, más elevada,
en pureza moral labra su nombre,
y la tierra va bien en su jornada.

Aquesta evolución tan meritoria,
marcando el alto paso del progreso,
cubrirá Nuevo México de gloria
poniendo una mujer en el Congreso:

Habilidosa, competente honrada,
de alma gentil, de corazón sincero,
¡héla ahí, la del pueblo proclamada,
la dama típica, Adelina Otero!

Vástago noble de español linaje,
y más aún americana pura;
pero ¿que importa el exterior ropaje
del que amerita distinguida altura?

No es exclusiva la grandeza humana,
que no limita con nación ninguna,
del alto cielo su poder dimana
y a quien le place su belleza aduna.

Mas no es ésta lisonja que motiva
el servil interés del egoismo,
que sólo encierra mi intención altiva
teñir en la justicia un idealismo.

Salud! Salud! Un brindis de alegria
placer del progresivo ciudadano,
os manda junto con la trova mía
el saludo de un pueblo soberano
                    F. M. CHACON.

"Acróstico a don Felipe Chacón," *La Bandera Americana*, Albuquerque, New Mexico, February 8, 1924 (facsimile).

Acrostico a Don Felipe Chacon.

Léanse las letras maysúculas al principio de cada línea de arriba para abajo.

El día menos pensado
Nosotros los suscritores,
O todos los ciudadanos
No olviden estos honores
Oro y plata les deseo
Rogándole a mi Creador
De que Dios le preste vida
En compañía de su amor.
Felicidad le deseo,
El editor y gerente
Le dé Dios buena memoria
I que sea muy prudente,
Para sacar su papel.
En todo este continente
Chanza no le ha de faltar,
Algunos dicen que es noble
Como ya lo están mirando
Otros amigos de Hubbell
Nunca les reclama el doble.
Señores pongan cuidado
Ustedes los suscritores,
Suscríbanse a "La Bandera."
Es purite americana,
Rosas y flores despide,
Verdad que es republicana,
I los demócratas dicen
Dos pesos por cada broma,
Oh! que ley tan favorable,
Responden de mala zona,
Republicanos, demócratas
Amigos, conciudadanos,
Mañana y hoy serán ayer,
Otro será el hortelano,
Nomás vámonos uniendo,
Bondosos republicanos,
Ora pagamos dos pesos,
Reflejen con atención,
Bondadoso pueblo y fiel.
Ora el hombre y la mujer
Adeuda capitación.

Image of Felipe Maximiliano Chacón from *Poesía y prosa* (1924).

Cover of the original edition of *Poesía y prosa* (1924).

Title page of the
original edition of
Poesía y prosa (1924).

OBRAS DE
FELIPE MAXIMILIANO CHACON
"EL CANTOR NEOMEXICANO"

Poesia y Prosa

Con un Prólogo por el
HON. BENJAMIN M. READ
Autor de "Illustrated History of New Mexico".
"Sidelights on New Mexico History, etc., etc."

Publicado por F. M. Chacón,
Albuquerque, N. Mex.
EE. UU. de A.

www.ingramcontent.com/pod-product-compliance
Lightning Source LLC
Chambersburg PA
CBHW051202300426
44116CB00006B/411